Software Deployment, Updating, and Patching

OTHER INFORMATION SECURITY BOOKS FROM AUERBACH

802.1X Port-Based Authentication
Edwin Lyle Brown
ISBN: 1-4200-4464-8

Audit and Trace Log Management: Consolidation and Analysis
Phillip Q. Maier
ISBN: 0-8493-2725-3

The CISO Handbook: A Practical Guide to Securing Your Company
Michael Gentile, Ron Collette and Thomas D. August
ISBN: 0-8493-1952-8

Complete Guide to Security and Privacy Metrics: Measuring Regulatory Compliance, Operational Resilience, and ROI
Debra S. Herrmann
ISBN: 0-8493-5402-1

Crisis Management Planning and Execution
Edward S. Devlin
ISBN: 0-8493-2244-8

Computer Forensics: Evidence Collection and Management
Robert C. Newman
ISBN: 0-8493-0561-6

Curing the Patch Management Headache
Felicia M Nicastro
ISBN: 0-8493-2854-3

Cyber Crime Investigator's Field Guide, Second Edition
Bruce Middleton
ISBN: 0-8493-2768-7

Database and Applications Security: Integrating Information Security and Data Management
Bhavani Thuraisingham
ISBN: 0-8493-2224-3

Guide to Optimal Operational Risk and BASEL II
Ioannis S. Akkizidis and Vivianne Bouchereau
ISBN: 0-8493-3813-1

How to Achieve 27001 Certification: An Example of Applied Compliance Management
Sigurjon Thor Arnason and Keith D. Willett
ISBN: 0-8493-3648-1

Information Security: Design, Implementation, Measurement, and Compliance
Timothy P. Layton
ISBN: 0-8493-7087-6

Information Security Architecture: An Integrated Approach to Security in the Organization, Second Edition
Jan Killmeyer
ISBN: 0-8493-1549-2

Information Security Cost Management
Ioana V. Bazavan and Ian Lim
ISBN: 0-8493-9275-6

Information Security Fundamentals
Thomas R. Peltier, Justin Peltier, and John A. Blackley
ISBN: 0-8493-1957-9

Information Security Management Handbook, Sixth Edition
Harold F. Tipton and Micki Krause
ISBN: 0-8493-7495-2

Information Security Risk Analysis, Second Edition
Thomas R. Peltier
ISBN: 0-8493-3346-6

Investigations in the Workplace
Eugene F. Ferraro
ISBN: 0-8493-1648-0

IT Security Governance Guidebook with Security Program Metrics on CD-ROM
Fred Cohen
ISBN: 0-8493-8435-4

Managing an Information Security and Privacy Awareness and Training Program
Rebecca Herold
ISBN: 0-8493-2963-9

Mechanics of User Identification and Authentication: Fundamentals of Identity Management
Dobromir Todorov
ISBN: 1-4200-5219-5

Practical Hacking Techniques and Countermeasures
Mark D. Spivey
ISBN: 0-8493-7057-4

Securing Converged IP Networks
Tyson Macaulay
ISBN: 0-8493-7580-0

The Security Risk Assessment Handbook: A Complete Guide for Performing Security Risk Assessments
Douglas J. Landoll
ISBN: 0-8493-2998-1

Testing Code Security
Maura A. van der Linden
ISBN: 0-8493-9251-9

Wireless Crime and Forensic Investigation
Gregory Kipper
ISBN: 0-8493-3188-9

AUERBACH PUBLICATIONS

www.auerbach-publications.com
To Order Call: 1-800-272-7737 • Fax: 1-800-374-3401
E-mail: orders@crcpress.com

Software Deployment, Updating, and Patching

Bill Stackpole

Patrick Hanrion

Auerbach Publications
Taylor & Francis Group
New York   London

CRC Press is an imprint of the
Taylor & Francis Group, an **informa** business

CRC Press
Taylor & Francis Group
6000 Broken Sound Parkway NW, Suite 300
Boca Raton, FL 33487-2742

International Standard Book Number-13: 978-0-8493-5800-5 (Hardcover)

Library of Congress Cataloging-in-Publication Data

Stackpole, Bill.
   Software deployment, updating, and patching / Bill Stackpole and Patrick
Hanrion.
      p. cm.
   Includes bibliographical references and index.
   ISBN 978-0-8493-5800-5 (alk. paper)
   1. Configuration management. 2. Software maintenance. 3. Computer security.
I. Hanrion, Patrick. II. Title.

QA76.76.C69S74 2007
005.1'6--dc22
                                                  2007027309

Visit the Taylor & Francis Web site at
http://www.taylorandfrancis.com

and the CRC Press Web site at
http://www.crcpress.com

Dedication

To my wife, whose constant dedication never ceases to amaze me.

Bill Stackpole

To my wife Tabitha and my son Broc, who allowed me to spend the time on the weekends to complete this book.

Patrick Hanrion

Dedication

Contents

About the Authors

William "Bill" Stackpole, Lead Security Architect, Microsoft Corporation

Bill is a 20-year veteran of information technology (IT) infrastructure, management, and security. His expertise includes network-based and host-based security design, implementation, and assessment; incident response and computer forensics; security architecture and governance; and secure software development. At Microsoft, Bill has served as a senior security analyst for Microsoft IT Operations, a senior security consultant in National Services, a security engagement manager at the Microsoft Security Center of Excellence, and now serves as the lead security architect for the western United States. Before coming to Microsoft, Bill was the principal consultant for the software security practice at Predictive Systems in Santa Cruz, California. Prior to that Bill worked as a network manager for the U.S. Department of Defense, as a voice and data manager for a Washington-based investment company, and senior network engineer for a Seattle-based consultancy.

Bill is a former CISSP Test Development Committee chairperson and Computer Security Institute Advisory Board member, as well as a current member of the (ISC)² CISSP and ISSAP Common Body of Knowledge committees. He has written and spoken on a number of topics, including application security protocols, secure software development, wireless security, security governance, and compliance management. Bill holds a bachelor of science in management information systems; he is a certified information systems security professional (ISC)² with an information system security architecture professional endorsement, and a certified information security manager, ISACA.

Patrick Hanrion

Patrick is a senior security consultant for Microsoft IT's Application Consulting and Engineering (ACE) group. Patrick has more than 15 years of experience in IT and information security and is involved in many large ongoing security initiatives and projects. Patrick has also worked at many recognized information security–focused companies, including Baltimore Technologies and Cylink. Patrick spoke at the 2006 and 2007 RSA conferences, and in 2006 he presented Microsoft's WS-federation technology. In 2007 he was a panel member discussing Balanced Scorecard and its use in presenting information security metrics.

He has a bachelor's degree in business management with an information management emphasis. Patrick is a certified information system security professional (ISC)^2 with an information systems security architect professional emphasis. He is a certified information security manager, ISACA. Patrick is a board member on the ISACA Academic Relations Committee.

Chapter 1

Introduction

A number of different factors have converged in recent years to elevate the importance of sound information technology (IT) management. The principle driving factor has been the growing dependence on information systems for business operations. The increase has been so significant, it has been suggested that IT should, in fact, be called business technology (BT) because businesses can no longer function without it. The 1992 bombing of the World Trade Center in New York City proves the point. According to *Disaster Recovery Journal*, 80% of the companies housed in the towers sustained unrecoverable losses and more than 60% of those businesses ultimately failed. The cause was not a result of lost data, but a result of lost access. The bombing did not destroy any information systems, but ensuring safety prevented access to those systems for almost a month. Dependency on IT systems has increased substantially since then and so has the importance of good disaster recovery planning.

Security concerns were another major factor. Red Code, Blaster, Slammer, and other forms of self-propagating worms and viruses had devastating effects on system availability, bringing airline reservations, communications, and other services to virtual standstills. Once again, the issue was not the loss of data, but the loss of access to critical processes and data resources. The distributed denial of service (DDoS) attacks against Amazon, Yahoo, and eBay in 1999 serve as another good example of data availability losses. But these examples pale in comparison to actual data losses. In 2005, the Privacy Rights Clearinghouse (http://www.privacyrights.org) chronicled more than 100 million instances of personally identifiable information (PII) being lost or disclosed, including social security, bank account, and credit card numbers. These disclosures, coupled with Securities and Exchange Commission (SEC) reporting concerns, led to the third major contributing factor:

1

dial-in. In addition, hypertext transfer protocol (HTTP)–based protocols like the service oriented architecture protocol (SOAP) and peer-to-peer applications like instant messenger can be used to circumvent these controls and expose internal systems to potentially dangerous content.

Connectivity for portable and remote systems also poses significant challenges for patch deployments. Systems may be attached to the network only for short periods of time and the connections may not have sufficient bandwidth to support efficient patching. Portable systems also have the potential to be infected while attached to other networks and to pass that infection along when attached to the internal network either directly or via a VPN.

Once an attack is on the internal network, the effect of the attack is often intensified by the sophistication of the worm and the lack of internal controls. Hydra worms use multiple vectors to proliferate themselves, including copying to open file shares, mailing to internal messaging systems, or attempting to exploit various vulnerabilities. Unmanaged systems provide easy targets for these attacks. An unmanaged/rogue system is a system that is attached to the network but unknown to operations/support personnel, and consequently do not get patched. Common examples include development systems, test boxes, third-party systems, and embedded systems.

Unfortunately the situation is not getting any better—in fact, it may be getting worse. Companies are deploying more servers than ever before and supporting more versions of OSs, applications, and hardware platforms, further exacerbating the issue. Complexity continues to increase patch quality and quantity issues, connectivity continues to increases the attack vectors, while reduced time to exploit and exploit sophistication are overwhelming network defenses.

More Work, Same Staff

All these factors boil down to what is undoubtedly the second biggest challenge to IT shops: workload. As dependence on IT for business operations has increased, so has the workload on IT staff, but in many IT organizations this has not translated into increases in staffing. IT is a big overhead expense, consequently organizations are more prone to cut IT costs than increase them. Workload increases have demonstrated the need for repeatable processes and automation. While these are desirable, many organizations are still operating on ad hoc manual processes. A recent Microsoft survey discovered that despite the availability of automated tools, most organizations depend on manual processes to retrieve, test, and deploy patches to Windows-based devices throughout their networks. Manual patching is so resource intensive, organizations quickly find themselves trapped in a costly, labor-intensive, and time-consuming process that just seems to go on and on. Research from the Aberdeen Group estimated that businesses and government entities would spend in excess of $2 billion in 2006 to investigate, assess, and deploy security patches. It is not hard to justify that figure if manual patching is being used, considering the number of vulnerabilities reported annually.

If the technical aspects of patch management weren't challenges enough, organizations and government agencies have come under increasing regulatory pressure regarding system security and maintenance. The Sarbanes-Oxley Act of 2002 requires public companies to report on the internal controls they use that can impact the timeliness and accuracy of financial reports. According to the Institute of Internal Auditors, this includes patch management: "Organizations must run supported operating systems and software and stay current with security patches" (http://www.theiia.org/itaudit). Financial institutions have similar requirements under the Gramm-Leach-Bliley Act of 1999, and health care providers and insurers under the Health Insurance Portability and Accountability Act of 1996 (HIPAA).

This book offers prescriptive advice on how to deal with these issues through the application of good configuration and update management processes facilitated by efficient and effective automation.

Configuration Management Solution

Good system operations and management begins with a good understanding of what needs to be managed. This includes the device or system as a whole, as well as the component configurations of those systems. Configuration management is the term used to describe the people, processes, and technologies used to discover, catalog, and maintain devices and device configurations throughout the system life-cycle (Figure 1.1). Configuration management is a fundamental IT management process designed to accurately track and coordinate changes to systems within the IT infrastructure.

The purpose of configuration management is to maintain the functionality, reliability, and security of IT systems. However, it is not possible to manage something you do not know about, nor can you accurately assess the impact of threats or changes to your IT infrastructure without an accurate record of its current state. Configuration management addresses these two critical elements by identifying infrastructure components and cataloging their configuration structures in a configuration management database (CMDB). The CMDB becomes the authoritative source of information for system management tasks, including system changes, repairs and upgrades, risk/vulnerability reduction, and compliance measurement.

The ability to prove compliance is often one of the biggest drivers for configuration management, but system dependability and security are also major factors. The impact on business operations and end-user productivity continues to increase as reliance on IT systems increases. Liabilities for security breaches, including recovery costs, regulatory fines, lawsuits, and loss of customer confidence, also continue to climb, making the need for consistent, accurate, and timely system management essential. Beyond cost and regulatory compliance, good configuration management

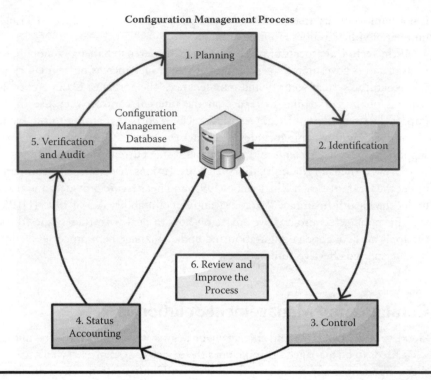

Figure 1.1 Configuration management process.

processes benefit companies by reducing the days of risk from worms, viruses, and other malware, reducing downtime for all components, improving response and resolution for security and component failure incidents, reducing operational errors and rework, and validating component effectiveness and return of investment. One of the major beneficiaries of good configuration management is update management—the ability to quickly and accurately update a system with critical security and reliability patches.

Update Management Solution

Update management is the second major topic of this book (Figure 1.2). It is really a subset of configuration management, but because of the security implications of many updates, it has also become a risk management function.

The importance of update management is really a result of "time to exploit." Time to exploit is the period of time between the release of a security update and the release of the exploit for the system vulnerability the update repaired. If a system is not updated within this window, it becomes susceptible to compromise. In recent years, time to exploit has become so short that failing to apply updates in

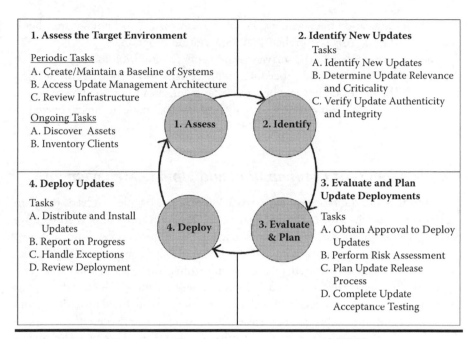

Figure 1.2   Update management process.

a timely fashion creates huge risks to business operations and IT infrastructure integrity. These potential risks never go away; in fact, automated tools are actually increasing the number of flaws hackers are finding, making good configuration and patch management essential throughout the lifecycle of the system.

Perhaps the greatest value of configuration management is the ability to move IT operations from a reactive to a proactive function. The information maintained by configuration management not only makes system management tasks easier, it improves coverage and facilitates automation. And automation reduces workload, giving IT engineering and operations staff the time needed to proactively plan and execute IT initiatives, improve existing processes, and support new business opportunities.

Goal and Scope of This Book

The goal of this book is to provide the information, processes, and guidance required to build an effective configuration management program, including good build, inventory, update, and compliance management practices. To this end the authors have taken a top-down approach to configuration management, beginning with the people aspects of configuration management—governance, strategy, policy, roles, and organization—progressing to the processes and procedures required to build, baseline, maintain, and retire systems, and concluding with the technologies that facilitate configuration management. People, processes, and technology are what it takes to produce a truly comprehensive configuration program.

The book is focused on the software aspects of configuration management, but the principles, processes, and procedures apply equally to hardware configuration structures. The key teachings and best practices from the authors' own experiences are included. The following sections briefly describe the scope of topics covered in the book.

People Aspects of Configuration and Update Management

Programs live and die based on the participation of the people involved. Program participation is driven by authority, that is, the program must have the executive backing necessary to require people to participate. A program without enforcement authority is a lame duck at best. Second, participation is driven by participant support. People involved in the program must understand their roles and responsibilities, have clearly defined tasks and timelines, and receive consistent and timely program communications. Clear expectations, well-defined procedures, and consistent communications make it easier for participants to execute their responsibilities and helps produce consistent results. You will find these people elements emphasized throughout the book.

Process Aspects of Configuration and Update Management

A sustainable consistent process is the cornerstone of a successful program. It simply is not possible to assign participants roles and responsibilities without understanding the program processes. Nor is it possible to achieve consistent and reliable results without well-defined processes. No IT event made this clearer than the worm attacks (Red Code, Blaster, Slammer) in early 2000. The success of these attacks did not result from unknown vulnerabilities, but from poor update processes that failed to close those vulnerabilities. Well-defined processes result in good procedures that provide program participants with the information they need and keep them on track for the tasks they must perform. You will note a considerable emphasis on process throughout the book. The authors have endeavored to provide both the processes and timelines present in configuration and update management.

Technology Aspects of Configuration and Update Management

Programs rely on technology to extend the coverage, effectiveness, and reliability of program processes and to improve the efficiency and productivity of program participants. Technology is a facilitator of program goals by reducing the number of manual tasks that must be performed. One of the best examples of this is tax preparation. The U.S. government estimates that it takes the average taxpayer 14 hours to manually fill out their tax return. Automating it with TurboTax, the process takes on average 3 hours, and there are no calculation errors either. This book uses the same approach—technology as a facilitator rather than a problem solver. The goal is to improve the process with technology, not replace it.

Measurement Aspects of Configuration and Update Management

This section is a brief discussion of the measurement terms used in this book and their application in the measurement process. Throughout this book, measurement is used to determine compliance with technical and process requirements. The ability to consistently and accurately measure key processes and technical solutions is essential to the success of IT programs for a number of reasons, the most basic being that measurement is a standard business process. Business management has three basic components: risk management, reporting, and accountability. It simply is not possible to report results without measuring. The results of good measurement can be used to:

- Demonstrate the effectiveness or value of a process or technique.
- Justify the cost of an existing or proposed solution.
- Show compliance with regulatory or audit requirements.
- Initiate improvements to an existing process or technique.

Unfortunately measurement has not been a strong point for many IT departments, and the consequences have been the loss of budget and personnel. After all, if you cannot demonstrate the value of what you are doing, it is difficult to justify the cost of doing it, and if you are a cost center (and most IT departments are), this makes you a prime target for cost cutting. This is the primary reason why this book places so much emphasis on measurement. Good configuration management is essential to successful IT operations, but without good measurement it is difficult to accumulate the resources necessary to create and sustain a successful program.

Measurement involves boiling down established policies, standards, and processes into a series of requirements and establishing metrics (measurement points) around those requirements. For example, a software update process includes intelligence gathering, compatibility testing, deployment timelines, and status reporting tasks. These tasks reflect a set of minimum requirements such as "vendors must survey daily for new patch or update releases" or "the status of patch deployments must be reported daily to system owners and monthly to the CSO." The baselines (minimum requirements) are used to establish measurement points (metrics). To meet the reporting requirements above, two measurement points must be established:

one for the daily and one for the monthly reports. Metrics simply define what will be measured; they do not define how because different systems require different techniques to gather the required information (e.g., determining the password length in Windows and UNIX OSs). The results (actuals) from each measurement techniques (test) are compared to the baselines to determine compliance. In most instances compliance is a simple yes or no answer; in other instances a number of results may be combined to determine a level of compliance. For example, if monthly update reports are consistently generated but daily reports are sporadic, the reporting process might be deemed "partially compliant" as opposed to "fully compliant" or "non-compliant."

The art of measurement is based on some straightforward steps: reduce policies, standards, and processes into baselines (minimum requirements); establish the metrics (measure points) for those baselines; create tests (measurement techniques) to gather the actuals (measurement data); and compare the resulting actuals against the baselines to determine compliance. Application of these steps is discussed further in Chapter 14.

Definitions and Terms Used in This Book

The book contains a glossary of terms. The intent of this section is to clarify the usage of some of these terms.

Actuals—Test results. Actuals are the information returned by a test or series of tests. The actuals are compared against system or process baselines to determine compliance.

Baseline—The basis for a measurement. In this book, baseline refers to the minimum acceptable value for compliance with a specific requirement; values that equal or exceed the minimum are considered compliant.

Compliance—Conformance to a requirement. Compliance can be expressed as a binary result (i.e., "met" or "did not meet" a requirement) or a level result (e.g., fully compliant, partially compliant, noncompliant). Compliance is used to determine subsequent remediation actions.

Configuration management—The policies, processes, and infrastructure used to control updates to system hardware, firmware, software, and documentation.

Managed system—A system that is actively managed and maintained by the operations group, for example, servers or workstations that the operations group inventories, monitors, updates, or repairs.

Metrics—Measurement points. A metric defines what will be measured based on established requirements. Metrics can apply to multiple and disparate processes or systems, therefore metrics do not define how the measurement is accomplished.

One-off system—A system that the operations group is aware of but cannot manage with existing techniques and tools due to special performance, availability, or confidentiality requirements. A medical system used for life support is a good example.

Patch/update—A patch is an update to a piece of application code. For the purposes of this writing the terms patch and update are synonymous and are used interchangeably throughout this book.

Procedure—A series of tasks designed to achieve a particular goal for a specific situation or technology. For example, a backup procedure consists of configuration, scheduling, execution, and verification tasks designed to protect data from destruction. The tasks are based on the specific requirements of the backup application, system hardware, and the computer OS.

Process—A series of high-level tasks designed to accomplish a particular goal. Processes are generic in nature so they can be applied across multiple situations and technologies. Change management, for example, is a process consisting of change requests, evaluations, approval/deny decisions, scheduling, and verification tasks designed to implement changes with minimum risk or impact to business operations.

Program—The totality of people, processes, and technology employed to achieve a specific purpose; for example, a configuration management program.

Remediation—An action taken to comply with a requirement. Remediation includes identifying the cause of the noncompliance and determining an appropriate course of action (solution) to resolve the issue. Remediation can include direct changes to the process or system, changes to surrounding controls or processes (e.g., addition of a firewall access rule), or acceptance of the risks associated with the noncompliance.

Rogue system—A system attached to the production network without the knowledge or consent of the operations group and not actively managed or maintained by operations. Examples of rogue systems include test machines, vendor and contractor laptops, home machines, etc.

Solution—The process, technology, training, and guidance used to resolve a problem.

Test—A measurement technique. Tests are the methods used to gather the actual data for a specific metric from a specific process or system.

Unmanaged system—A system the operations group is aware of but does not actively manage. Examples of unmanaged systems include systems located in testing facilities or staging areas, systems supplied and managed by third parties, and one-off systems.

Update management—The policies, processes, and infrastructure used to control updates to system software.

Chapter 2

System Lifecycle Overview

System lifecycle management is the management of information technology (IT) systems, and the people and processes required to ensure IT success. Lifecycle management defines systems from their initial introduction into an IT infrastructure to their removal. A system can be either a single computer or multiple computers that are required to provide a specific IT service.

The system lifecycle can be broken into six different phases: envision, system engineering (plan/design), test/stabilize, deploy, operate/maintain, and retire. All of the phases are an integral part of the system lifecycle process. The system lifecycle process must be understood and supported by executive management for an IT organization to be effective. Without management support, the funding will not be made available to make the program complete. The job of IT is to make sure that the IT system lifecycle is aligned with an organization's business objectives, otherwise it will be difficult to gain management support for all of the required phases.

The system lifecycle process is a linear process that will be used to bring software and hardware into and out of an organization:

- Envision—The initial envision phase is crucial for the success of all IT projects. This is where budget and management support are garnered. High-level strategy, business alignment, and risk management are all considered in this phase. A vision document should be built in this phase that can be used to convince the management team. The document must contain the high-level business justification for any new IT projects. It should not be too specific.

The specifics need to be left up to the IT architects that are familiar with the operational environment specifics.

■ System engineering (plan/design)—This phase is where all of the new projects are designed and planned. The design includes selecting the technical details of a solution and answering the "what" component of the project. The planning piece is where the "who" and "when" components of a project are decided. This is an exciting phase for the IT staff. Management would be well served by making sure that all the IT staff has an opportunity to be a part of the system engineering phase. When staff is always assigned to maintenance tasks, it is easy to get into a rut and become bored. A bored IT staff is a prime target for system attacks. All of the operation's teams need to get involved. Functional teams need to be formed to decide on the technical architecture, deployment, daily management, change management, and support infrastructure. All of the above processes need to be put into place and staffed at appropriate levels to ensure the continued smooth systems operation.

■ Test/stabilize—The newly formed teams must create their reference architecture here and begin to understand how they will move forward with their new systems. The team can create their test lab and prototype the solution. When a design is constructed in a test lab it allows the operations staff to learn and understand what will be required of them. New solutions will need to be integrated into the organization's disaster recovery and incident response plans.

■ Deploy—The tested architecture is rolled out at this point. Depending on the deployment there may be specialized deployment teams to ensure the process happens quickly and without interruption. The deployment specialists may also consist of the future system management team. If an upgrade is being deployed, the deployment team must make sure that there is no interruption in service.

■ Operate/maintain—Once the system is deployed, the management and support teams will need to manage the system. Support procedures need to be defined. Incident response, ongoing compliance, and risk management are processes that need to be in place for successful system operations. A security program will also be required to monitor the system to identify security issues. The maintain phase is the longest phase for all new solutions brought into an IT infrastructure. If a solution is successful the maintenance phase can continue for decades. Many of these processes will be explored in greater depth in the configuration management chapters of this book. System maintenance is a circular process that is contained within the linear process of system lifecycle management. Applications and hardware that provide business value enter this phase and leave the phase once they are no longer needed by the organization. The maintenance phase is also where the greatest amount of management discipline is required. Without good management practices in place the maintenance of systems can easily degrade and become the downfall of IT management.

■ Retire—All systems that are deployed must be managed and their retirement expected. The easiest way to retire systems is to follow the vendor lifecycles and be sure to retire systems that will fall out of vendor support. The largest drain on IT resources is the failure to successfully retire hardware and software. Many organizations are running hardware and software that no longer has vendor support. If there are any issues on these systems, an organization is without recourse to resolve them. Usually the only way to solve problems with out-of-date systems is to pay large additional costs for the vendor to back-port fixes. This is a no-win situation, where the vendor wastes money supporting one-off fixes and the organization spends more money on outdated equipment than it would on new systems that could improve efficiency.

Configuration Management Throughout the Lifecycle Process

Configuration management is a subset of the overall system lifecycle management process. Configuration management focuses on the creation and maintenance of system component (hardware and software) configurations. Many IT organizations call this build management, but configuration management also includes hardware and firmware configurations as well as system build management. Figure 2.1 shows how configuration management fits into the overall system lifecycle process.

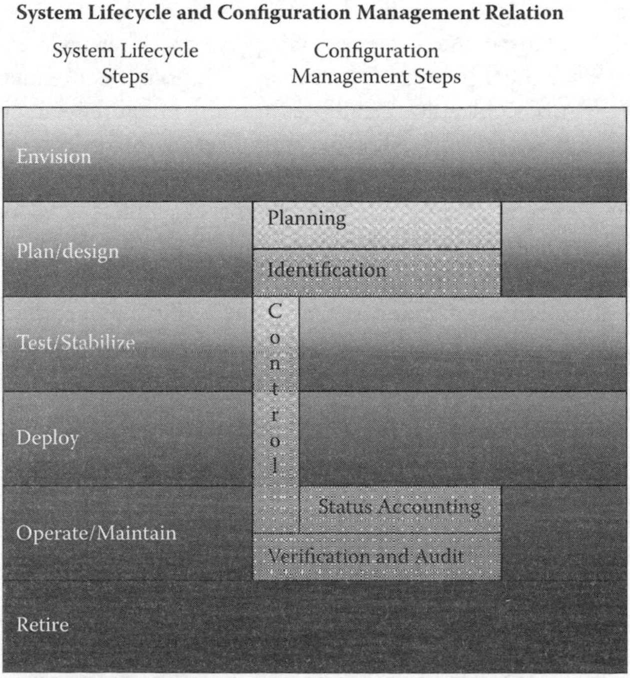

Figure 2.1   System lifecycle and configuration management relation.

All of the phases of configuration management and system lifecycle create outputs that will be consumed by subsequent phases. These output products can be used to measure one's progress. Only the envision and retire phases will be covered in depth in this chapter because they are the only two phases that are not repeated as part of system maintenance and operations.

Envision Phase

Envision is the initial phase where strategy, organization, and budget requirements are set. Each function of the envision phase of a system lifecycle requires greater upper management involvement than the latter stages.

The strategy process is where policy and functional requirements are decided upon. The outputs of the strategy sessions should include functional requirements that are aligned with the company's business objectives and policies. Policies must be supported by the management team and executive board in a formal manner, such as a memo or directive to all employees, voicing support for the policies created in the envisioning process. If management support for IT policy is not absolute, all other IT processes will see varying degrees of success. Solid management support for the policy and compliance measures to ensure adherence also ensures the overall success of IT management.

When new strategies are executed, management needs to ensure correct roles and responsibilities are defined so that managers can either train current staff or hire appropriately skilled personnel. These organizational requirements should be based on the organization's culture and the functional requirements that have been created in the strategy sessions. Allowing staff to grow into new roles that employ new technologies motivates IT personnel. IT is a fast-moving sector; if staff is left to stagnate in their current skill set, the best employees will leave for positions where they have active career paths.

The organization component of the envision phase is a review of the organization to make sure it is ready to take on a new service. To make sure that the company is ready for a service, the service should be understood, and a review of the current organization should take place to make sure that any organizational changes can take place at the proper timeframe. Organizational reviews should consider the training needs of IT staff. In addition to internal resources, many companies are now outsourcing or using contractors in some capacity. A part of reviewing organizational requirements should be to ensure that service level agreements (SLAs) with third parties are in line with business objectives and the IT and security strategy. An organizational review should be created to list the gaps between the current organizational structure and what is required to meet the new strategies.

The IT budget should be based on both technical and organizational needs. The functional specification should help enumerate the software and hardware budgetary requirements needed to realize the strategic goals. The organizational review must identify all organizational gaps in the operations and support staff. The overall budget for the lifecycle management of the system must include both the technological and staffing requirements needed to execute the IT strategy.

Strategy

Organizations will have one or more strategy groups. These groups should be brought together to create the policies and functional requirements that will drive future projects based on the needs of the business. The strategy group should consist of representatives from the following functions: business operations, IT security, IT management, human resources, finance, and legal. The primary purpose for involving these functions as part of the IT strategy group is to create comprehensive policies and technical requirements for IT that improve operational efficiency and align IT with the organization's business objectives.

Policies

Policies are the written minimum requirements that allow the business to meet compliance requirements. Without policies, many organizations tend to be unorganized, with disparate measures in various places. Policies need to be broad enough to work for 90% of all situations, yet direct enough to ensure that certain auditing criteria are met. Policies in most cases will be aligned with regulatory requirements such as the Health Insurance Portability and Accountability Act (HIPPA), the Sarbanes-Oxley Act of 2002 (SOX), or the Gramm-Leach-Bliley Act (GLBA).

Action items that come out of the strategy sessions become part of the functional requirements. Functional requirements identify, at a high level, the requirements that will allow a project to successfully meet the business needs of an organization. This includes the specific executive-level requirements that the project teams need to meet, executive goals, as well as system roles, applications, and integration. Functional requirements need to define all business requirements and technical needs of a specific IT project. The functional requirements do not need to include developmental or infrastructure details unless there are specific technologies that must be used in an identified area, otherwise the technical details must be left to the technical architecture.

IT System Roles

This section defines the system roles that will be used throughout this book. System roles are a way of placing systems into manageable groups. This allows system administrators to focus on specific skill sets and develop expertise in specific knowledge areas. There are a number of possibilities, but most systems will ultimately fall into one of the following classifications or roles: application, file and print, test and staging, infrastructure, database, Web, or other.

Application Role

The application role covers a large number of very diverse systems and, based on business requirements, may need to be further broken out into subcategories. These could include line of business applications, email, document management systems, portals, customer relations management (CRM), and so forth. Many times, application systems involve middleware and a requirement for developers with intimate knowledge of the system to make changes as business needs shift. Effective application system management requires more forward thinking and planning then some of the other system roles because of the possible requirement to build or update software. Managers need to follow the company's business trends and anticipate the changes required in application software. As these goals emerge and are understood, action in the application development environment can be instituted to meet specific requirement timelines. Depending on the environment, application systems managers need to consider system fault tolerance and load management as well.

File and Print Role

File and print role requirements are based on the types of data the system will be hosting. This determination is based on the organization's data classification policy. Document classification is a Federal Information Security Management Act (FISMA) requirement that follows the Federal Information Processing Standards (FIPS) publication 190 specifications. File servers should be in a data center location and, depending on the document types it will host, may require both redundancy and varying levels of system backup. Printers and print servers should have similar controls to the file servers based on the document types they will be printing. Printers need to also consider physical location and the access one may have to freshly printed documents.

Test and Staging Role

The test and staging role is focused on managing the test environment and test lab. The role includes the required ability to model various working environments. Test and staging systems need to be managed separately from the production system and isolated from the production network so they do not cause issues with business critical applications. There can be portals or other ways of accessing these systems from a production network as long as they are segmented off and their changing environment cannot interfere with day-to-day business operations.

Infrastructure Role

Infrastructure systems such as the domain name system (DNS), directory, Dynamic Host Configuration Protocol (DHCP), time, public key infrastructure (PKI), Remote Authentication Dial-In User Service (RADIUS), etc., normally need to be accessible to all other systems and users. These systems are the core of IT operations and must be both secure and highly available. Systems requirements must include redundancy and, where needed, load balancing. Effective infrastructure system management can be challenging; in addition to availability requirements, the systems are often dispersed across geographical locations and time zones.

Database Role

Database systems either manage data elements or develop database-specific code. Database system management is very specialized and storage centric. Database development involves traditional development languages, and usually includes in-depth knowledge of database-specific application programming interfaces (APIs) in addition to database-specific code like Structured Query Language (SQL) or one of the many SQL variations. Database management systems (DBMSs) need to be managed based on the systems they support. In some cases they can be stand alone, while in other instances database systems must be redundant, backed up, and fault tolerant.

Web Role

Web systems include portals, Web services, and static and dynamic content servers and are an entry point for many system attackers. Web systems need to be managed in a secure manner so that they do not become larger company problems. More than other systems, update management and system hardening is a heavy consideration in Web system configuration management. Development for Web servers also needs to be very security conscious.

Other System Roles

This category covers voice integration systems, manufacturing and production control devices, embedded OSs, and so on. These will be referred to as one-off or specialty systems throughout this book. The management requirements for one-off systems can vary considerably depending on their function and the criticality of that function to business and IT operations.

The bottom line is, all systems, regardless of their role, need to be managed according to their specific technical and business functions. Both aspects need to be considered to make the correct management decision about how to operate and maintain these systems.

Organization

In the envision phase of a project or system, management must ensure that system envisioning includes all of the stakeholders that will be involved with the system. The organization should be modeled to correctly manage the systems and needs of a company. The roles and responsibilities must be molded around what individuals actually do. Skills need to be managed in a manner that allow administrators and operators to stay ahead of the technical needs of the organization. As new skill set requirements emerge, personnel must be trained so the people supporting the systems are happy with their continued role in day-to-day operations.

Organizational Reviews

Regular yearly organizational reviews need to be conducted. Some aspects of the IT organization to be reviewed include:

- Is the correct organizational structure in place?
- Do individuals in the organization feel they are correctly placed in the organization?
- Do IT staff have management backing to correctly do their jobs?
- Do administrators and managers have the correct skill sets to proficiently do their jobs?
- Do the job descriptions actually match what the people in the organization do?

Budget

Budgeting is the process of funding both current operations and new projects. The process usually involves the corporate accounting team. Accounting skills are required in IT management so that requests for new projects can be put into accounting terms. Budgeting seems like a pretty simple accounting function at face value. Do this year's projects have adequate funding to be successful? The simplicity goes out the door when organizational politics are involved, and most of the time they will be. The organizational difficulty is determined by corporate culture, size, etc.

Planning and Design Phase

The planning and design phase of the system lifecycle is where the technical team is allowed to sort out the details of a specific solution. Once the technical details are determined, personnel and logistical planning can occur.

In this phase, executive management can step out of the picture. This is where specialists and subject matter experts are asked to step up and begin to model the specifics of a system. Not only is the system architecture addressed, but staffing, on-going maintenance, and system lifetime must be addressed as well. System installation is important, but the complete lifecycle should be planned out so that there are no surprises over the 5- to 10-year life of the system.

Determining Configuration Requirements

The technical specialists must determine all of the system's technical specifications (hardware, firmware, software, and security), including both the local system and interfaces to other devices in the computing environment needed to make a system successful. This process takes some time and requires a team of individuals with specific knowledge of current internal company systems, and at times, external subject matter experts. This architecture team must perform a comprehensive review of the project to make sure that no technical requirement is left out of the project plan. Any missed aspect in the architectural phase will probably result in budget overruns or even project failure.

Determining Test Requirements

The architecture and management team must determine the test requirements associated with the new system (Table 2.1). Testing should use a set of checklists to make sure that each release of software or update applied meets the minimum requirements and that all stakeholders are aware of the pass or fail status of the components being deployed.

Determining Deployment Requirements

When a system is being deployed, environmental requirements and interoperability with other applications residing on the same client system must be considered. Power, cooling, and fire suppression requirements, as well as network bandwidth utilization, must also be considered, especially for distributed applications. Bandwidth is always an important consideration for distributed databases and infrastructure applications like Active Directory and Lightweight Directory Access Protocol (LDAP). The deployment timeline must also be considered. Automated installation applications will have very different management needs. Software distribution and the location of the software will also have to be considered in the application area. Larger application deployments can cause network issues if the software deployment infrastructure is not adequately distributed for the operational environment.

Table 2.1 Component Test Requirements

Component	Description
Localization	When applications are built in more than one language, testing in each language should be performed for linguistic integrity.
Performance	A system should be tested to make sure that it meets its minimum functionality requirements. In addition to the marketed requirements there will be end user expectations that need to be addressed.
Interoperability	A system must be tested for interoperability with other applications that are deployed in the production environment.
Access control	When new applications have access control components it is best to integrate the access control mechanism with existing user stores, for example, a current directory store.
Provisioning	Provisioning of new software needs to be researched to ensure that it will fit in with the current software setup strategy.
Load	Any required software load must be packaged and tested in the current deployment infrastructure.
Criticality	Critical systems may have their testing escalated to the top of the testing cue.
Security	Any tested system must go through a security review to ensure compliance with the corporate security policy.

Determining Operation and Maintenance Requirements

Operation and maintenance requirements are an integral part of the planning process. This is crucial in planning for proper system staffing. The planning stage must consider personnel needs so there are no surprises when a system is finally rolled out. If existing staff is going to assume new responsibilities, then training needs must be identified and scheduled before system rollout. Management tools and software updates need to be a part of the planning process so the new system can be integrated with the existing tools or new management tools can be brought online as part of the overall rollout plan. Automation and system management tools help minimize the impacts new system deployments can have on existing staff. Compliance needs to be considered as well so that the systems can be monitored correctly and appropriate policy constraints can be put in place. Acceptable uses for the system must be defined and documented in the organization's "acceptable use policy." New systems introduced into an existing architecture need to be evaluated for compatibility with existing systems. Ideally new systems should be designed to fit into the existing system's management infrastructure. By ensuring compatibility, IT organizations can reduce the costs and resources needed to manage new systems. When reviewing system administration tools one should look at consolidation and multiuse tools. Many

Table 2.2   System Operations and Management Requirements

Number of systems	Management tools
1–50 systems	Shell scripts
	Scripting languages
	Open source tools
51–500 systems	WSUS
	hfnetcheck pro
501–1000 systems	SMS
	Altiris
	Openview
	Tivoli

organizations purchase and deploy tools that are only partially used. A well thought out tools strategy can save both money and resources for an IT organization.

When systems are brought into an organization's infrastructure, management decisions need to be made about how those systems will be maintained. The optimal situation is where a well-understood management tool like Microsoft SMS, IBM Tivoli, or HP Openview is already in place. Many organizations fail to have well-trained personnel running these systems and they become a huge waste of money and resources. When systems management systems are well run they can save resources, time, and money. The success factor for running management applications is well-trained personnel. In smaller organizations there may not be a need for a full-blown systems management application. However, in these organizations there still may be a place for some forms of automated management, including admin-built scripts, software update systems (e.g., Microsoft WSUS), and monitoring tools such as Microsoft Baseline Security Analyzer (MBSA). The management options that one chooses will depend on the size of the organization, the number of systems being managed, and how available resources are dispersed. There are a number of vendor-based examples of when management systems should be deployed. Table 2.2 provides a generic breakdown.

Managed and Unmanaged Systems

Managed systems are systems that are actively operated and maintained with existing tools and management procedures. Unmanaged systems are systems that are not actively managed by the operations and support teams and in some instances are entirely unknown to these teams. Unmanaged systems may be intentionally malicious or susceptible to compromise because of missing updates and security fixes. In either case, unmanaged systems are a significant security risk. Many organizations have no plan to deal with unmanaged systems. By coordinating between IT compliance and other groups, IT should have a plan on how to bring systems back into compliance and into a managed state. The biggest issue with unmanaged systems is how to detect systems you do not know about. This can be resolved by running network-based compliance tools. There are also ways of identifying unmanaged systems that are built into many management tools. There are new technologies on the horizon, such as Network Admission Control (NAC) and Network Access Protection (NAP), that tackle the unmanaged system problem. These new technologies restrict unauthenticated systems to a network with limited scope. On NAC or NAP networks, systems can be brought into compliance and then allowed back onto trusted corporate networks. See Chapters 10 and 16 for further information on unmanaged system operations, detection, and remediation.

Determining Training and Skill Requirements

Skills management is crucial to a healthy IT organization. From the management perspective, the organization's skill set needs to match the current and future needs of the technology deployed in the environment. Organizations need to have a formal skills management process that is ahead of their technology planning and design cycles by at least a year. This way personnel can be trained in emerging technologies and be a part of the technology planning process. From the personal contributor perspective, an organization must invest in skill and career growth. Without skill growth the IT organization will lose most of the individuals with the drive to obtain new skills.

Determining Performance and Compliance Baselines

Organizations need to define system performance and security compliance baselines during the planning and design phase. Baselines provide the metrics for future performance and security measurement. System baselines should be based on the business needs of the organization and established policies, standards and regulatory requirements, as well as the performance and availability goals the various deployed applications are expected to meet. There must be one team within the IT organization that creates the various system baselines. This team should include representatives from security, audit, marketing, customer relations, and business operations to ensure team results meet the expectations of everyone who will be using the applications. In addition to performance and availability baselines, compliance baselines need to be defined so that users do not violate corporate policy or inadvertently open security holes that can be exploited by an attacker. Compliance baselines need to be employed to keep the organizational assets in a manageable state. Compliance is a difficult thing for many organizations to gain control of. There are many new products that claim to be compliance software, but compliance is more about the policies and baselines that are set by management. The software is only there to check whether the systems meet specific requirements. The human aspect of compliance is where the policies are set and the remediation of noncompliant systems is carried out.

Determining Organizational Requirements

During the planning stage it is recommended that an organization review its structure. When going through a large system rollout, it may make sense to realign the organization to better match the new environment. It also provides the organization with an opportunity to assess the old structure and evaluate whether it was effective or not.

Determining System Retirement

Many organizations fail to set end-of-life plans for systems and software. The result is that systems and software accumulate until the inventory is hundreds if not thousands of items long. With that many different systems in an environment, it becomes an unmanageable mess. Even with good software management tools, an environment with too many software packages becomes unmanageable. Table 2.3 presents end-of-life variables that should be considered when planning for system retirement.

Table 2.3   System Retirement Factors

Factor	Description
Vendor lifecycles	Vendor lifecycles should be a huge consideration for any manager tasked with system retirement. Software and hardware that has been retired by the vendor should be phased out. Any issues that require support can be very costly.
Supportability	As systems age they become more costly to support. System retirement will reduce both organizational support and paid support to vendor costs.
IT technology trends	Retiring systems allows for new technology and improved business efficiency by bringing in new faster systems and removing old inefficient programs.
IT staff and skill set	Older systems can stagnate IT staff. IT positions have historically been forward-thinking jobs. Staff that is stuck supporting an old technology without being allowed to learn new skills will become disgruntled.
Organizational structure	The organizational structure should be reviewed when systems are retired. Many times the removal of an old system is an opportunity for a staff member to grow.
Operational costs	Older systems, over time, become more costly to support and operate.
Corporate policy	Corporate policy must mandate a general timeline for all systems. This way system retirement will become an integrated part of how IT functions.

Documenting System Plans and Designs

The outcomes of all planning and design sessions need to be documented. The initial draft documents that come out of these meetings become the guidelines for the overall system architecture. From the drafts should come more specific and complete documents that lay out all of the required components, including the technical pieces as well as the people and process components of the overall design. Table 2.4 presents sample documents from the planning and design phase.

Table 2.4 System Planning and Design Documentation

Document	Description
System technical design	A document that describes the technical specifications of the design that needs to be deployed.
Support plan	Once a solution is in place there must be a plan on how an IT organization will support the solution. This should include the organizational structure and the expectations that end users should have for support.
System operational processes	This document includes the operational instructions and procedures that the operations staff needs to follow to be successful.
System compliance baseline	The compliance baseline document lists the basic security compliance measures that the new system will be tested against. It should also include the countermeasures that will be employed when noncompliance is detected.
System performance baseline	The system performance baseline document describes the minimum performance measures for the new system. It should also include the measures taken when the performance numbers are not met.
Roles and responsibilities	The roles and responsibilities document contains a list of the roles required to support a new service. It also defines the responsibilities of the staff roles required to provide a quality service.
Skills required	The skills document is a list of specific technical and management attributes required for smooth operation of the new service.
Test plan	The test plan document is a detailed plan of how the test group will go about testing a service. It must include a checklist of specific features to test. It should also include the consequences of test failure.
System deployment plan	The system deployment plan is a plan that details the methods of system deployment. It includes the individuals needed and the tasks they will be required to perform.

Test and Stabilize Phase

The test and stabilize phase of the system lifecycle process is where systems begin the verification process. In this phase, if a system does not pass verification the whole project can be turned back to the plan phase. In some cases the system may need to be rearchitected based on some unforeseen issue that was brought to light during testing. This phase also incorporates various checks to ensure the system is resilient under failure and heavy load conditions.

Verifying System Configurations

When testing a system, one should first verify that the system configuration is correct and meets the defined specifications. All aspects of the system must be checked for correct configuration to eliminate the unnecessary duplication of test efforts that can result by running tests that will be invalid because of misconfiguration. System testers should have configuration checklists that enumerate configuration requirements for hardware, software, firmware, security, and applications, as well as the configuration settings of any other components the system may have, such as the Distributed Component Object Model (DCOM), distributed transaction managers, communication proxies, and so on.

Verifying System Interfaces

When testing a system, the tester should test all of the system interfaces. This means that the tester should go through each functional scenario that an operator may possibly encounter. Testing each scenario can be an exhaustive process. There is software that can be used to automate an extensive test cycle. This can also be used when vendors release software updates. Existing test programs can simulate a user going through various interface operations.

Verifying System Performance

The performance of the system must be tested against defined expectations. Performance testing helps the organization plan for the amount of system resource that will be required to meet the organization's business needs. Performance is more than a system's CPU speed; it can encompass many other factors, including memory, network bandwidth requirements, bus speed, storage requirements, software optimization, redundancy, and fault tolerance.

Verifying Security Requirements

Security accreditation is the process used to verify system security functionality. It can vary widely depending on system usage, data sensitivity, location, and the installed line of business applications. Publicly traded companies, government agencies, banks, and small business all have very different security requirements. For large publicly traded companies and financial institutions there are usually a number of government and industry regulations that must be met. It is best for these organizations to have both internal security checks and external auditors to verify the compliance of the system with all defined and imposed security requirements that may need to be in place. For government organizations, there may be additional checks. A government agency may need to meet certain common criteria (ISO/IEC 15408, FIPS 140) standards in addition to all of the normal government regulatory requirements. Most often an external (independent) audit is required. In some instances the governing bodies may conduct these audits; for example, the Federal Deposit Insurance Corporation (FDIC) provides audits for banking institutions. For a small business, security accreditation may be a simple IT manager sign-off.

Verifying System Interoperability

Before deploying a system into the production environment, tests must be conducted to ensure the new system does not adversely impact or break any of the existing relied upon systems. This is where testing becomes difficult and the availability of automation tools invaluable. Even in a small computing environment with few applications, the testing load can grow exponentially based on a number of different variables. For example, 2 applications with 20 test components on 2 systems means that a total of 80 tests need to be conducted. In some environments, testing is so resource intensive that it is just forgotten. There are a few different methods for conducting interoperability testing. Exhaustive testing (verifying all conceivable scenarios) is the ideal, but many IT organizations do not have the time, resources, or knowledge required. More often a small group of advanced users becomes the "beta" test team. The system is rolled out to them first. If the beta team sees no problems then the system is made available to the rest of the user community. While not ideal, a test community is better than having no testing at all. Interoperability testing improves overall IT stability by ensuring that there will be no issues with existing applications. This significantly reduces unexpected outages and associated support costs. For additional information on test methodologies and technologies see Chapter 14.

System and Support Documentation Updates

Once testing is concluded, the documents that were initially created in the planning and design phase need to be updated. In addition, deployment guides need to be created showing how to deploy the system (Table 2.5).

Table 2.5 System and Support Documentation

Document	Description
Site deployment plan	A plan for the deployment of software and hardware per site.
System configuration guides	Guides that detail how systems need to be configured.
System sizing guides	Guides that recommend the hardware and software needed to support a specific task. This is usually x clients require x servers to y capabilities.
System networking guides	A networking guide states the network needs of a system. It is usually based on the number of clients that need to be supported.
System readme that may include issues with existing IT software packages	A document that contains technical changes and last-minute technical details from the software developers.
Deployment automation tools	A guide that describes the method of deployment for a specific software package.
Initial user community	A document that profiles the user community and their specific needs from the solution being deployed.
Phase plan (if rolled out in phases)	A document that describes the various phases of system rollout. This document is created by the deployment team.

Deploy Phase

The deploy phase is where the system is made available to the user community. Depending on the user community, this may require additional IT resources. The deployment process must be well planned so that it minimizes downtime and impacts to end user productivity. This not only includes hardware and software rollouts but end user and help desk training. The deployment phase includes the following tasks:

- System build
- Hardening
- Installation
- System compatibility testing
- Change control
- Operations verification
- Security verification
- System support documentation

System Build

The system build process includes creation of software and automated deployment packages, and putting the system into the configuration management database (CMDB). The CMDB will be covered in much greater detail later on, but for now let's define the CMDB as the place where system build images are stored for upcoming deployments. This can be simple or very complicated, depending on the number of systems and operating environments that an IT organization manages. The CMDB can be a build system or even a deployment or management system; it depends on how your IT organization chooses to manage systems.

Hardening

System hardening is the process of enhancing the security of a system by adding security measures and turning off or removing unnecessary ports, software, and services. The amount of hardening performed on a given system should be based on a risk assessment that includes the criticality of the system and the value of the information the system processes or stores. Overhardening a system can render the system unusable for its intended purpose. Underhardening a system can lead to system compromise, loss of data, and extensive recovery costs.

Installation

The build process covers the creation of standard system images. The installation process deploys those images to production systems. Installation includes creating and configuring new systems, introducing new software to an existing system, updating the configuration of an existing system, and creating and tracking change management requests, approval, and closures. The installation process can be extraordinarily complicated when the scope of an IT organization spans more than a few thousand systems, especially if those systems are geographically dispersed. When managing a large installation base, companies should employ software management products to manage deployment and system configuration.

Systems Management Software

There are many different systems management packages available to address various organizational needs. The most important aspect of a management software product is the ability of the organization to operate and maintain it. There should be processes in place to govern how the system is utilized, staffed, and maintained. Many companies purchase management software without addressing the organizational overhead that is required. A well-trained team of system support personnel will be needed to get the most out of any system management software.

System Compatibility Testing

The interoperability testing in the test and stabilize phase looks for incompatibilities between interrelated system components. Compatibility testing looks for incompatibilities with unrelated components. When installing new software or systems, a test team should be commissioned to verify the compatibility between existing software packages and the upgrades. Compatibility testing is especially important in organizations with a large number of deployed applications.

Change Control

All IT organizations should have a change control program in place. Change control is a way for all of the interconnected people and processes to be aware of and approve changes made to systems that effect the organization. During deployment, the system implementation team will need to apply for, track, and close one or more requests for change (RFCs). RFCs are disbursed, reviewed, and approved by the organization's change management program. See Chapter 13 for a detailed explanation of change management. For major deployment projects, the project manager is usually an active participant on the change control board and may be granted change approval authority for changes under his purview.

Operations Verification

Once systems are deployed there must be a way to verify that they are performing to the expected levels. This can be measured by a combination of compliance and management software tools. Systems should perform as expected and discovered issues should be addressed as soon as possible. A system in the infrastructure that is too outdated to keep up with the changing needs of the organization should be retired or repurposed to a more suitable task.

Security Verification

System security controls need to be verified separately from operational verification. There are multiple ways for an organization to verify the security functionality of their systems, including penetration testing, compliance testing, risk assessment, and threat modeling. Any combination of the above measures can be employed based on the operational or regulatory requirements of the company.

Penetration Testing

Penetration testing is where an internal or external team of security professionals attempts to circumvent system security controls to gain unauthorized access to system resources. Larger IT consulting and auditing firms provide "pen test" services. The team must try to leverage technical vulnerabilities in the system software, applications, and configurations, as well as flaws in physical security controls and operational procedures. An organization must be careful when hiring penetration test services; there is a fine line between ethical hackers and not so ethical hackers. It is best practice to perform a background check on the person or organization you intend to use for penetration testing within your organization. A clear definition of what is in and out of scope for the test must be created, and all management stakeholders should be aware of the testing and scope so there are no surprises should the tests raise alarms with IT staff or end users.

Compliance Testing

Regular compliance testing should be conducted by the IT/security organization to ensure that systems are adhering to the organization's security policies, standards, and requirements. While the overall level of compliance is an indicator of how well the company is doing as a whole, the compliance details can be used to verify the operational effectiveness of the security controls on individual systems. There are many commercial compliance tools that can be used to conduct compliance testing (for a detailed discussion of compliance management see Chapter 16; for a review of compliance tools see Chapter 17).

Risk Assessment

Risk assessments should be a part of the overall security verification program. External parties should conduct the assessment to ensure that there is no bias in the assessment findings. Assessments should focus on identifying risks that could lead to system compromise or failure. The risks can be technology, process, or people based. An assessment should also identify ways to mitigate the risks that are identified.

Threat Modeling

Threat modeling is an integral part of the security verification process. Threat modeling is the process where a team of security professionals reviews a specific application and tries to identify possible attack points. The outcome is a list of attack points that IT security should protect against.

System Support Documentation

Once the system is deployed and operational the system documentation should be corrected and updated with the final operational configuration parameters as well as any "lessons learned" from the installation and configuration process. The types of documentation produced will vary based on its use and the organization. End user documentation should be provided to all users of the system. The end user documentation can be the standard vendor documentation for standard consumer software. More customized applications may require documentation that is personalized to the configurations deployed within the company. System administration and development documentation as well as help desk procedures should be provided to the IT personnel supporting and managing the deployed software. This documentation should be periodically reviewed, especially for customized software (e.g., human resource systems, billing systems, etc.). Frequent changes to these applications will warrant updates to the documentation. This must be a planned activity when any system upgrades or changes are deployed.

Operate and Maintain Phase

The operate and maintain phase covers aspects of system operations, support, and audit. This phase constitutes the bulk of a system's lifecycle. Operations and system support have been described as the grunt work of IT; not glamorous, but absolutely essential to company productivity and operations. The management of operations and support has seen many significant improvements in recent years, including a number of new strategies and methodologies that can be employed to greatly reduce the amount of grunt work so IT people have time to focus on strategic and growth management initiatives. This has led to a more proactive IT function where operational issues are identified and resolved before they can adversely impact business operations. The following sections cover a number of these operations, including hardware and software changes, additions, and deletions), account provisioning, security management, performance tuning, and storage management.

Adding New Software, Hardware, or Firmware

Adding new software, hardware, or firmware to the current install base should be managed with caution. The key to the successful introduction of new components into the install base is thorough testing. In modern systems there are many dependencies; thorough testing ensures critical impacts, such as bringing down the billing system when deploying the latest collaboration software, are avoided.

Changing Software, Hardware, or Firmware

Updates and changes to systems are inevitable, but they must be properly managed to avoid unnecessary impacts to user productivity and business operations. All changes

Baseline System Measurement

Baseline measurement is a monitoring function designed to collect usage, performance, security, configuration, and audit information for comparison to established requirements and to track system operational characteristics over time. Measurement is often overlooked by IT departments, but good measurement practices can be invaluable. Measurement can be used to demonstrate operational effectiveness and return on investment, and to justify new IT projects and spending. IT management should ensure that measurement is a part of the overall IT strategy so that an ongoing baseline is known.

Remediate or Repair Noncompliant Baselines or Failed Hardware, Firmware, or Software

Misconfigurations and unauthorized changes are the most common support issues, followed by hardware failures. When systems break or fail there must be procedures in place to quickly identify and resolve the problem. This is equally true of systems that fail baseline security checks. Clear procedures, including problem escalation, are necessary to ensure the operational integrity of the IT infrastructure.

Retire Phase

Every system reaches the end of its life at some point in time. Software requirements outstrip hardware capabilities, users requirements outstrip software capabilities, functions are eliminated, and line of business applications are transitioned to newer more capable technologies. IT organizations need to do a yearly review of the applications they manage and support. Most organizations do not take the time to correctly manage the removal of systems or applications from their infrastructure. Systems that are running on retired operating systems should be upgraded or retired. Systems that no longer meet the minimum performance requirements should be upgraded or retired. When there is a system that performs the same or similar function of another system, they should be combined and one system retired. Maintaining obsolete systems unnecessarily wastes IT resources and ultimately can lead to system failures that are difficult and costly to recover from. System retirement helps IT consolidate and simplify the number of systems they manage, thus reducing costs.

Retirement Notification

Retirement notification must be part of the overall retirement plan. Everyone that uses or consumes information generated by the system must be made aware of the retirement and the plans for transitioning new applications, services, etc. Retirement planning and notification should begin well before a system reaches its end of life.

Verification of Nonuse

The notification process must include a feedback mechanism to identify any parties still using system resources or outputs. When all users have been adequately warned of the end of life timeline, their accounts should be removed from a system. The IT operations group must verify the nonuse status of the system before performing system power down to minimize issues.

Power Down

Once the nonuse verification has taken place, the system can be shut down and recycled. Decommissioning a system for one use does not mean the system cannot be repurposed for other tasks. Older systems are frequently repurposed for testing purposes where system load and performance requirements are minimal.

Remove from CMDB and Infrastructure Services (DNS, Directory, etc.)

The final step in system retirement is to remove the system from the configuration management database, all system management and monitoring systems, and infrastructure services (i.e., active directory, DNS, DHCP reservations, etc.).

Conclusion

System lifecycle management is the major assignment of IT personnel. A system's lifecycle includes the following phases: envision, system engineering (plan and design), test and stabilize, deploy, operate and maintain, and retire. IT management must be aware of the full process so they can ensure that their infrastructure is a healthy environment for business to flourish. By ensuring that each of the phases is executed in a manner required for their business, IT managers will be successful in their goals.

Chapter 3

Configuration Management Program Overview

Configuration management (CM) is an information technology (IT) term used to describe the management of changes to hardware, software, firmware, documentation, testing, and all aspects of IT. The purpose of CM is to ensure that the configurations of systems are well documented and tracked so that they can be used in support of all other IT operations, including incident response, support services, change management, release management, and patch/update management. All of these operational activities are used to ensure that an organization or business is able to maintain optimal operational efficiency. The CM function is critical to business continuity. When an organization has a highly mature CM program most of the functions are automated. CM is highly connected to system lifecycle management, but does not cover the initial envisioning or retirement of systems. When reviewing CM we need to consider the Information Technology Infrastructure Library (ITIL) best practices around CM.

The ITIL defines the basic activities of CM (Figure 3.1) as:

- Planning—Defining the purpose, scope, objectives, policies, and procedures, as well as the organizational and technical content for CM.
- Identification—Selecting and identifying the configuration structures for the entire infrastructure's configuration items (CIs), including their "owner," their interrelationships, and configuration documentation. It includes allocating

identifiers and version numbers for CIs, labeling each item, and entering it in the configuration management database (CMDB).

■ Control—Ensuring that only authorized and identifiable CIs are accepted and recorded, from receipt to disposal. It ensures that no CI is added, modified, replaced, or removed without appropriate controlling documentation (e.g., an approved change request and updated specification).

■ Status accounting—The reporting of all current and historical data concerned with each CI throughout its lifecycle. This allows changes to CIs and their records to be traceable (e.g., tracking the status of a CI as it changes from one state to another; for instance "under development," "being tested," "live," or "withdrawn."

■ Verification and audit—A series of reviews and audits that verify the physical existence of CIs and check that they are correctly recorded in the configuration management system (Office of Government Commerce, *Service Support*, Norwich, England: The Stationery Office, 2000, p. 121, ISBN 0113300158).

Beyond the five CM activities, to have a truly mature CM program there must also be a process improvement step. Process improvement must be considered at every stage of CM and not just once in the cycle. For this review of configuration

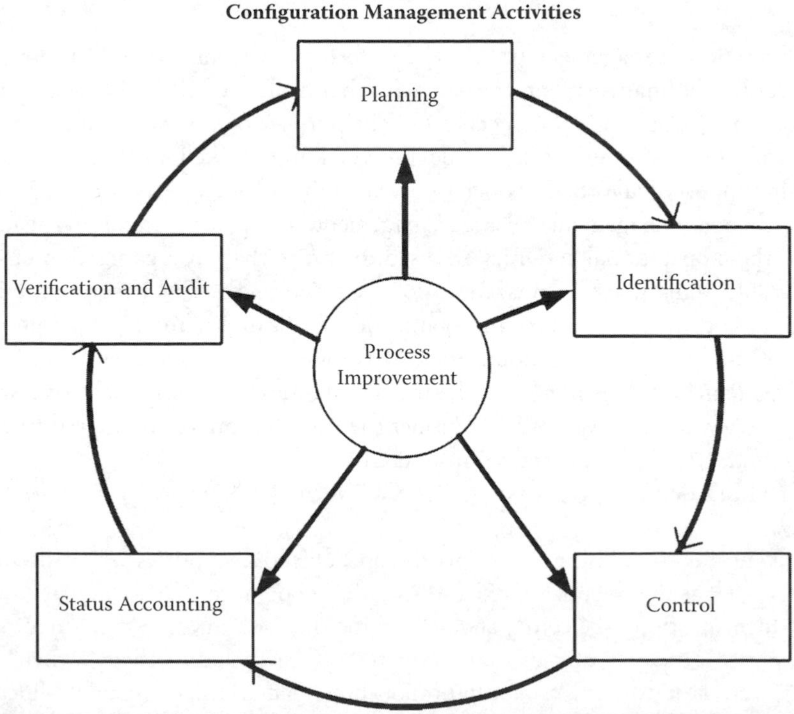

Configuration Management Activities

Figure 3.1 Configuration management activities.

management, the authors would like to expand on the ITIL definition and look at CM in a broader prospective.

Configuration Management Roles and Responsibilities

The first step in creating a CM program is to assemble the correct team. When initiating a CM program, all of the roles may not be required for the initial phases, but people are required for the initial stages of setting goals and creating program requirements. The team must contain the correct individuals so that the team not only creates an appropriate strategy and program, but the team must also have the authority to execute the plan. This team will eventually be required to include stakeholders in the various systems. Appropriate management personnel will need to sign off on any changes, including management, testing, the CM librarian, administrators, support, and strategy.

Management

The correct management needs to be a part of the CM team. The decisions that are made by the CM team need to be supported by the highest levels of management. The management team must contain a broad range of management personnel so that all groups are represented in decisions that effect the entire company. A sample of management representation could include board members, accounting, legal, sales, production, marketing, and IT. When dealing with management, care needs to be taken to make sure that their involvement is not abused. The higher up the management chain decisions need to be made, the more important it is to be brief and precise with their inclusion.

The management team that will be most involved in the process is IT service management. Every service that IT provides to the organization will have multiple configuration components that will be included in the CMDB. The service team will then rely on the stored configurations to perform various critical IT functions.

Testing

Information technology configuration testing must be involved in the CM team. They will need to determine system compatibility. A precise testing plan and strategy needs to be in place to ensure that all configuration changes will not adversely affect future business operations and IT integrity. The test organization needs to be aware of all system changes so they can duplicate those changes as needed. The need to duplicate the live system environment is critical to the test organization's ability to be effective. When the test organization does not mirror the live environment it leaves the organization vulnerable to unforeseen problems.

Librarian

The librarian for the CM team is the person that takes care of the CMDB. The librarian must be a part of the CM team and have input into the overall process. The CMDB librarian must be skilled in both the tools that the organization has selected to manage their configurations and in how to correctly document all of the configurations. The librarian determines the CIs and eventually teaches others how to use and input data into the CMDB. Initially the format and attributes stored in the CMDB should be agreed upon by the CM team as a whole, but once the format is established, the librarian is responsible for day-to-day changes and usage enforcement. Many times the CMDB tool can be configured to enforce input standards and require fields to be filled out.

Administrators

The CM team should also include IT system administrator representatives. They need to be a part of the team so that their various real-life experiences in configuring systems are utilized. Administrators will be the everyday users of the CMDB and the CM processes that are in place. They will benefit greatly from providing input into the initiation and ongoing management of the CM process. The administrators that are the representatives in the CM process group must be very active in the process to represent the real-life situations that they face while doing their daily tasks. Their jobs will be most affected by changes in the CM process.

Support

Information technology support must always be a part of the CM team. They can expose various configurations that are causing support issues. Support issues, if not resolved, can significantly raise IT costs. Support must understand the CM process and how the CM processes intersect with their own support process. If they are not integrated, there will be issues in how support incidents are resolved. Support relies heavily on CM data and can use it to greatly improve the support process and the satisfaction level of their customers. Support can use the CMDB as a remediation reference. When working on problem systems, they can always use a configuration to a known CMDB-supported configuration and troubleshoot from there.

Strategy

Information technology strategists need to be a part of the CM team. They need to make sure that the CM team knows about all future IT directions and what they need to be ready for. The strategy team must be integrated into the CM planning

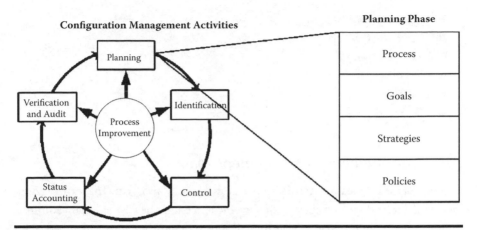

Figure 3.2 Configuration management planning.

process. By being inserted at the planning level, they can make sure that all of the strategy is realized in the planning of new service initiatives.

Planning

Planning is the start of the CM process (Figure 3.2). Any new initiatives need to start in the planning phase. Any ongoing service should be part of periodic planning exercises to make sure that the service continues to meet the needs of the organization. Planning should be focused on initiating and improving operational efficiency and effectiveness. The planning phase of CM is where an IT organization must focus on realizing its goals. The planning phase consists of goals, strategy, policies, and processes.

Each of these topics needs to be thoroughly reviewed so that the CM plan for the year is aligned with the business. The plans must be on budget and strategically aligned with the overall organizational strategy.

Processes

When building a plan for CM, the CM team needs to make the process work for the businesses that it serves. The processes involved in the creation and maintenance of a CM program include:

- Form a CM team
- Define the CM strategy
- Define the CM architecture
- Create the CM policy

- Create the CM baseline
- Create the CMDB
- Test
- Compliance
- End of life
- CM metrics

Form a Configuration Management Team

Creation of the CM team is the first step in creating a CM program. The team needs to include the roles discussed above—management, testing, the CM librarian, administrators, support, and strategy. The team will consist of mostly advisory members, with a few people that are dedicated to the CM program (e.g., the CM librarian).

Define the Configuration Management Strategy

The CM strategy is the action plan for CM execution. The CM team must work on the strategy that will be put in place. The strategy must improve the management of the defined baseline configurations. The CM strategy needs to ensure that the CM program and systems are robust and ready for use when needed.

Define the Configuration Management Architecture

The CM architecture is very important in the execution of the CM program. The architecture needs to consider the main system—the CMDB. Around the CMDB there needs to be processes that will enable communication and operation of the CMDB's output and input. The CM architecture needs to define all of the communication channels. The CM architecture must define the processes that are required to ensure a successful program.

Create the Configuration Management Policy

Once the team has been created, the entire team must meet to create the CM policy. The CM policy needs to be in line with the overall IT policy. The policy must outline how the CM program will be governed. The policy must be monitored for compliance and enforced when the policy is not followed. The policy should include device policy, user policy, software policy, security policy, policy timelines, and policy exceptions.

Create the Configuration Management Baseline

With the staff and policies in place it is time to create the configuration baseline. Each computer or device in the IT environment will need to be configured with a base configuration. The baseline configuration is a starting point that in many environments can be automatically deployed. The CM baseline configuration for each system can be deployed and then the baseline can be changed based on role and user needs. In most environments there will be multiple baselines or core platforms. Even though there will be a need for multiple baselines, the CM team must try to keep the number of configuration baselines to a minimum.

Create the Configuration Management Database

To create the CMDB the CM team needs to meet and decide what will be included in the CMDB. It will obviously be a storage location for configurations, and there may be endless discussion around every CI attribute. The team must focus on making sure that the needed attributes are included, but they also need to ensure that attributes that will never be used in CM or CM-supported activities are eliminated.

Testing

The CM test process needs to be focused on configuration validation. The process must be automated in larger environments. In smaller environments there may not be the budget for automation tools. All configuration settings need go through an approved test process before they can be entered into the CMDB. The test process is critical to building confidence in the CM program. If the CM stakeholders do not trust the configurations that come from the CMDB, the program will fail.

Compliance

Configuration management compliance is the function of checking systems in the IT environment for compliance with the CM baseline. The key to a successful compliance program is the use of automated tools to check for compliance. The automated tools should recognize systems that are out of compliance and alert administrators to them. The administrators must have the authority to enforce policy and bring systems back into compliance.

End of Life

Within the CM framework, the end of life process is focused on retiring a specific configuration. Configurations need to be retired so that the CM system does not become overloaded with dated information. The removal of configurations is always a cost-saving measure. The cost-saving aspect of CM end of life should be emphasized to raise process visibility and importance.

Configuration Management Metrics

Configuration management metrics need to focus on the success or failure of the CM components. The process must be specific about identifying the data points to measure and what the output from those data points mean. The metrics will allow the overall CM program to improve itself and show where changes need to be made.

Goals

A CM program must have well-defined goals so that the direction of the CM group is clear. CM goals need to support an organization's operation. They should focus on making the business stable and efficient. Any newly introduced services should enhance the ability of a business to execute on its corporate vision. CM goals should include:

- Configuration simplification
- Centralized management
- Application consolidation and reduction
- Policy unification
- Standardize security
- Minimize support costs
- Improve security
- Reduce training needs
- Ease of system rollout
- Support business and IT functions
- End of life for obsolete software and hardware

By achieving all of these goals an IT organization will have a very successful CM program.

Configuration Simplification

Configuration simplification will reduce the IT workload. IT organizations are already under great pressure to reduce costs, and making configurations simpler will reduce the time spent on configuration maintenance. IT organizations seem to add configurations without viewing the overall picture. Overly complex configurations are difficult to manage and change. Removing unused configurations reduces management overhead.

Centralized Management

Centralized management allows an organization to go to one authoritative place for all configuration information. CM must be centralized in a CMDB. This is one of the key CM elements that has been introduced to IT by the ITIL best practices books. There are a few vendors that are now selling CMDB products. The few that come to mind are Computer Associates, BMC, IBM, Symantec, and nLayers. There are other organizations that have built their own home-grown CMDBs with internal developer resources. The concept of a CMDB makes it possible for organizations to greatly reduce the errors that are caused by having configuration information stored in multiple locations.

Application Consolidation and Reduction

Application consolidation and reduction reduces IT costs by minimizing the number of applications an organization is tasked with supporting. CM can facilitate application consolidation by identifying applications that can be removed from an IT infrastructure. CM tasks can also identify applications that are not being used. Once redundant or underused applications are identified a plan can be created to remove them from the environment. Application consolidation is a difficult task for organizations that are in a reactive mode. Application consolidation is something companies that are underfunded or understaffed can turn to in order to reduce the number of supported applications they are required to manage. Application consolidation and reduction makes good sense and can exponentially reduce the workload of an IT organization.

Policy Unification

Configuration management is focused on centralized management of configurations. The centralized management concept should be applied to policy creation as well. The planning group needs to make sure that policies are aligned with each other. IT policies must be aligned with human resources and all other company policies. Policy unification across all IT groups is essential to the business. Unified policies can help ensure that the solutions that are deployed work together toward a single business goal.

Standardize Security

Information security must be aligned with industry security standards and regulations. By following industry standards an IT organization can be secure in the knowledge that they have done their due diligence in securing corporate assets. CM simplifies the deployment of standardized security because it needs to be added only once in the configuration baselines. When the standards are a part of the base configuration they become a normal part of any system deployment. Certain industries have regulatory compliance requirements that they must follow in addition to the standard information security measures they take. Companies may be audited for compliance and need to be prepared for audits targeted toward their industry.

Minimize Support Costs

Configuration management minimizes support costs by reducing the amount of in-depth troubleshooting that needs to take place. By creating a CMDB and a support knowledge base a company can shorten support calls and therefore reduce costs. The CMDB makes it easy for support personnel to find any configuration information needed in the support process.

Improve Security

Configuration management can improve security for a company by reducing the number of misconfigured systems. By improving overall system management, the number of unknown and rogue systems is reduced. Rogue systems are one of the greatest security issues for company internal networks.

Reduce Training Needs

Configuration management can help an organization reduce training needs by reducing the requirement to train certain configurations. CM can help identify the most misused applications. This information can help IT organizations target training where it is needed. Planning for the future can ensure that IT organizations are trained on the technologies that will be brought into the environment. These early trainees can then cross train others in the organization.

Ease of System Rollout

Configuration management will give an IT organization confidence that systems that are deployed have been through a comprehensive testing program. The configuration baseline exists in the CMDB. This baseline configuration allows all other deployments of a specific application to be a mirror of the first. A goal of CM should be to make system rollout easier than if CM did not exist. CM can make rollout easier by automating many of the functions of system deployment.

Support Business and IT Functions

Configuration management supports IT configurations by maintaining a store where all configurations exist. The CM store is the baseline that all other deployments can be based on. CM must look toward IT's role within the business and further the goals of the business. Within IT organizations people may become focused on specific technologies that are trendy, but the bottom line is, if the business does not exist, the IT organization does not either. IT must look for ways to automate business functions and make the business more efficient.

End of Life for Obsolete Software and Hardware

Configuration management maintains all configuration information. Correct management of configurations mandates that at some point they should be removed. The removal or retirement of configurations is essential to minimize costs, complexity, and IT bulk. The CM group within an organization must make sure that they include an end of life program for software and hardware. Many organizations miss this step and end up supporting too many system configurations. When you consider the number of variations of software packages that can be deployed on multiple versions of hardware, the number of configurations can quickly become unmanageable. Making sure that an end of life program is in place will help reduce the amount of work IT groups will have to do when deploying configurations.

Strategy

Configuration management strategy is the action plan to ensure CM success. The strategy must note the actions that need to be executed to fulfill the organization's vision. CM strategy is the approach you take toward CM to ensure that your CM plan meets your business needs over a period of time. The actions need to be realistic and the timeframe for completion needs to be met. Strategies can be broken up into short-, mid-, and long-term focuses. An organization's strategy must always be evolving as the business changes.

Short-Term

Short-term configuration management strategies must be quick actions that enable CM. Short-term strategies cover a 1- to 3-month time period and resolve specific urgent issues. A short-term CM strategy is usually more urgent when the CM program is being initiated. The short-term strategy can also contain the initial steps of longer term projects, initiatives, or focuses for the IT organization. When building a new strategy, the short term usually contains "quick wins" and urgent needs. In a more mature CM program, short-term strategies are more likely to be enacted in emergencies.

Urgent Needs

Urgent needs are CM items that come up in a risk assessment or incident response exercise. The action items that come from these processes need to be addressed immediately. And when they are addressed, the changes touch on components of CM. The CMDB will need to be changed to reflect the changes required to address any incident.

Budget

When building a CM strategy, the immediate budget must always be considered. All changes and enhancements need to be thought out in the context of the current budget. The greatest plans can be useless without adequate funding. Short-term strategies need to be inserted into the existing budget cycle and use as little of the budget as possible.

Midterm

Midterm CM projects involve any new services that are introduced during the year. The CM components of new service rollout projects include configuration baselining, application compatibility testing, configurations added to CMDB, and adding configuration signatures to compliance tools. Midterm CM strategies usually fall into the 6-month to 1 year time frame. Midterm projects can be prepared for in the short term and executed in the midterm. Midterm strategies need to address any new planned projects.

Yearly Projects

Many of an IT organization's yearly projects are the executions of strategic plans. This is true not only for CM, but for all groups, standards, and methodologies that an IT organization employs. Yearly projects will always be one of the main functions of an IT organization. CM must be a consideration in these projects. CM operations will help ensure that projects continue to be successful.

Identified Needs

In the midterm, projects come up that need to be completed quickly. When these projects are identified, they need to be addressed and a strategy created. IT must have processes that can identify needs for specific projects. Some activities that may reveal specific IT needs include risk assessments, end user reviews, management reviews, and business reviews. The output from these IT activities initiate CM needs and changes. The new CM components need to be collected in the CMDB for use in the future.

Long-Term

Long-term configuration management strategy needs to be about improving the CM process. A long-term CM strategy may be to improve or upgrade the CMDB. Long-term strategies must be forward thinking and be more research focused. Long-term strategies must solicit business leader needs and must consider IT methodologies and industry best practices. Long-term strategies must set the direction of the IT organization and identify strategic directions.

Improve Manageability

Long-term CM strategy will improve manageability by continuing to streamline and simplify the CM process. The strategy must further the CM goals of giving the IT organization more control of configurations via automation and sound management principles.

Enhance System Lifecycle

Long-term CM strategy will improve the system lifecycle by streamlining and improving the CM process. Something to consider when building a long-term strategy is that any strategy must meet all policies and lifecycle time lines that are already in place. It does not make sense to embark on a 5-year project when the hardware will be obsolete in 2 years.

Improve Security

Configuration management improves security by grounding all configurations in a known good baseline. The long-term strategy to improve security should be that the CMDB and CM resources are always available to all IT resources. CM must always remain security conscious.

Policies

Policies are the documents that define the specific actions that need to be taken by the CM team. Policies must not be too technically specific, but actionable and enforceable. The success of a policy is based in whether upper management accepts and follows it. With upper management support, the IT CM team is empowered to enforce policy. By enforcing policy, the CM team can be sure to realize the benefits from CM. It is ideal if all policies are accompanied by a management letter or memo in support of the specific policies.

Device Policy

Configuration management policy needs to cover all devices that are allowed into a corporate infrastructure. This is a difficult task and leans on the IT compliance function. This function is critical to all policies. Policies are just pieces of paper if there is no review for compliance. When compliance checks find out-of-compliance machines the policy allows the CM team to take measures to enforce compliance.

User Policy

User policy affects the CM program by enabling CM to track user-specific CIs that may need to be in the CMDB. CM policy must cover any users that have access to corporate resources. These products can also be considered an extension to the compliance product arena.

Software Policy

Software policy is important to CM because all software components and configuration settings need to be part of the CMDB. Any change beyond a default software installation will be tracked and documented by the CM process. CM policy must cover all software that is deployed on company resources. This may even extend beyond company resources; for example, contractors using their computers on a company's internal network may be required to have a current antivirus image.

Security Policy

Security policy must be very specific to the organization and its security needs. The security needs will vary greatly depending on the business. Security policies are very lax in environments that are creative and looking to foster collaboration and sharing. Security policies can be locked down and extremely rigid in a government top secret situation.

Policy Timelines

Configuration management policies need to have timelines assigned to specific tasks. The timelines must be aligned with system lifecycles. Many policies will have timelines that are specific; for example, the password timeline should be set at a specific interval of 90 days.

Policy Exceptions

Configuration management policy needs to allow exceptions. When creating exceptions to a policy there must be a time when the exception is released and no longer exists. Many organizations have an exception policy where the exceptions go through a rigorous process before they are accepted. This process must have the correct people involved so that exceptions are given when needed but not handed out so easily that corporate security is diminished.

Identification

The CM identification phase is focused on determining the resources that should be included in the management program (Figure 3.3). Identification needs to frame the CM environment so that it is understood and managed. CIs are the attributes that are monitored by the CM process. Identification can be the function of an automated system that also identifies systems that fall outside the realm of CM. The identification program includes the following tasks and elements: infrastructure and facilities, network scanning, and procedures.

Infrastructure and Facilities

When identifying CIs, leveraging the IT infrastructure and asset inventory is the way to go. In a managed IT environment there are usually many different tools that can be used to identify systems on the network. The tools can acquire all kinds of information from the computers on the network. The task of the CM group is to identify which CIs they will manage within the CM framework.

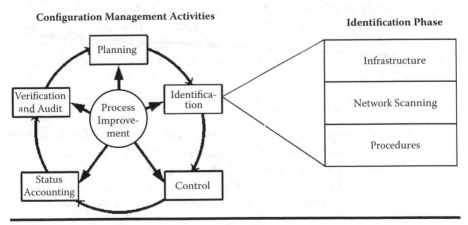

Figure 3.3   Configuration management identification.

Hardware and Software Owners

Configuration management requires the identification of various components. The owners of various systems need to be identified so that they can be notified of changes that will affect them. Users, user groups, hardware groups, and software groups all need to be identified so that the correct services can be deployed to the correct user and hardware groups. Many times these groups correspond with the business functions of the various groups. All of this information must be contained in the CMDB so that the configurations can be standardized to accelerate system deployment.

Naming Standards

Naming standards need to be created to simplify the CMDB. This will make database queries quicker and more understandable. The name must be descriptive of the object it is identifying. A typical naming convention includes items such as function and location.

Base Architecture

It is important to create an architecture and system baseline. This is the start of what will eventually be the CMDB. The base architecture must include normal system configurations, security parameters, and software, hardware, and firmware versions. The architecture must include system owners and the people responsible for the various IT services that are being provided.

Platform Standards

A set of standards must be in place for system hardware and networking gear. There must be minimum performance and security parameters. These standards need to be documented and well understood by the IT staff. The standards can be used as parameter checks for the various CI components that will be entered into the CMDB.

Software Standards

Standards for software must also be in place. This is something that all of the IT staff must be well trained in. The software standards must be documented and reside in a place that is easily accessible; for example, the corporate IT portal. Software standards can also be used as CI parameter checks. The standards can frame various CI components and ensure that the CIs are not beyond the standard's scope.

Network Scanning

Network scanning must be an integral part of the CM team's toolbox for identifying systems and their active state. There are many tools that perform general detection services and there are others that specialize in particular areas that may not be covered by the general tools. A CM group must decide on the CIs they will look for and whether they will require the use of specialized tools.

Identifying Systems on the Network

A method for cataloguing and identifying system health needs to be deployed in environments with more than 100 systems. Over a certain number of systems, an IT organization usually does not have the capacity to scale and manually manage systems.

Identifying Rogue Systems

The same method that is used to identify systems on a corporate network can also be used to monitor for systems that are not managed. Systems that are either intentionally or unintentionally unmanaged are known as rogue systems, and are a real problem for many IT organizations. Unknown or unmanaged systems on the corporate network are the greatest security problem in most organizations.

Procedures

Procedures go beyond the policies and standards that the IT organization has created or adopted. Procedures are the specifics for a certain organization. A governmental organization will have very different procedures from a Silicon Valley startup. Procedure specifics come down to how IT is aligned with the organization to make it function more efficiently. CM procedures are the documented operation functions of CM.

Installation and Configuration Guidance

There is an obvious need for specific installation and configuration guidance. For most organizations this goes beyond the documentation provided by a vendor. The IT organization must maintain documents specific to the environment that helps end users customize their systems to the company's environment.

Configuration Change Procedures

Configuration management documentation must contain procedures on how to initiate or modify a configuration. This can flow into the change management process which will be discussed later in this book.

New Product Introduction Procedure

Documented procedures for introducing new software and hardware configurations into the CMDB must exist. Introducing new software or hardware configurations into an environment can dramatically increase the amount of complexity, testing required, and overall work for the IT organization.

Control

Configuration management control needs to be in place to ensure that CIs are managed in a way that the integrity of the attributes is maintained (Figure 3.4). In the case of CM, control over who has access to the CMDB and what goes in is crucial. This is a task that is delegated to the CM librarian. This individual needs to maintain control over the input and output of the CMDB so that the information is reliable and used in the correct manner.

Policies

A policy must be in place to define the CMDB input and output process. It defines who has access to the information, when it is used, and how it is changed. When

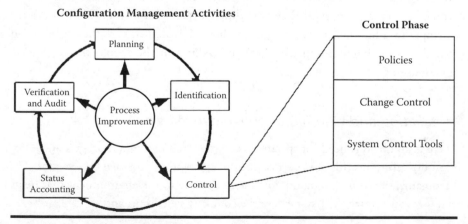

Figure 3.4 Configuration management control.

creating policies for control, the focus needs to be on making sure that hardware, software, and users are in compliance with organizational policies. These can be controlled and managed by the automation systems that IT has in place. The policies that a CM team needs to ensure are in place include change policy, identification policy, system software policy, system lifecycle policy, system usage policy, and system security policy.

Change Control

Change control in the context of CM is a tool that can ensure that configurations stay in their baseline state. With tight change controls in place, an organization takes control of their environment and ensures that systems will only be changed with proper validation checks. Change control is very interested in the management of CIs and changes to specific CIs. The change control process include the following steps:

- Change approval—Once the change review board has been notified they are given a timeframe in which to approve or reject the change. The approval process involves all of the change stakeholders. They make sure the changes do not adversely affect existing systems. If the change is approved, the request moves on to the next level.
- Change implementation—With the change approved, it is then assigned a timeframe in which the requester can make the change. The change operations need to follow the documented procedures in the change request. Any deviation from the change request procedures will invalidate any assurance given by the approval committee. The requester needs to make the change in the assigned timeframe and also provide any required reporting metrics.
- Change reporting—The change reporting process includes listing the change in the change management system. Automated change management systems are much easier to use than manual systems. An automated change management system includes the required individual involvement per its setup.
- Change review—After the change has been implemented, mature change control programs review the change to see if there is anything that can be done to improve the process. The change review should ensure that the process was followed per the change request. If there are any issues with a change, the change review will help a company identify where the process broke down and how to fix it.

System Control Tools

There are CMDB tools that automate many of the management functions. The controls on a CMDB can also be as simple as field constraints in a form. Field constraints are typical in most forms-based programs. They make sure that a specific form field follows specific parameters. In the case of a CMDB, a form parameter might ensure that a server name follows the organization's naming conventions.

Status Accounting

Configuration management status accounting focuses on ensuring that machines in the management process are monitored throughout the entire process (Figure 3.5). The status of machines and other components needs to be tracked through the CM process to ensure control is maintained.

Configuration Management Lifecycle

The CM lifecycle is a component of CM. The CM lifecycle is the movement of CIs throughout the CM process. Tracking of components through the lifecycle is important to ensure that the operations people are ready to perform the tasks when they need to be executed. Lifecycle tracking can help with resource planning.

Configuration Management Change Status Modes

When reporting the status of CIs it is important to use terms that are clear to all involved and reading the reports. When accounting for CM status, an organization needs to look at each component within CM and list the status of each. In addition to status modes, the processes can also be ranked in a maturity model. The status of the various CM components must be reported to IT management so that they can

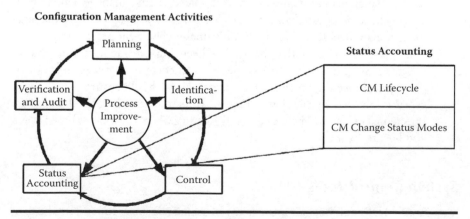

Figure 3.5   Configuration management accounting.

correct any problems. Terms that are generally used when noting CI status include in development, tested, live, and retired.

Verification

Configuration management status can be an automated process that is integrated into the overall system monitoring process (Figure 3.6). There are tools that can report system versions, types, etc. These tools can help make the overall monitoring process simple. Verification is the verification of CIs.

Compliance Checking

Configuration management relies on compliance checking to ensure that the approved system configurations are in place. There are many compliance tools that can check for a wide variety of configuration parameters. These tools must be deployed to manage systems. By using compliance management tools, organizations can increase their security.

Compliance Remediation

Compliance remediation is about enforcing the compliance policy set by IT management. This is important to CM because when systems are out of compliance it means they are also not running CM-approved configurations. The CM team needs to know about systems that are noncompliant so they can review the situation and resolve the problem. There will be times when the CMDB is missing a

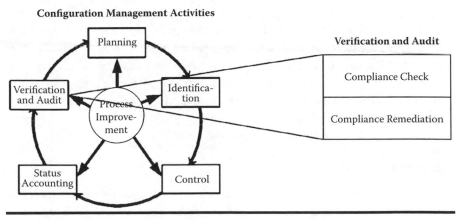

Figure 3.6   Configuration management verification and audit.

configuration, and if the CM and compliance team are synchronized they will be able to resolve any discrepancies.

The remediation steps can be tiered so that if a system cannot be resolved by one method it can be moved to the next level There are many things that can be done when a system is found to be noncompliant: automatically remediate, quarantine, terminate network connectivity, terminate the user account, or lock the user out of the system.

Configuration Management and Its Relationship to Other Programs

Configuration management affects many programs that exist in an IT organization. CM touches most of them in some way. Good CM either enhances related programs or has direct inputs and outputs that feed other programs.

Risk Management

Risk management is related to CM by the risk management and risk assessment processes. Risk assessments are needed to review configurations for risk. The risk management process takes the risk assessment and works toward risk reduction using different methods. This can include changes to configurations that greatly reduce risk.

Incident Management

Incident management uses CM processes and output when dealing with incidents. One of the first troubleshooting procedures is to look at what has changed from the original configuration. In most instances something on a system changed and caused the incident. If there was a hardware failure, CM is used to bring a system back to the IT standard baseline configuration. A subset of incident management is incident response. Incident response is a set of procedures that an organization uses to react to threats. The incident response process needs to be tightly integrated with the business continuity process.

Change Control

Change control and CM are probably the most closely tied processes. There are multiple inputs and outputs that flow between the two processes. Any change must be entered into the CMDB.

Information Technology Strategy

Configuration management must be aware of the IT strategy so that it can plan for the strategic changes that IT is planning. An organization's IT strategists must be aware of the CM process and the organization's specifications for the CM system. When the strategy is being created it must be CM aware so that it can seamlessly support the existing CM process.

Update Management

Configuration management relies on update management as one of the automated methods of deploying changes. The changes need to go through the change management process, but the update management system will ultimately roll out any patches to the system. The update management system can also be tightly integrated with the CMDB.

Compliance and Audit

Configuration management uses many compliance and audit reports. These reports can help the CM team identify items that should be managed by the CMDB. The CMDB can be used by the compliance team to create their compliance baseline. When the compliance team finds any discrepancies in compliance they can make sure that the CMDB is not missing anything that is in the IT production environment.

Operations

Information technology operations is the group that will consume all of the CMDB data and use it in deployment scenarios. They also provide valuable feedback to the CM group about issues that arise. The operations staff are the individuals that will eventually put the CM program components in place.

Information Technology Security

Information technology security is enhanced by CM. One of the greatest security issues is unknown and unmanaged systems. CM is a program that can bring unknown systems out of obscurity.

Conclusion

This chapter discusses all of the various CM concepts. Later chapters will delve much deeper into the details of CM. CM activities are shown in Figure 3.7. The

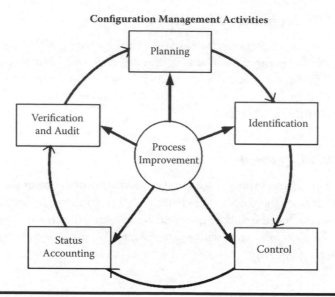

Figure 3.7   Configuration management activities.

CM activities are circular processes that need to be continually repeated. By repeating these activities, an IT organization will become increasingly efficient at performing them.

Chapter 4

Configuration Management Planning

Planning

The planning phase of configuration management (CM) ensures that the correct processes, goals, strategies, and policies are in place (Figure 4.1). Initial planning requires a large amount of time to ensure the program is successful. Without correct planning for CM the program will fail. Once the program is up and running, periodic reviews and changes will be required. In this chapter the planning phase of CM is reviewed in depth.

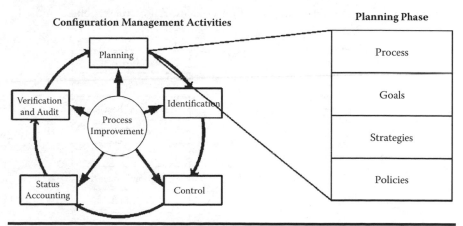

Figure 4.1   Configuration management planning.

Processes

Configuration management processes govern normal CM operations. The processes that are listed here are now to plan for a CM program. The phases of identify, control, status accounting, and verification audit all need to be considered when creating processes. Each phase of the operational process associated with running a CM program must be documented.

Form a Configuration Management Team

The first step in creating a CM program is the creation of a CM team. The CM team includes management, testing, the CM librarian, administrators, support, and strategy. The team members should be split into two different types: CM focused employees and advisory members. The CM focused employees focus on CM functions and applications. Advisory members provide input to the overall program.

The CM employees include the CM librarian, CM software administrators, and the CM program manager. CM advisors include IT testing, support, management, and strategy personnel. For a CM program to be successful, all of these roles need to be filled. Every role is important so that all of those affected will have a say in the program.

Create the Configuration Management Policy

Once the team has been created, they must meet to create the CM policy. The CM policy needs to be in line with overall IT policy. The policy should outline how the CM program will be governed and should include the CM baseline, timeline, compliance, lifecycle, and communication policies. All of these policies must be

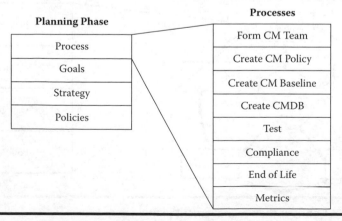

Figure 4.2 Configuration management planning processes.

in place to create a framework for the process. The CM stakeholders then perform specific tasks within this framework.

Create the Configuration Management Baseline

With the staff and policies in place, it is time to create the CM baseline. In most environments there will be multiple baselines or core platforms. Even though multiple baselines will be needed, the CM team must try to keep this number to a minimum. There are many tools the CM operations team can use to baseline systems. If a system management program is deployed, the operations team can use the output to create system baselines. Baselines can also be created manually, but then human error can come into play. The system baselines need to be well documented so that they can be duplicated in both an automated and manual fashion. The baseline configurations should be maintained in the lab.

Create the Configuration Management Database

To create the configuration management database (CMDB), the CM team must define the configuration items (CIs) (Table 4.1). Defining CIs is one of the most important operations the CM team will perform. The CIs are items that can be used to correctly configure a system in a specific IT environment. CIs need to be created for various devices, software packages, and components that are critical to business operations.

The CMDB implements and uses all of the CIs that are created by the CM team. The team must focus on making sure that needed attributes are included; they also need to ensure that unneeded attributes are eliminated.

Testing

The CM test process should focus on configuration validation. The process should be automated in larger environments, but in smaller environments there may not be the budget for automation tools. The test process must include:

- Configuration validation—The test group performs configuration validation to make sure that all accepted configurations are compatible with the production environment.
- Baseline creation—The test group creates the system baselines for the CM system. The baselines should be robust configurations that are considered stable. Baselines will be used later for troubleshooting starting points.

■ Application compatibility—The test group performs application compatibility testing. This operation will take up most of their time. Application compatibility is a huge task that continually cycles through the test organization.
■ New system validation—The test group validates new systems when they are brought into the environment. New systems need to meet minimum requirements, including compatibility with the existing environment.

Compliance

Configuration management compliance checks for compliance with the CM baseline. The key to a successful compliance program is the use of automated tools. Compliance and CM intersect in many different functions. The CM team needs to have access to compliance system output. The compliance output allows the CM

Table 4.1 CMDB CI Selection

IT component	Possible configuration items
Hardware	Firmware, configuration files, firmware settings
Operating system software	Installation configuration files, configuration settings
Business software	Installation configuration files, configuration settings
Other software packages	Installation configuration files, configuration settings
Databases	Database configuration, database setup files
Environments	Environment variables
Database connectors	Database connector settings
Configuration baselines	System baseline settings
Software releases	Software update settings
Configuration documentation	Documentation
Change documentation	Documentation
User information	User settings
Contractor information	Contractor information
Service level agreements	Service level agreements
Network components	Network settings, configuration settings
Service management components	Service software setup
Records	Records
Workflow	Workflow settings
Procedures	Procedure documentation
Business processes	Business process documentation
License information	License documentation

team to understand how the configuration core settings are working. The compliance team can then use the CM baseline to gauge compliance, and when noncompliant systems are discovered, they can take action to remediate the issues.

End of Life

Within the CM framework, the end of life process is focused on retiring configurations. Configurations need to be retired so that the CM system does not become overloaded with outdated information.

Configuration Management Metrics

Configuration management metrics focus on the success or failure of the CM components. The process must be about identifying specific data points to measure. The CM metrics process defines what the output from those data points means. The metrics allow the overall CM program to improve and provide an understanding of where change needs to occur. The key to making metrics an integral part of the CM IT process is to make sure that the metrics output is presented in a way that can influence management. The operations team should learn what is important to management and then work to convert raw data into valuable business data. The data should help IT management make decisions that will improve IT performance and operations.

Goals

Configuration management should have some well-defined goals so that the direction of the CM group is clear (Figure 4.3). The goals need to ensure that the CM program is operational and efficient. CM goals should include:

- Configuration simplification
- Centralized management
- Application consolidation and reduction
- Unified policy
- Standardized security
- Minimize support costs
- Improved security
- Reduced training needs
- Ease of system rollout
- List supported and tested configurations
- End of life for obsolete software and hardware
- Support business and IT functions

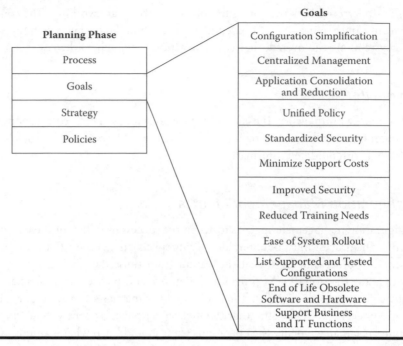

Figure 4.3 Configuration management planning goals.

Configuration management goals may include other targets. Listed are some of the things that will happen automatically when a well-run CM program is implemented. The goals of the CM program must be focused on the control of system configuration. The CM program owner should hold a kickoff meeting with representatives from the following groups: management, testing, CM librarian, administrators, support, and strategy. All configuration meetings should be very open and interactive.

Configuration Simplification

Configuration simplification should be a goal of the CM group. IT organizations seem to add configurations without viewing the overall picture. The more complex a configuration is, the more difficult it is to troubleshoot. Trying to troubleshoot a system with too much software or a machine that is tasked with too many services is almost impossible. The main technique in troubleshooting issues is to remove all of the layers of software until the system is in a known working state and then to dig through the remaining log files to identify the offending component. Simpler configurations make this process much simpler. Things that one can do to simplify configurations include:

■ Improve your software and hardware retirement system.
■ Remove unused configurations.

- Automate processes.
- Simplify scripts.
- Choose software that is simple to configure.

Centralized Management

Configuration management must be centralized in a CMDB. This is one of the key CM elements that has been introduced to IT by the Information Technology Infrastructure Library (ITIL) best practices. Many vendor-based systems provide centralized management tools, including IBM Tivoli, CA Enterprise System Management, Symantec ESM, EMC/Nlayers CMDB, Microsoft System Center suite, BMC Atrium, and HP Openview. All of these are well respected products for managing systems. The eventual selection needs to be based on the company's IT needs. When considering deploying a management suite, an organization should make sure the vendor addresses the following:

- How many users (minimum and maximum) can the software handle?
- Make sure the software solution is not too small or too large for the organization.
- Do you have a list of CIs that the software manages?
- Check this list against the list of CIs you are looking to monitor.
- What do you consider the technical strengths of the software?
- Ensure their focus is yours. Some software may be security or storage centric and may not be a good fit for your organization.
- How long have you been producing management software?
- The more mature systems will have many more CIs and options. More can be good or bad, depending on your organization. Organizations should make sure they are not purchasing a $500,000 desk warmer. A correctly sized management system is critical to the system's success.
- Which database types do you support?
- If the system supports a database other than what you run in your organization it may require you to incur the additional costs of training staff on a new database type or hiring new staff.

Application Consolidation and Reduction

Application consolidation is a difficult task for organizations that are in a reactive mode. Application functionality is being combined into stronger, more effective solution suites. It is in the best interest of both IT and the end user to reduce the number of applications that are required to do one's job. IT must always be looking for ways to consolidate applications. User stores are an area that all IT departments should strive to minimize. With the boom in applications over the past 10 years, user information has become a huge security risk. Metadirectory technology is something that has helped IT departments consolidate user stores and user information.

Unified Policy

Policy unification across all IT groups is essential. Unified policies can help ensure that the deployed solutions work together toward a single business goal. When the CM group creates and reviews policies that effect CM, the group needs to ensure that all policies are aligned with the organization's overall objectives. A company that has lax human resources and company policies may not be able to enforce strict CM policy. In this case, CM staff need to be creative in their authoring of policy. When dealing with difficult operating environments, the best approach is automation. Automation can help the IT group accomplish its mission without the end user being affected.

Standardized Security

Information security must be aligned with industry security standards and regulations. Some organizations must comply with various governmental regulations, including the Sarbanes-Oxley Act of 2002 (SOX), Basel II, Committee of Sponsoring Organizations of the Treadway Commission (COSO), and the Federal Information Security Management Act of 2002 (FISMA). The mandated measures are usually prescriptive and do not specify a method or technology to achieve compliance. IT must work to define its compliance with regulations. The best way to achieve this and prove that an organization has done its due diligence is to adopt industry standards and best practices. Information security best practices include International Organization for Standardization (ISO) standards, National Institute of Standards and Technology (NIST) standards, Information Technology Infrastructure Library (ITIL) best practices, and IT Governance Institute (ITGI) best practices.

Adopting the above standards shows an IT organization is well informed about industry standards and the latest management techniques. Standards should be used by organizations as a framework for their own method of meeting compliance obligations. Because standards are written in broad language with room for interpretation, they can be adapted to meet specific business needs. Most organizations will need to adapt the standards to fit in their business framework.

Minimize Support Costs

This is an obvious goal for most companies, but the use of CM to achieve this goal is not always as clear. If CM is not in place, the initiation of CM will incur costs.

Once the CM program is up and running there are numerous aspects that will help organizations minimize support costs. Some ways that CM can reduce support costs include:

- A single point for configuration information—A CMDB can greatly improve service efficiency. By giving the support staff a place to gather information on configurations they can identify application incompatibilities.
- A baseline troubleshooting platform—The baseline improves service by reducing troubleshooting time. With a baseline, support can easily track changes to a system by using simple commands like sysdiff. Sysdiff will perform a check and report the differences between two systems.
- Change management—Change management reduces the number of errors that could occur when changes are made. There must be a quality process of checks to ensure that all aspects of the changes are considered before they are made.
- Compliance information—Compliance checks will quickly identify systems that are out of compliance. By understanding when a system becomes noncompliant, IT can be proactive in remediating issues. In addition to remediation, it is important for IT to understand why the system became noncompliant.
- Automation—CM is focused on automating as many of the CM processes as possible. By increasing automation, service calls and the need for manual processes will be greatly reduced. This will allow service staff to focus on more complex issues instead of dealing with simple fixes that can be automated.

Improved Security

Configuration management can improve security for a company in many different ways, including:

- Management of base configurations—Security is enhanced by the existence of a base configuration. Configuration consistency always improves security by allowing security scanners to look for changes in the baseline. Any behavior different from the baseline will alert information security to trouble.
- Automation—Automation allows IT to check the configurations once and then be secure in the knowledge that the remaining systems that are automatically administered will be the same. This allows more scrutiny in the test lab of the initial image.
- Improved policy adherence—All of the automation and additional checks on any changes ensure that the information security policy is strictly followed. Information security must be involved in the CM process so that they can ensure that information security policy is addressed in the process.

Reduced Training Needs

Configuration management can help an organization target its training budget. This targeted training will ensure that needed skills are available. Other requirements for training can be reduced with the use of automation.

Ease of System Rollout

A goal of CM should be to make system rollout easier than if CM did not exist. The automation and asset management systems that come with a mature CM program will greatly enhance the rollout experience for both IT management and end users. Using management systems to push all software reduces the need for IT to physically touch systems. When the hands-on work is minimized, staff can focus on improving process and quality.

Support Business and Information Technology Configurations

Configuration management must look toward IT's role within the business and further the goals of the business. Within IT, many times the people become too focused on specific technologies that may be trendy, but if the business doesn't exist, the IT organization doesn't either. IT must look for ways to automate business functions and make the business more efficient.

End of Life of Obsolete Software and Hardware

The CM group within an organization must include an end of life program for software and hardware. System retirement is one of the most overlooked programs in IT. Improving the way an IT organization retires systems can produce huge gains in productivity. Some of the benefits of a mature end of life program include:

■ Less work—By successfully retiring old software and hardware, a company reduces the amount of work needed to support old systems. IT organizations should look very hard at new systems and work hard to reduce them. Each new hardware or software component should be looked on as a work multiplier. If a company supports 20 applications and 5 versions of hardware in their environment, testing, support, etc., will need to consider 100 different possible configurations. If they also support multiple operating system (OS) versions, say 3 OS variations, then 100 configurations becomes 300 configurations. That does not even consider the possible multiple ways that each application can be configured. In the above scenario, if the supported options are reduced so that only 2 OSs are supported with 10 applications and 3 hardware options, the number of supported configurations is reduced from 300 to 60.

- Simplified operations—Retiring systems will simplify operations. This is another easily demonstrated benefit from the previous example. A reduction in configuration options makes the job of operations much easier.
- Ease of support—Retirement will simplify support options also. Support needs to have an intricate familiarity with all of the possible configuration options, and a reduction in the number of possible options will make support easier and improve the quality.
- Improved system performance—A reduction in system requirements will free hardware resources to be used by the existing software components. Every system administrator knows that to increase system speed you can always add more memory, but reducing the load on a system frees up system resources for use by existing programs.

Strategy

Configuration management strategy is the plan of execution (Figure 4.4). The strategy is one of the outputs of CM planning meetings. The strategy addresses how to deliver a working program. The strategy is an evolving entity that needs to change as programs change.

Short-Term

The short-term strategy covers the tasks that need to be completed in the next 3 months. The short-term strategy must also contain the initial steps of longer term projects and anything the CM program needs done immediately. The short-term strategy should include urgent needs, quick hits, impacts, and budget.

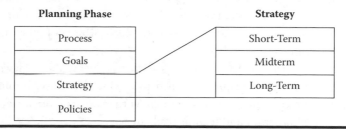

Figure 4.4   Configuration management planning strategy.

Urgent Needs

When building a CM strategy, one must look at what the missing pieces are in the overall strategy. Urgent CM needs include:

- CM program—If a CM program does not exist, that should be the first task on the strategy list. The CM program must be well planned and focused on providing a framework that will manage the configuration information within the organization.
- Incidents—Incidents should always be given a high priority and inserted into the short-term strategy. Large-scale incidents can spin an IT department into a reactionary mode that will halt all other activity. Well-planned incident response processes need to be followed so that the team can recover from the incident and execute a strategy to resolve the incident.
- Changes—Changes will hopefully be short-term needs that can be taken care of quickly.
- CM team—When building a CM program, one of the first things that needs to happen is to select team members. The team members can then be part of planning and strategizing.

Quick Hits

The short-term strategy for CM must contain any quick, easy-to-resolve issues. Any missing component that can easily be added to the CM program must become part of the short-term strategy. Any quick program successes will help boost team spirit and allow it to continue on to more complicated tasks. A fledgling CM program should consider the following quick hits:

- CM overview documentation—When a CM program is new, the complete program needs to be documented. Documentation can change over time, but getting that initial revision out to guide the implementation process is crucial.
- CM organizational structure—The CM organizational structure must be posted as soon as the team has been solidified. This will allow interaction among team members to begin.
- CM strategy plans—When creating a strategy, once it is reviewed by the team, the strategy must be published to a wider audience. Publishing the strategy is an easy quick hit that will allow the entire IT organization to see that the CM program and team is ready to act.
- CM policies—CM policies must be published once the newly formed CM team has them hammered out. This is another step in the creation of the CM program that shows the rest of the organization that CM is coming.

■ CM process documentation—The CM process needs to be documented and inserted into the broader IT and corporate process flow. The process publishing task allows the team to set timelines for implementation.

Impact

The short-term strategy needs to contain projects that will have the greatest impact on the program in a short period of time. This can include missing CM components or things that will address a change in an organization's business model.

Budget

When building a CM strategy, the budget must always be considered. The greatest plans can be useless without adequate funding. Short-term strategies need to be inserted into the existing budget cycle. Short-term strategic projects need to use as little budget as possible.

Midterm

Midterm CM strategy includes those items that need to be taken care of in the 6-month to 1-year timeframe. This is where projects that are not short term, but are still required, can be addressed. Midterm projects can be prepared for in the short term and executed in the midterm. Midterm projects may be critical but require more planning and time then a short-term project. This is where the bulk of IT is executed. The midterm strategy includes plans for yearly IT projects. The midterm strategy must consider long-term strategy goals.

Yearly Projects

Many of IT's yearly projects are the execution of strategic plans. This is true for not only CM, but for all groups, standards, and methodologies that an IT organization employs. Yearly projects will always be one of the main functions of an IT organization. CM yearly projects can include CMDB deployment, CMDB upgrading, CM baselining, and CM process improvement.

Identified Needs

In the midterm, projects come up that need to be completed quickly. When these projects are identified, they need to be addressed and a strategy created. IT must have processes that will identify needs for specific projects. Some activities that may apply to specific projects are risk assessments, end user reviews, management reviews, and business reviews.

Long-Term

Long-term strategies must be forward-thinking and be more research focused. Long-term strategies must set the direction of the IT organization and are determined by the needs of the business. The long-term strategy must take into account the metrics that are reported to the IT department. These metrics can identify areas for improvement. Long-term strategies should focus on improving manageability, enhancing the system lifecycle, improving security, and improving the CM process.

Improve Manageability

The long-term CM strategy needs to improve manageability. The strategy must further the CM goals of giving the IT organization more control over configurations via automation and sound management principles. The strategy can identify specific technologies or standards that are of particular importance.

Enhance System Lifecycle

Something to consider when building a long-term strategy is that any strategy and solution must meet all policies and lifecycle timelines that are already in place. It does not make sense to embark on a 5-year project when the hardware will be obsolete in 2 years. The long-term CM strategy should consider vendor system lifecycles in their plans.

Improve Security

Configuration management must always remain security conscious. Strategies should not diminish security, and if possible, the best situation is to have security improve as an IT organization progresses. The CM goal of justifying changes and controlling configurations will always improve security because when changes happen within the CM framework they are controlled.

Improve the Configuration Management Process

Long-term CM strategies must always include how to improve the CM process. Improving the CM process includes:

- Tool upgrades—Upgrading to the latest tools will ensure that the CM program is able to grow and keep up with new technologies.
- Policy changes—Over time, policies will need to be changed to compensate for overall program changes. These changes need to be reflected in the policies so that the CM program remains effective.
- CI changes—As a program grows, there may be new requirements that need new CIs. The CIs need to reflect the organization and the things that it needs to monitor.

Policies

Policies are the documents that define how CM will occur in an organization (Figure 4.5). Policies should be not too technically specific and should be enforceable. There will be some CM-specific policies, but there will be other general IT policies that are influenced by CM.

Device Policy

Most IT organizations will already have a device policy, but before a CM program is initiated a CM-specific policy will be needed. The CM stakeholders need to ensure that CM policy specifics are inserted into the device policy. The device policy should include the following CM attributes:

- Device CIs—Device CIs must be noted in the device policy. A policy for the CIs will help CM make sure that the CIs exist and are noted.
- Device lifecycle timeframes—The device policy must include device lifecycle timeframes. The policy can be as simple as company x will retire devices when the vendor support lifecycle is up. It can also be more difficult: system type x must be supported by vendors for x number of years. IT organizations can negotiate support lifecycles with vendors. Many times a company can extend support for programs that are retired for a fee.
- Mandated device configurations—The device policy must mandate specific device configurations. Newer operating systems for devices are beginning to add management software that can automate device configuration. The device policy should also indicate the device configuration location.
- Recommended hardware list—The device policy must include a recommended hardware list. By following the recommended hardware list, the selected devices can easily be supported by the support staff. There should be consequences for deviating from the recommended list.

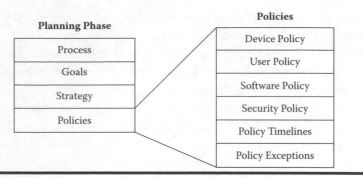

Figure 4.5 Configuration management planning policies.

User Policy

The CM policy must cover any users that have access to or use corporate resources. This can be considered an extension of the compliance product arena. The user policy may also include user behavior mandates that force specific actions. User policy should include password restrictions, usage policy, and authentication methods.

Software Policy

Configuration management policy must cover all software that is deployed on company resources. This may even extend beyond company resources; for example, contractors using their computers on a company's internal network may be required to have a current antivirus image. Software policy should contain the following:

- Authorized software—The software policy must contain an authorized software list.
- Software usage policy—The software usage policy needs to note how company software should be used. The policy must state the consequences for noncompliance.

Security Policy

The security policy must be very specific to the organization and its security needs. Security needs vary greatly depending on the type of business. CM stakeholders must influence security policy makers to ensure that the security policy has CM-specific policies to help CM be effective. The security policy should include:

- Compliance policy—The compliance policy will help CM by ensuring that configurations are maintained. The policy must include a definition of compliant and noncompliant systems.

- Business continuity policy—The business continuity policy describes where CM will be used to bring systems online in case the business continuity plan needs to be executed.
- Change control policy—Change control policy should be very heavy with CM mandates. The policy should contain the following components:
    All changes must be entered into the CMDB.
    Changes must be tested by CM.
    Changes must be packaged into the CM system.
    The CM system will deliver packages.
- Access control policy—Access control is very configuration heavy. The access control policy should ensure that programs use only authorized access methods. The policy must include access levels based on asset value.

Policy Timelines

Configuration management policies need to have timelines assigned to specific tasks. The timelines must be specific so that the guidance provided to end users will be understood. Many times the timelines for tasks can be automated and made compulsory.

Policy Exceptions

Configuration management policy needs to allow exceptions. When creating exceptions to a policy there must be a time when the exception is released and is no longer in effect. Many organizations have an exception policy where the exceptions go through a rigorous process before they are accepted. This process must have the correct people involved so that exceptions are given when needed, but not handed out too easily to protect corporate security.

Conclusion

The planning phase of CM is about setting up the framework for a successful CM program. With proper planning, the CM program will be successful.

Chapter 5

Configuration Management Identification

Configuration management (CM) identification is focused on determining what resources will be included in the management program (Figure 5.1). Identification needs to frame the CM environment so that it is understood. Identification can be a function of an automated system. The identification program contains the following parts: infrastructure, network scanning, and procedures.

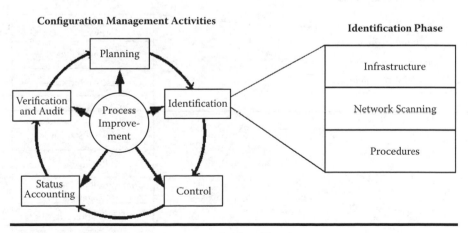

Figure 5.1   Configuration management identification.

Infrastructure

When identifying configuration items (CIs), leveraging the information technology (IT) infrastructure is the way to go. In a managed IT environment there are usually many different tools that can be used to identify systems on the network. These tools can acquire all kinds of information from the computers on a network. The task of the CM group is to identify which items to manage within the CM framework. The CM group also needs to build the architecture and systems required to manage configurations. The identification infrastructure includes the following components (Figure 5.2):

- Hardware and software owners
- Naming standards
- Base architecture
- Platform standards
- Software standards
- Intelligence
- Configuration management database (CMDB)
- Classification filtering
- Generalized risk and threat analysis

Hardware and Software Owners

Configuration management requires the identification of various components. Users, user groups, hardware groups, and software groups all need to be identified

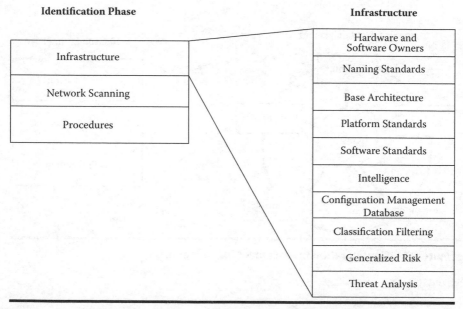

Figure 5.2   Configuration management identification infrastructure.

so that the correct components can be deployed to the correct groups. Many times these groups correspond with the business functions of various groups. All of this information must be contained in the CMDB so that the information can be duplicated and used for various additional operations. The system owners need to be determined so that they can be held accountable for any changes that are made to their systems. Changes to a single system are not quite as critical as changes made to systems that interact with other systems.

Naming Standards

Naming standards need to be created to simplify the CMDB. This will make database queries quicker and more understandable. The name must be descriptive of the object it is identifying. Some of the attributes to be considered when creating a naming standard are:

- Physical location
- Logical function
- Version number
- Software or hardware
- Users
- Backup or primary

Optimizing a naming convention can make the name descriptive enough that it contains all of the pertinent information one needs to know. An example of this is shown in Figure 5.3. The figure is a graphical example of a possible naming convention that indicates location, application, function, and building/room number. There are many other things that one can use in creating naming conventions, but they need to be targeted toward the item's use. The naming conventions that are

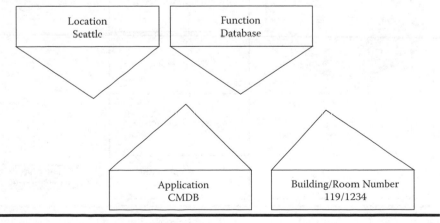

Figure 5.3   Identification naming convention.

adopted by an organization should be specific to that organization. This will allow users to easily understand a components attribute solely by its name.

Base Architecture

It is important to create an architecture that defines the CM operations and communications plan. The architecture must be specific to how the team will execute its strategy. This is the beginning of the design process for what will eventually be included in the CMDB. This architecture is what will drive the main design for the CM function. The base architecture should include CMDB design, a communications plan, CM architecture strategy, and the relationship of CM to other processes.

Configuration Management Database Design

Figure 5.4 is a sample CMDB design diagram. A key thing to note in the CMDB design is the connection to other applications. Most CMDB applications contain the components that are listed in Figure 5.4. They will need to be reviewed by the CM team to make sure that the provided components meet the organization's needs. Areas that usually require additional development work include reporting

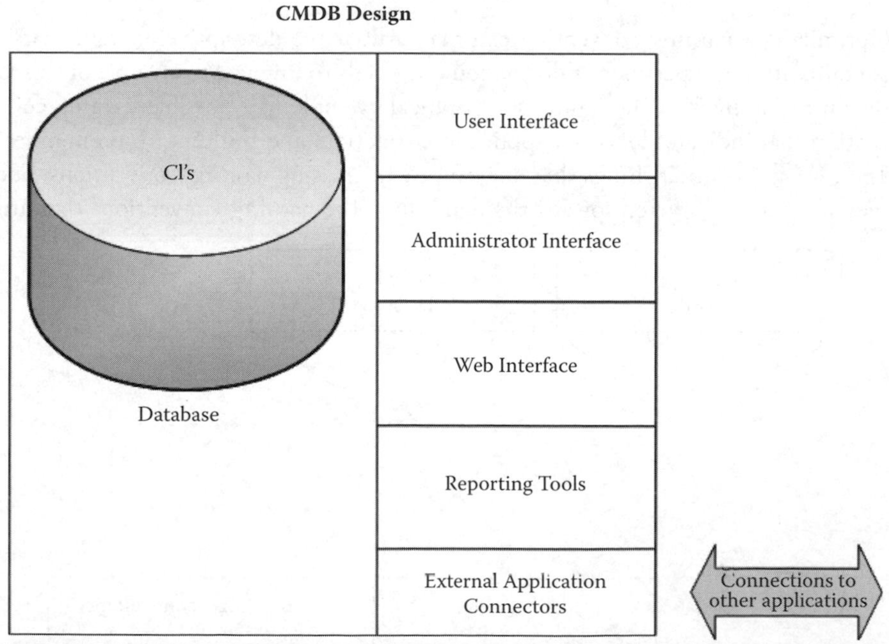

Figure 5.4 Configuration management database design.

tools and any connections to external applications. There are many applications that contain CIs, and creating connectors to other applications will greatly reduce the amount of manual data entry.

Communications Plan

A communications plan is critical to the smooth operation of a CM program. The CM communications plan is similar to the change control plan. CM communications enable the introduction and removal of configurations into the process. The CM communications plan should also be able to deal with any exceptions or errors that may exist in the system.

Configuration Management Architecture Strategy

The CM architecture strategy is the action plan that executes the architecture. The architecture must identify the individuals needed to fill the CM roles. The architecture should include the communications and operations components. The CM architecture strategy should be specific to the organization rolling out the CM process and to that team's specific timelines and intricacies.

Configuration Management Relationship to Other Processes

When designing the CM architecture, there should be an emphasis on how CM affects other IT programs and processes. CM will affect most programs positively by streamlining troubleshooting and operations in general. Some operations will be affected by longer test processes and more formal procedures for operations. These minor difficulties should be accepted when they are weighed against all of the positives that come from the overall CM program.

Platform Standards

A set of standards must be in place for system hardware and networking gear. There must be minimum performance and security parameters. These standards need to be documented and well understood by the IT staff. The standard that should be closely reviewed when building out a CM program is the Information Technology Infrastructure Library (ITIL) service and support best practices document. An organization must also review its regulatory requirements. If there are any regulations that the organization needs to comply with, the CM program must include this information.

Software Standards

Standards for software must also be in place. This is something that all of the IT staff must be well trained in. The software standards must be documented and reside in a place that is easily accessible; for example, the corporate IT portal is a good place to store corporate software standards.

Intelligence

An organization should understand the information they will be managing and processing so that the correct controls can be put in place. Information needs to be both secure and available. Information about systems and controls also needs to be maintained in a controlled manner. Detailed documents about system architecture and configurations should be controlled so that only people that need the information have access to it. All of the gathered information should be placed in a centrally managed location. Configuration intelligence can be gathered from many locations. Automated technical tools can gather most of the technical information, but there are other components that may require manual methods. Questionnaires should be created for users of corporate systems. These questionnaires can gather information that software programs cannot. There are questions that should be asked of both IT administrators and managers as well as end users. Some questions that should be asked on a CM questionnaire to end users include:

- Do you use corporate systems?
- What do you use IT systems for?
- Do you memorize your password or write it down?
- If you have issues with your system, what is your next step?
- Have you installed software on your system?
- Where did you get the software you installed?
- Does this software work well?
- Was the software packaged by the IT department?
- Are you aware of the IT usage policy?
- Do you feel your system is secure?
- Do you think your system is adequately supported by the IT staff?
- Do you know what CM is?

Some questions that should be asked of administrators include:

- Are deployment policies followed?
- Do you think you have management support for your job?
- Do you feel security policies are followed?

- Do you feel the CM team is adequately staffed?
- Do you think that CM has the correct CIs selected?
- Do you feel the CMDB is managed correctly?
- Does the CMDB service have enough hardware to do a good job?

Some questions that should be asked of IT management include:

- Do you feel the IT staff has adequate support in performing CM operations?
- Is compliance with CM policy enforced?
- Do you feel you have adequate budget to support the CM function?
- Do you have enough staff on the CM team?
- Do you feel the CMDB is managed correctly?
- Does your staff have the correct skill set to do their jobs?
- Do you think end users are satisfied with the CM service?
- Who are the CM end users?

There are many other questions that can be asked to gather intelligence from staff and users of the CM system. This intelligence process is a way management can gain insight into operations beyond software-based approaches.

Configuration Management Database

The CMDB is an emerging area on which more organizations are beginning to focus. CMDB is a concept that was first introduced by the UK's Office of Government Commerce in the ITIL, however, it has not been standardized beyond the loose definition ITIL initially created. This leaves CMDB open to some broad vendor-based interpretations. The products that are available vary broadly in function and form.

All of the product-based issues aside, the idea of a CMDB is pretty simple. It is a place to store configuration setting details so that they are easily accessible. This simple information can then be used by many other IT functions. Change control, help desk, etc., can all be enhanced by access to a central repository of configuration information.

Configuration Items

Determining the CIs that are managed by a CMDB is where there will be considerable work when an organization is ready to deploy a CMDB. There may be hundreds of components to store when it comes to system setup. A way to simplify this is to ensure that the CMDB vendor you select has organizational CI lists that mirror your own. The CIs should also be built based on the configuration baseline. These baselines are extremely useful in troubleshooting support issues. An example is when a system comes from HP, the system will have basic elements installed and configured. IT may modify the system by adding and removing software. A user then adds some personal identification information. All of this information can be stored in the CMDB so that if the system has problems, IT can track changes to the system and make the necessary corrections.

Populating

Populating a CMDB should be done when a system is brought into the infrastructure and when any changes are made to the system. By populating the CMDB when a system is created or changed, the loss of information can be reduced. It is imperative that the information in the CMDB be correct. Otherwise, any troubleshooting on problem systems could be in vain. There should be a very precise and followed process for populating the CMDB. All systems should be double-checked so that there are no problems after configuration.

Updating and Maintenance

The maintenance of the CMDB is all about the change management process and how it is integrated into the CMDB. Any changes to the system need to be reflected in the CMDB. Any deviation from this will render the CMDB useless.

Classification Filtering

There are many ways of classifying and grouping various components. The major groupings are usually by operating system (OS) and application. This can be modified based on the business or organization. An example would be a service-oriented business, which would probably have a homogeneous environment and not need an OS classification. This organization would be best suited to organize their systems into either applications or job functions. An engineering organization would probably have systems that are very specialized, with many different types of OS builds and highly specialized configurations. Classification should invariably come down to a decision based on what an organization is tasked with doing. Figure 5.5 presents a graphical representation of filtering techniques.

By using filters, the larger configuration groups can become easily managed subgroups. In larger organizations there may be multiple CMDB administrators who focus on specific subgroups. Most management software will support multi-layered subgroup creation.

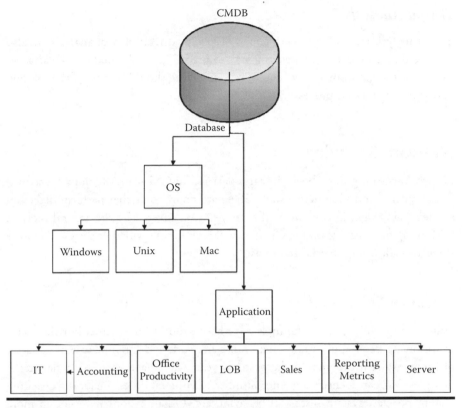

Figure 5.5 **Configuration management database filtering techniques.**

Compilation and Storage of Information

Management systems, and ultimately the CMDB, should be considered high-value information. With this information an attacker can penetrate most systems. Thus organizations should take every precaution to protect this information. These controls should make sense based on the organization's need.

Generalized Risk

Risk is something that all IT organizations must always think about. In the context of CM, risk analysis should be completed on a regular basis. Risk analysis is a review of the risks that a specific application or system is vulnerable to. Many times the risk analysis is performed by a consultant who can then suggest controls that can be applied to reduce the risk. The controls can be either technical solutions or some other measure, including physical, procedural, or insurance. In addition to controls, one can also accept risk as part of the system.

Threat Analysis

Threat analysis is a more in-depth review of specific threats. Threat analysis can also include threat modeling, which is a way to predict possible methods an attacker might use to compromise a system. Threat modeling should be part of the solution and application build process.

Network Scanning

Network scanning must be an integral part of the CM team's toolbox for identifying systems and their active state. There are many tools that perform detection services; some specialize in areas that may not be covered by the general tools. A CM group must decide on the CIs they will look for and whether they will require the use of additional specialized tools.

Vulnerability Scanning

System vulnerability scanning tools have been around for a while, but they have traditionally been applications that scan a network and attempt to execute a set of known system exploits. In the past few years there have been many new technologies that can identify a greater number of vulnerabilities, including checking system policies, system historical behavior, etc. Organizations have gotten more sophisticated in their system scanning and will continue to evolve as additional technologies are adopted (e.g., Network Admission Control [NAC] and Network Access Protection [NAP]). In addition to the tools that are there to stop specific security threats, there are new tools emerging that take a compliance approach to scanning. These tools may not be focused on a specific threat, but review overall compliance and infrastructure health. Some of these tools are listed in Table 5.1.

Table 5.1   Vulnerability Scanning Tools

Health check systems	Intrusion detection and prevention	Security scan	Hacker tools
Microsoft NAP	Internet Security Systems (ISS) BlackICE	ISS	L0phtCrack
Cisco NAC	Symantec IDS	Symantec Security Check	Password Probe
	eEye Blink	eEye Retina	John the Ripper

Types of Systems and Scanned Vulnerabilities

A system scan policy should be in place before the system is initially scanned. The scan process can be very intrusive and, depending on the global location, may need to be disclosed to end users. In many countries, full disclosure of network user rights must be posted before a user connects. The policy should include the types of systems and vulnerabilities being scanned. This is a policy that should be reviewed frequently so it evolves with all of the new features that software makers are packing into their scanning tools. An interesting area is rogue systems. How do you tell someone that may not want to be controlled that they will be scanned and controlled on your network? At some point there will need to be some rules created to deal with rogue situations. System scan selection can be separated into groups that make sense for the organization. A possible breakdown is shown in Figure 5.6.

Frequency of Scans

The frequency of system scans depends on the organization's needs. There are some organizations that scan very frequently—every hour—and some that will randomly scan only once a week. New network protection technologies are evolving into quasi-real-time scans. The frequency will depend on the scanning solution's ability to assess a system's state and the volume of information it can handle. This will be determined by the technical design of the solution.

Frequency of Updates

When identifying information and systems for CM needs the tools that an organization uses should be considered. Most modern software can be updated directly

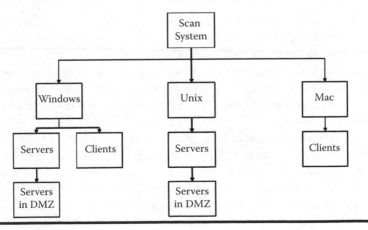

Figure 5.6   System scan selection breakdown.

from the software manufacturer or to some organizationally managed server. Direct update from the manufacturer works for most home consumers and small businesses that use off-the-shelf software. For large organizations, it is better to setup and push updates to managed devices; this way the organization can do their own tests on internal line of business applications. Application compatibility is one of the biggest issues that organizations face as they grow. There are many application and OS patch management programs; some of these are free, such as Microsoft's software update service. As the number of applications grows, manageability decreases. By maintaining control of the update process, organizations can maintain a high level of application compatibility.

Actions to Take Based on the Information Obtained

The remediation measures that one takes based on a system state can also vary greatly based on the solution deployed. Newer technologies are being designed to remove a threat in real time. Many of the current systems are dependent on human intervention to physically disable a network port or remove individual user access. In the area of remediation, newer systems are becoming increasingly automated. This reduces some of the cost, but it can also cause some difficulties when a user's access is based on a yes or no type of question. The fear many administrators have is that they will turn on enforcement policies and in one stroke turn off the CEO's access to the network. Fortunately most of the new access control technologies have a monitor mode where they can monitor noncompliance without taking any action. Another feature of some of the new technologies is the ability to fix a problem and then grant access.

Reporting and Alerting Requirements

The reporting mechanisms for system scanning should be well defined. The scan data, in a summarized form, should be available to those that need to make decisions based on the scans. The scan data can be used by security operations people to remediate specific vulnerabilities. The data can also be used to help with information security trending. Some specific threat reporting should be automated so that if critical systems are affected by a specific incident the correct staff is alerted immediately.

The identification process in most enterprise environments includes some form of system management software. Organizations may have a broad policy regarding reporting, in addition to specific policies for certain systems. System monitoring software usually has highly configurable reporting tools. By using these reporting metrics, IT management can create figures regarding return on investment (ROI) for specific systems, projects, and solutions. In addition to ROI, reporting can be used to trend system, staff, solution, and efficacy.

Escalation and Remediation Requirements

As issues are reported, there is a need for an escalation process based on the type of incident, its severity, etc. The process should define who is involved and in which stage of the incident they need to be included in the incident process. As with other escalation processes, there should be multiple classifications for incidents so that, based on severity, the correct individuals are involved. In the case of identified vulnerabilities, there should be a process for the remediation of vulnerabilities. This process should be able to handle all levels of vulnerability classification and exceptions.

Identifying Rogue Systems

The same method that is used to identify systems on a corporate network can also be used in many cases to monitor for systems that are not managed (i.e., rogue). Rogue systems are a large issue for many IT organizations. Unknown and unmanaged systems on the corporate network are the greatest security risk in most organizations.

Testing Facilities

To greater control the environment within an organization, a test lab is required. A test lab should be able to duplicate the live infrastructure. The test lab can be used to test all changes before they go into effect. A test lab can be used to test all new software and hardware in a live environment.

Receiving Updates

All IT departments should monitor the software they manage for updates. In addition to monitoring for updates, the person who manages software updates should make sure the updates are received from a trusted location where the software downloads can be verified in a secure manner. One of the greatest attack points for hackers is the downloading of software that has been tampered with.

Testing Updates

Before installing updates to systems in your environment, all updates should be tested in a test lab. This will allow you to determine if there are any application incompatibilities. In the lab, the back-out procedure should also be tested, but by doing the initial testing, most problems can be caught before the updates are installed.

Packaging Updates

Once the updates are ready and tested, they should be prepared in a way that they can be distributed to the environment without being tampered with. The packages and distribution process should be tested as well. The initial distribution should be a stepped process so that if there are any issues they can be caught and resolved before the package is distributed to the total environment.

Procedures

Procedures go beyond policies and standards that the IT organization has created or adopted. Procedures are the specifics for certain organizational functions. A governmental organization will have very different procedures from a Silicon Valley startup. The procedure specifics come down to how IT is aligned with the organization to make it function more efficiently.

Installation and Configuration Guidance

There is an obvious need for specific installation and configuration guidance. For most organizations this goes beyond the documentation provided by a vendor. The IT organization must maintain documents specific to its environment that help end users customize their systems to the company's environment. IT documents should include company recommended configurations, additional software, step-by-step guidance, company support information, and screen shots of each step.

Configuration Change Procedures

Configuration management documentation must contain the procedures for modifying a configuration. The change process is something that should be emphasized and noted as important. This can flow into the change management process, which will be discussed later in this book.

New Product Introduction Procedure

There must be documented procedures for introducing new software or hardware configurations into the CMDB (Figure 5.7). Introducing new software or hardware configurations into an environment can dramatically increase the complexity,

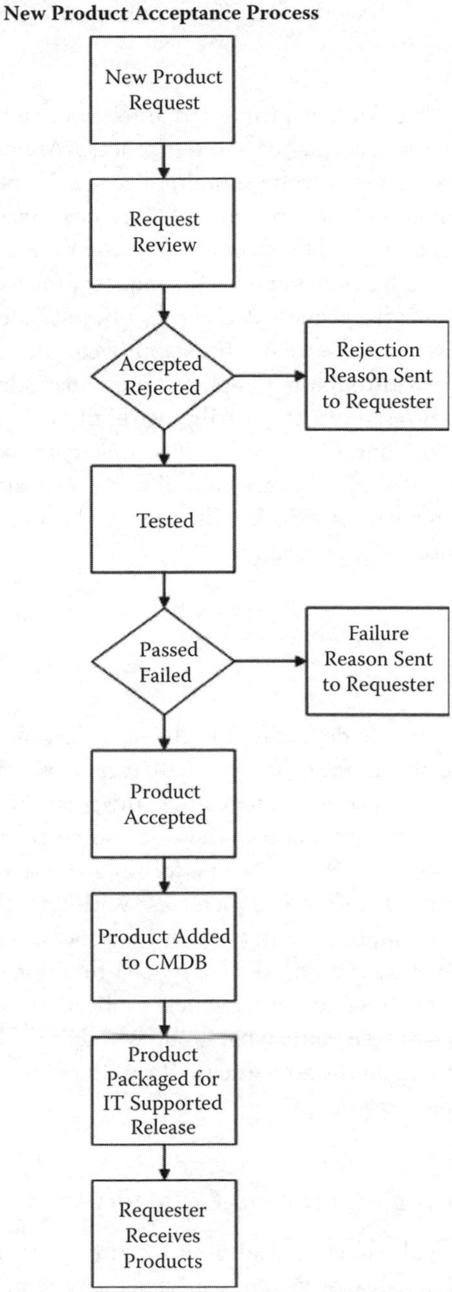

New Product Acceptance Process

```
          ┌─────────────┐
          │ New Product │
          │   Request   │
          └──────┬──────┘
                 ▼
          ┌─────────────┐
          │   Request   │
          │   Review    │
          └──────┬──────┘
                 ▼
             ◇─────────◇                ┌──────────────┐
            ╱ Accepted  ╲───────────────▶│  Rejection   │
            ╲ Rejected  ╱                │ Reason Sent  │
             ◇─────────◇                 │ to Requester │
                 ▼                       └──────────────┘
          ┌─────────────┐
          │   Tested    │
          └──────┬──────┘
                 ▼
             ◇─────────◇                ┌──────────────┐
            ╱  Passed   ╲───────────────▶│   Failure    │
            ╲  Failed   ╱                │ Reason Sent  │
             ◇─────────◇                 │ to Requester │
                 ▼                       └──────────────┘
          ┌─────────────┐
          │   Product   │
          │  Accepted   │
          └──────┬──────┘
                 ▼
          ┌─────────────┐
          │Product Added│
          │  to CMDB    │
          └──────┬──────┘
                 ▼
          ┌─────────────┐
          │   Product   │
          │ Packaged for│
          │IT Supported │
          │   Release   │
          └──────┬──────┘
                 ▼
          ┌─────────────┐
          │  Requester  │
          │  Receives   │
          │  Products   │
          └─────────────┘
```

Figure 5.7   New product acceptance process.

testing required, and overall work of the IT organization. Below is an example of a new product procedure:

> New products that will be introduced into company *x* need to go through an extensive acceptance and test process. Any request for new services or software needs to be submitted to the IT planning group. The request should include what the software or services will be used for and how they will benefit the company. If you have pricing information, please include it in the request. The request process could take up to 2 months. Once the request decision has been made an email will be sent to you. If the software has been approved, the software will be purchased and put through the application compatibility testing process. This process tests for compatibility with all of the currently supported software options. Once the test is complete, the software will be available for installation. If you would like the software added to the automated deployment process it will require additional time to have the automation package created.

Risk Assessment

Risk assessments vary greatly depending on the organization. A risk assessment is part of the risk management process (Figure 5.8). A risk assessment is a process that needs to consider CM components. There are many small organizations that may never perform a risk assessment because they are too costly and the organization may be willing to assume the risk of not performing the assessment. As an organization's value goes up, the risk of loss increases. Within the IT space, risk assessment is a security function, but many tasks in the process are of interest to CM, and the output information can be valuable to CM functions. Organizations that perform risk assessments need to define which applications they will assess, how often the assessments will take place, what group will do the assessments, and what action will be taken based on the assessment. The policy should be understood and accepted by upper management.

Objective Basis for Determining Criticality

One of the more difficult issues to deal with when performing a risk assessment is how to assess the criticality of various aspects of a system. There are a few different methods for leveling maturity. The Carnegie Mellon Capability Maturity Model (CMM) can be used by organizations to assess maturity. The Information Systems Audit and Control Association's (ISACA) Control Objectives for Information and Related Technology (CobiT) tools have a process for assessing maturity.

The maturity leveling process is when someone assigns a maturity number to a specific aspect of an application or system; another person assessing the same situation may number the situation differently. When performing risk assessments, consistency is important to ensure the assessment output can be reviewed year after year and relate to each other. The consistency should be driven by both the individuals involved in the assessment and the methods used to assess a specific application.

Assessment Timeframes

An organization that does make risk assessments a part of their IT strategy should make sure the strategy includes a timeframe for how often and when the assessments occur. Assessments take time and people, and each enterprise should understand the time cycles and make sure assessments happen regularly but do not interrupt normal business cycles. For example, assessments should not happen at the end of a financial cycle so that system engineers are able to devote time to the assessment. The frequency of assessments should be part of the risk assessment policy so that there is consistency in the reviews and credibility in the data. Having two reviews in 2 consecutive years and then lapsing for 3 years would probably indicate a lapse in IT governance, in addition to possible deterioration of information security.

Appropriate Actions Based on the Level of Criticality

When performing a risk assessment, there is the task of deciding what to do when the assessment is over. The actions taken are always tied to a budget. The

Risk Management Procedures

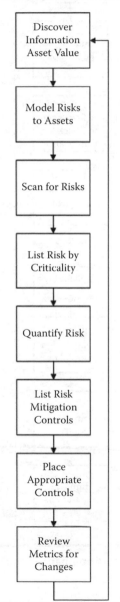

Figure 5.8 Risk management procedures.

Compliance Procedures

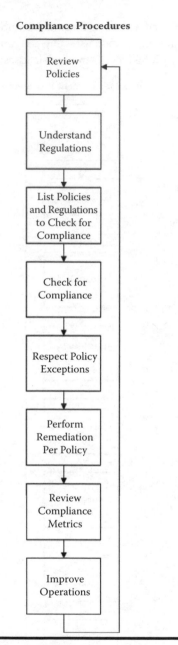

Figure 5.9 Compliance procedures.

best approach is to use the assessment as a way to determine which tasks need to be adopted first. The actions taken usually become more difficult as an application or solution becomes more mature. With the easy remediation tasks out of the way, difficult decisions need to be made.

Compliance Monitoring

Another area that is evolving rapidly is compliance (Figure 5.9). There are new tools being released that look at the various aspects of compliance. New vulnerability and health solutions can also be considered compliance tools. Compliance is usually thought of as the monitoring of systems once they are configured to a desired state to make sure they remain that way. Compliance is critical in situations where there are regulatory issues that an organization faces and they need to prove compliance. Compliance may also be as simple as the need to keep a certain version of a particular software off of a system because of application compatibility issues.

What Information Will Be Tested for Compliance?

When creating a compliance policy, the critical definition is, what is a compliant system? For many organizations this may be a very difficult process. There needs to be a process for exceptions. In many cases there will be a need for multiple definitions based on job role or some other identifying user or system characteristic. The thing to remember when building compliance baselines is simplicity makes a compliance program much more manageable. The more variations there are, the more difficult it will be to determine whether systems are compliant.

How Often Should Scans Occur?

Systems should be scanned frequently. Most organizations that have a compliance checking tool usually check compliance at least once a day, if not more frequently. This can vary based on what is being checked. Even small changes can cause compliance issues. If a user installs a noncompliant application that shuts down a line of business application, that user will probably look for help desk assistance. If the compliance checking tools identify these changes in advance, the help desk personnel can then be ready to back out the changes.

What Actions Should Be Taken Based on the Information Obtained?

When a system is discovered to be out of compliance there may be specific actions based on the collected data. A compliance system can be an integral part of IT operations. Most out-of-compliance issues eventually lead to the involvement of either help desk or information security personnel. In the most extreme cases, information security may need to involve an organization's legal or human resources department.

How Is the Information Reported?

There should be a well-defined method for reporting and managing out-of-compliant systems. The information itself should be protected so that it can be trusted. In many cases the information is trivial, but there may be the occasional instance where IT security needs to conduct a legal or criminal investigation based on the compliance data collected.

Conclusion

The identification phase is where the CM program identifies and catalogs systems to put them under the management infrastructure. Figure 5.10 is an overview of the identification phase and where it fits into the overall CM process. The identification process is where all of the infrastructure components of CM are designed and deployed. Once the infrastructure for CM is in place, the components are used to identify systems in the infrastructure and their current state.

Policies

A policy must be in place to define the configuration management database (CMDB) input and output process (Figure 6.2). The policy defines who has access to the information, when it can be used, and how it is changed. When creating policies for control, the focus needs to be on making sure hardware, software, and users are in compliance with the policies. The policies are created, controlled, and managed by the automation systems that IT has in place. The CM team needs to ensure that the following policies are in place:

■ Change policy
■ Identification policy
■ System software policy
■ System lifecycle policy
■ System usage policy
■ System security policy

Change Policy

The change policy governs all of the change control processes and procedures that relate to the CM process (Figure 6.3). The change control policy should contain the components discussed below.

Change Requirements

Change requirements are required by the change control committee for change requests. These requirements should be very specific and should be included on the change request form. Figure 6.4 shows a sample change request form. The change request form is a good way to drive change policy.

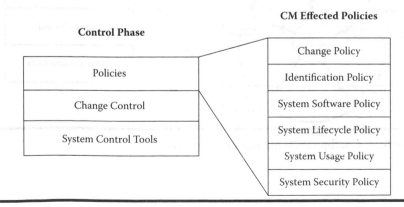

Figure 6.2   Control phase policies.

CM Affected Policies	Change Policy Components
Change Policy	Change Requirements
Identification Policy	Change Timelines
System Software Policy	Change Acceptance Process
System Lifecycle Policy	Change Test
System Usage Policy	Change Signoff
System Security Policy	Change Deploy

Figure 6.3   Change control policy.

The change request form is required by the Change Request Board. All fields in the form must be filled out for the form to be valid. Any forms that are not completely filled out will be rejected.

Change requester _____

Change requester manager_____

Change requester division _____

System to be changed _____

Reason for change_____

_____

Other systems affected (For every system that is affected, that system owner must sign off on the change)

  System owner 1 _____

  System owner 2 _____

  System owner 3 _____

  System owner 4 _____

  System owner 5 _____

Other change stakeholders_____

Change details _____

_____

Change diagram (please place a bmp formatted picture of the change diagram)

System test process_____

_____

System tester signoff _____

Change committee signoff:

  Signature 1 _____

  Signature 2 _____

  Signature 3 _____

  Signature 4 _____

  Signature 5 _____

Figure 6.4   Sample change request form.

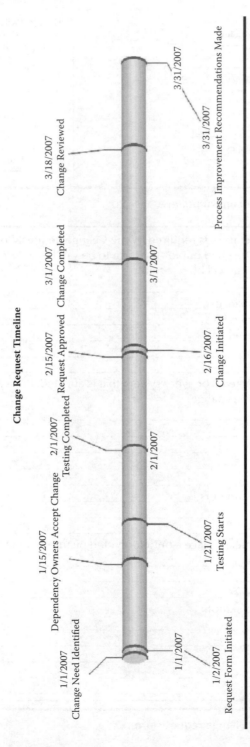

Figure 6.5   Change request timeline.

Change Timelines

Change timelines should be included in the policy so that the process is framed. Timelines provide some perspective. Many times requesters want changes to occur immediately and that is not the reality. If requesters are given a timeline they will understand the process better and know that a change could take weeks or months, depending on the complexity. Figure 6.5 shows a sample timeline. The change management timeline needs to include both small and large changes. There also needs to be an accelerated timeline for critical patches that are needed to protect corporate security.

Change Acceptance Process

The change acceptance process must be very well defined so that requesters know what to expect. The process should be posted on the change request Web site. The acceptance process also needs an accelerated process to deal with critical incidents and security breaches. There should also be a method for the requester to appeal either failed tests or failed acceptance. The change process is discussed in much greater detail in Chapter 13. The complete change process is shown in Figure 6.6.

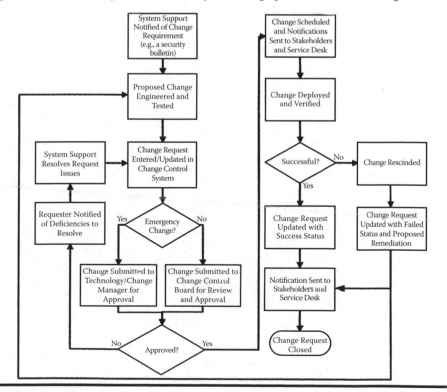

Figure 6.6 The complete change process.

Change Test

The change test process needs to be defined and needs to be understood by the requesters and the test team. The requesters create the test plans, so they need to follow the test process in the creation of the test plan. The CM team needs to be aware of the change process and ensures that changes are tested per the change management process. The test team needs to follow test protocol so that the test is valid and accepted by the change request committee. Communication between the CM and change control groups must be well documented and accepted. The test flow process is shown in Figure 6.7.

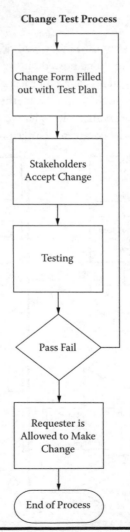

Change Test Process

Figure 6.7   Change test process.

Change Signoff

The change signoff process is critical to the integrity of the change control process. This section is a quick look at the change request process and how it relates to change management. This subject is discussed in greater detail in Chapter 13. Without the signoff process, there is no accountability for changes and the change control process becomes a mere documentation exercise instead of a process that can provide assurance that due diligence has been performed before a change occurs. This signoff process is a function of the Change Request Board (CRB). There are two signoffs that need to take place in the change control process: the stakeholder signoff and the CRB signoff. Both need to sign off before the change can occur. Each of the signoff groups must perform a series of checks before they can accept the change.

Stakeholder Signoff

The stakeholder signoff is the check that requires the most research. The stakeholder is anyone that owns an application that will be effected by the change. The decisions can be difficult. If the change will cause no issues for the stakeholder's servers it can easily be accepted. If the change will cause problems, decisions will need to be made and compromises reached. The stakeholder signoff process is shown in Figure 6.8.

Change Request Board Signoff

Members of the CRB may be service stakeholders, but they do not need to be. The CRB oversees the CM process and ensures that the process maintains its integrity. The CRB signoff is pretty straightforward and most of the responsibility lies with the requester to make the process go smoothly. The CRB signoff process is shown in Figure 6.9.

Change Deployment

The change deployment process is the most straightforward of the change processes. The requester simply follows the change as it was laid out in the change request form. The one thing that needs to be emphasized is that the change must be performed exactly as it is listed in the form; it is the only allowed change. Otherwise what has been added to the CMDB will be incorrect. There should be consequences listed in the process for deviating from the documented change.

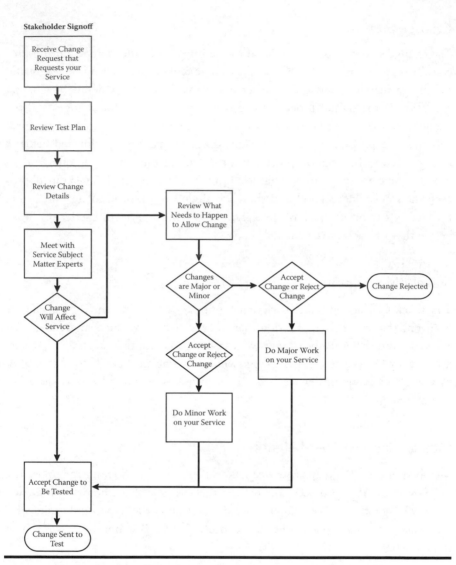

Figure 6.8   Stakeholder signoff process.

Identification Policy

The identification policy frames the methods by which systems will be discovered within the organizational IT environment. This policy needs to be described in broad language; the technology behind the identification process is not listed in the policy. By listing technologies in the policy, an IT organization binds itself to these technologies. Since technology is one of the fastest changing components of business, leaving technology out of the policy will allow the organization to change technologies without violating the policy. A sample identification policy is shown in Figure 6.10.

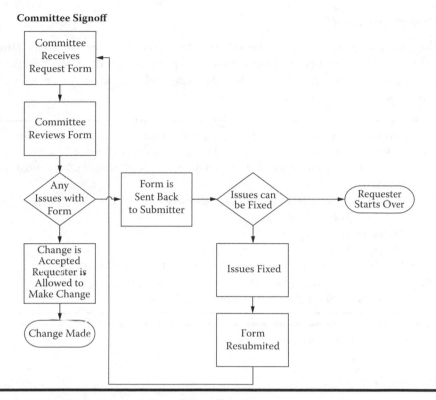

Committee Signoff

Figure 6.9   Change request board signoff process.

The company x identification policy describes the ways that company x will go about identifying both company resources and rogue systems within the environment. Company x will scan the internal networks for computers, users, devices, applications, and anything else that will communicate with company resources.

The scans will be conducted frequently for both informational and security reasons. Any information that is obtained by scans of company x's environment is considered company x's property and will be used in any way by company x for its benefit.

When any unknown component (an unknown entity is anything within the company x environment that is not managed by the IT department) is discovered, it will be brought into the company x management framework or removed from the environment.

Identified components will be scanned for compliance with all IT policies. If any components are noncompliant, they must be brought back into compliance. Compliance will be achieved by either automated or manual methods.

Figure 6.10   Sample identification policy.

System Software

The system software policy must be written in very general language so that quality software can be brought into the environment. The software policy must be written so that software will easily fit into the CM framework. A sample system software policy is shown in Figure 6.11.

The company x system software policy is a set of requirements that software will need to comply with to be allowed onto company resources. Any software that is discovered that does not meet system software policy must be removed immediately.

For software to be allowed on company resources it must be

- Purchased by the IT department
- Tested by IT testing
- Managed by IT
- Configured with configuration management approved settings

Any unapproved software that is detected on company resources will be removed either automatically or manually by IT staff.

Figure 6.11   Sample software policy.

System Lifecycle

The system lifecycle policy needs to describe how systems are brought into and removed from the IT environment. CM is concerned with how systems are integrated into and removed from the CMDB. A sample system lifecycle policy is shown in Figure 6.12.

System Usage

System usage policy governs how end users are allowed to use corporate resources. The usage policy needs to be in place to protect an organization from legal liability. A system usage policy helps protect the company from legal lawsuits that could occur if company employees use company resources for other than business uses. A sample system usage policy is shown in Figure 6.13.

System Security

All organizations should have a system security policy in place. The security policy contains many components that the CM program requires. CM staff must make sure that the security policy discusses compliance, use of CM systems, and security controls. A sample security policy is shown in Figure 6.14.

The company x system lifecycle policy is a set of mandates that govern lifecycle process. This policy defines requirements for systems to be brought into the company x environment, how they will be managed, and how to retire systems.

When systems are brought into the company x environment they must

- Be supported by a business need
- Be fully funded by the requesting business
- Be tested by the IT test organization
- Successfully complete a security review from IT security
- Be managed by IT management
- Have the configurations entered into the CMDB
- Require the use of corporate authentication methods

Systems that are in the company x environment need to comply with all corporate computing policies. Noncompliant systems will be brought back into compliance or removed from service.

At some point systems will need to be removed from the company x environment. The system retirement committee will make the decision to remove systems from the IT environment. Systems that are being retired:

- Need to be removed from the CMDB
- Need all hardware storage securely wiped
- Must have communication sent regarding the end of life timeline
- Must be removed from any management software
- Need to have any references to the software removed
- Must not effect other systems by their removal

Figure 6.12   Sample system lifecycle policy.

Company x's system usage policy is in place to frame end user behavior of systems. This will protect company x and its employees from intruders. The policy will also protect the company from any user indiscretion. Users must comply with all usage policies or face consequences, including termination.

Users of company x resources must

- Have antivirus installed at all times
- Not allow nonemployees to use their computer
- Follow the software usage policy
- Only install IT supported software
- Notify IT of any odd computer behavior
- Use appropriate protection on high-value information per the information security policy

Figure 6.13   Sample usage policy.

Adherence to the information security policy by all company *x* employees is mandatory. The policy is in place to protect company *x* employees and assets. Some security monitoring techniques will be used that will expose some user information. Users should not consider computer resources used or accessed from company resources as private. For security purposes, at times this communication nay be monitored by either automated or manual techniques. Systems on company *x* networks will be scanned for lapses in adherence to corporate policy. Any noncompliant systems will be brought back into compliance or removed from the network.

Users of company *x* systems must

- Use company delivered security software
- Use strong passwords (a strong password is at least 10 characters long with at least one number, one uppercase letter, one special character, and one lowercase letter)
- Protect company data with provided security techniques
- Allow resources to be scanned
- Allow all resources to be managed by management software
- Comply to all compliance measures
- Use approved proxy servers
- Not remove any corporate installed software
- Use only company approved software

Figure 6.14   Sample information security policy.

Change Control

Change control is an area that has entire books devoted to in-depth reviews of its process organization and execution. Chapter 13 goes into detail about the change control process. In the overall context of CM, change control is very important. Change control is usually put in place once an organization's IT department reaches a certain size. Change control is a way to manage changes to production systems or to reduce the risk associated with changes that are made to systems. There are some commercial off-the-shelf change control systems, but many of the systems in use today are home-grown line of business applications.

In essence, a change control system provided a policy for making changes and allows the people that will be affected by the changes ample time to review and respond to the changes. In the CM context, the changes need to be understood and well documented in the CMDB. When change control is in place, the policy should be fairly ridged. A ridged policy reduces the risk involved in changes. The change control process should include a step where changes are added to the CMDB. Issues almost always arise when the policy is subverted and changes are made too rapidly

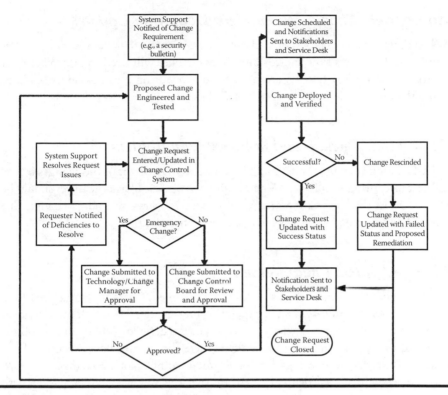

Figure 6.15 Change control process.

without allowing the entire organization to analyze a change's impact to the systems they manage. The change control process is shown in Figure 6.15.

How a Change Request Is Submitted for Each Update

When formal change control is deployed the process should be well defined. The time frame and reviewers are probably the two most critical elements of the change control process. On average, organizations allow a week of review time for changes. The CM team needs to be informed of changes that are submitted so that the CMDB and test groups can be prepared to ensure that the changes will work in the CM framework.

Exception Process for Emergency Updates

Even though the change management process should be fairly rigid, there should be an exception policy. This way, if there is an emergency situation, the company will be able to deal with the problem as soon as possible.

Appropriate Change Window for Deploying Updates

When a change takes place should also be well defined so that changes do not interrupt critical business functions. Many times changes will need to take place after hours so that critical systems are not shut down during business hours. Change times should be reviewed on a case-by-case basis.

Appropriate Backup and Rollback Requirements

When making changes, there should be a process to back out of the changes if they fail or cause unforeseen issues. When testing changes, rollback measures should be also tested so that there are no surprises if there is a need to undo a change. The CMDB will be relied upon when changes are rolled back.

Change Approval Requirements

Change approval requirements should be well defined. There may be a need for a conflict resolution process as well, depending on the organization. If an individual is going to refuse a change, the process should be defined so that information is provided to support the denial of change. There should also be a process to force changes if needed so one organizational group cannot block a change. The CM stakeholders will be relied upon to ensure that the changes are compatible with both current baselines and line of business applications that the change will affect.

Pre- and Postchange Notification and Reporting Requirements

Not only should changes be announced to all IT groups, but once a change is decided on it should be announced to all users. There should be a formal process and time constraints on this announcement process. Prechange and postchange messages should be sent to all users so that they can prepare for the change and be aware of any system downtime.

System Control Tools

Asset Inventory System

Many times an asset inventory system is an integrated part of the CMDB software. But the asset inventory system can also contain systems that need little or no configuration or change. Asset inventory is very important for the accounting of a company. An IT department is tasked with managing IT assets and therefore should make sure it can account for all of the devices it manages and purchases. An asset inventory is also important to identify systems that may be a part of the corporate network but not a corporate asset. This may be a violation of policy, depending on the organization.

Software

The software an organization owns should be tracked, and many software license tracking programs are available. There are also software tracking components built into some operating systems. If an organization does not track its software assets, it may be leaving itself vulnerable to lawsuits for licensing violations.

Hardware

Hardware assets can be easy to track if they are networked, but there may be some devices that are not networked (e.g., a personal printer). Most software asset tracking programs can identify devices by their IP address. For a complete inventory there will be some manual hardware entry required for nonnetworked devices. For a truly accurate inventory it is important to take this additional step to account for all devices.

Location

Asset location is an interesting attribute to track in the inventory system. This can be useful if there is a need to execute on a business continuity plan. In times of crisis, this asset location information will help greatly in the recovery process. Location information can be used to locate missing devices that are unintentionally moved around an office or campus.

Other Information Required to Determine Updating Requirements and Criticality

An asset inventory program should store information pertinent to the device as well as specific organizational attributes. These attributes are things that may be required for company-specific hardware or software. Company-specific information may be related to a specific organizational initiative or project. An easy way to think about the CIs that should be in a system management tool is to remember that they must facilitate repeatable installation and, if needed, removal.

Deployment Infrastructure

The deployment infrastructure in larger organizations should be reviewed to see if there needs to be alternative methods of distribution. Many times it makes sense to have multiple methods of software distribution. This can help reduce the need for manual or help desk intervention. Companies rely on system management tools to deploy software. Many modern operating systems contain built-in methods for receiving new software and changes automatically.

Primary Automation Methods

Even in smaller organizations there should be one automated method of software update distribution. This can be as simple as one of the low-cost, free offerings available, up to large, complex system management systems. It all depends on the needs of the organization. Smaller companies that do not have the resources for test organizations will be forced to trust system vendors and their pushed updates.

Secondary Automation Methods

A secondary automated deployment method could be one of the low-cost offerings. With Windows systems, you can also use group policy as a software push mechanism. A secondary method should be in place in case the primary deployment method is disabled in some way.

Manual Methods

Manual methods of installation should be understood by the IT technical staff in case there is a need to install or remove software outside of automated processes. These methods should be well documented and clear for technical staff who will be tasked with troubleshooting and help desk operations.

Communications Portal

In addition to systems that manage configuration information and software distribution, there should be a place for the IT staff and end users to communicate. This can include normal system status, software availability, training, etc.

Security Bulletins and Update Release Notification

All security bulletins and change notifications should be posted on the IT portal. Those changes can also be communicated in an email to all affected parties. Security bulletins and update release notifications are an important part of configuration and update management. These communications should be sent out in the deploy phase of update management. Update management components are discussed in greater detail in Chapter 15.

Update Binaries

Update binaries are pushed using the update management system. The updates can also be posted on a Web site for people to self-install. Having a self-install process is a great way to reduce IT strain and allow technically competent end users to take on update tasks.

Discussion and Feedback Lists

Discussion and feedback lists are ways for IT to gauge their effectiveness. IT should understand how the end user perceives their services so that they can continue to receive needed funding. All of the feedback needs to be compiled into reports that can help positively influence management to support IT initiatives.

Compliance Reports

Compliance reports can be posted on the IT communications portal to show how compliance is evolving within the organization. This makes it easier to promote the groups involved in the compliance effort or pressure them to improve their performance. Compliance reports also need to be reviewed by the CM team for any discrepancies. Noncompliant systems should be investigated by the information security organization, but CM should also be aware of the outcome of any compliance activities. When compliance issues are resolved, either the noncompliant systems are brought into compliance, or the CMDB may need to be updated to correct any errors in the database.

Other Communications

Any additional noncritical communications can be posted on the IT portal. This is a good place to advertise optional events such as application training and other projects that use IT services.

Incident Response and Forensics

All organizations of a certain size should have an incident response process. An incident response process will help an organization be ready in emergency situations. Information security incident response programs are very similar to any other incident response programs, be it fire, police, or other incidents. The plan should be in place so that, when needed, the response team can act quickly to reduce damage to organizational infrastructure. The plan should include a way to quickly assess and isolate the area in question. Once isolated, a plan can be devised on how to remove the attacker and rebuild the system.

Identifying Infected Systems

There must be a process for identifying systems that may have already been infected or attacked. Intruder identification is extremely difficult, especially when one is confronted with sophisticated attackers. Many times attackers will write their own exploits and exploit tools to gain access. The best way to identify an attacker is by network trending. An attack code usually uses already existing applications or emulates their activity so that no new applications seem to be installed. But for any connection to your system there will be some inbound and outbound activity. When this is different from your normal activity or to locations that you do not normally connect to, it could be cause for concern. Once you determine that a system has been compromised, you need to identify the scope of the intrusion. There are researchers working on network isolation projects, creating networking zones that can contain intruders to specific areas and quarantine the damage.

Once an intruder is identified the organization needs to determine if there is any exploit code left on their system. One way to do this is to take a complete system signature. There are software tools that can do this. There are also National Institute of Standards and Technology (NIST) image signatures that are available to check against. NIST is the U.S. government standards organization that creates many of the standards and guidance for government IT. Once the extent of the attack is understood, the organization can then isolate the incident.

Isolating or Quarantining Infected Systems

Once the exploit is understood, the organization should isolate or quarantine the affected systems. This can be done by changing passwords, adding firewalls, or disconnecting systems. Depending on the systems that are attacked, an organization may need to isolate these systems for forensic discovery. Continued vigilant monitoring is critical during this time to make sure that the incident is isolated to the contained area. The larger the infected area becomes, the more cleanup work will be required. Incident cleanup can be extremely expensive and disruptive to an organization's normal operations. In the worst cases, a complete infrastructure clean install may need to be performed.

Root Cause Analysis

The root of the exploit should be understood before the quarantined systems are rebuilt. Otherwise systems that have just been rebuilt may be compromised again. Once isolation and a greater understanding of the attack has been achieved, the organization can begin the recovery process.

Documentation and Feedback Requirements

It is necessary to document the incident and gather feedback to facilitate changes to the environment to prevent or minimize the impact from future similar incidents. After the recovery process is complete the organization should review the complete incident process, making sure the process that is in place was able to handle the incident in an organized manner. If there are changes that can be made to improve the process, initiate the changes and add them to the short-term strategy. Also, document the incident in case other organizations experience the same exploit. Sharing the resolution to a specific exploit helps the entire information security community.

Forensics

There are many new courses out there teaching forensics techniques to determine attack techniques and how investigators gather information from compromised systems. The way to think of systems once they are compromised is that they are like any other crime scene. Anything you do to the system is considered evidence tampering. Therefore it is best not to do your own forensics work on compromised systems. It would be similar to you attempting to help out the local police with gathering DNA evidence at a crime scene. If you have an understanding of IT forensics techniques you may be able to make suggestions to local law enforcement officers.

Conclusion

The control phase of the CM process is where resources are actually brought into the system (Figure 6.16). If the program is up and running, this phase is where systems that are brought into the framework are controlled. After the control phase, systems are officially considered managed.

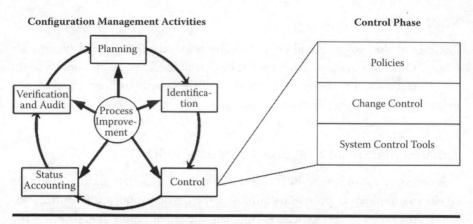

Figure 6.16   Configuration management control phase.

Chapter 7

Configuration Management Status and Verification

Once there are managed systems in place, the next thing to do is monitor the status of the systems and verify that the reported status is correct. Measuring status is a way to create metrics that can then be used to drive change and improvement. The complete configuration management (CM) lifecycle needs to be measured and the status of the various configuration items (CIs) should be monitored for effectiveness. Verification of the CM states by way of compliance checks can ensure that systems are supportable and sustainable.

Status

In the CM lifecycle, status and verification accounting are important to the continued success of CM (Figure 7.1). By checking status metrics the CM team will be able to create reports based on status numbers. The CM team use the results to report the successes and failures of the overall program. This will be the agent that will drive change and improvement in the overall process.

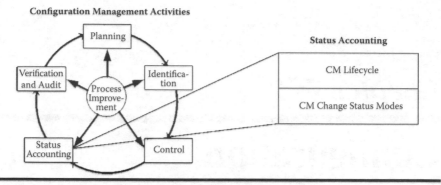

Figure 7.1   Configuration management status accounting.

Configuration Management Lifecycle

Gathering status metrics on the CM lifecycle can be a daunting task. There are many places to start pulling status information. The lifecycle is shown in Figure 7.2. When looking at the overall lifecycle, one can take any one of the phases and pull the feedback metrics. Metrics can be obtained from the following possible locations:

- People that use the CM process
- End users that are affected by the CM process
- System logs from computing systems that are part of the process
- Managers that have a say in the process
- System packaged reports
- System custom reports

In larger organizations there will be people tasked with gathering metrics. The operations measurement manager may have various team members that are focused on taking data and placing them in various reports for management. At the end of each of the CM activities the measurement manager must be there to gather metrics from all stakeholders involved in the process. The reports need to be focused to their target audiences. A status report about specific hardware may be very interesting to an operations manager tasked with keeping a service working. The same report may not provide a higher level manager the same level of insight. Upper management is interested in reports that prove strategy and business alignment, cost savings, and operational efficiency. Metrics should be modeled to help the management team understand whether IT is executing on the organization's vision.

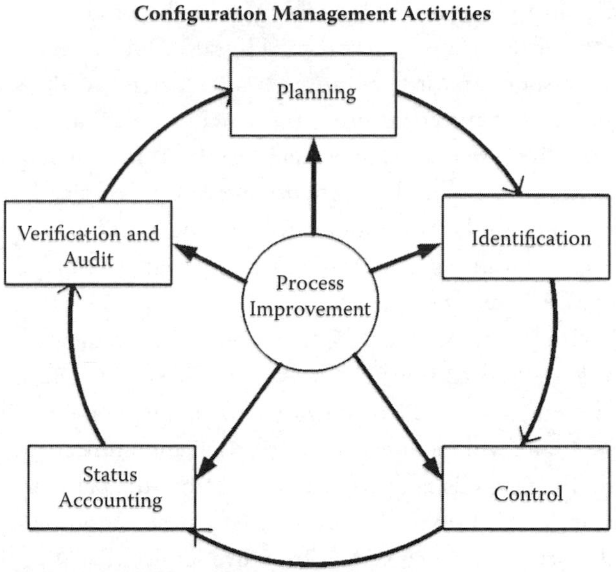

Configuration Management Activities

Figure 7.2   Configuration management activities.

Configuration Management Change of Configuration Item Status Modes

When reporting the status of CIs it is important to use terms that are clear to all involved and reading the reports. Standardizing CI terms allows everyone that views the metrics to understand the CI state. CI status modes should be published in the CI report legend. Terms that are generally used when noting the status of CIs are:

- In development—This is when the item or process is being created or built. It is a statement that is understood in the software development space, but in the operations function it can mean that the software is being installed and configured. It could also mean that hardware is being put in place. In development can also mean a system that exists only in a proof of concept lab.
- Tested—The tested status is when the solution has been through the test lab process but is not deployed into the production environment. The solution should be through the architecture design phase. The test lab phase will take some time, depending on how mature the product or solution is. It may be very quick if it is just a simple CI. This state is for solutions that are ready to be deployed and have completed all of the steps required to be officially released into the production environment.

■ Live—The live phase is when a system is in the production environment. Knowledge of this state is critical for IT staff. Once a service is in the live state, IT personnel must be aware that any changes to the service systems or any reliant systems could bring the system into an unwanted state. Any changes to a live system need to be made via the change management process. Live systems will, in any large environment, have service level agreements (SLAs) attached to their operations. All operations staff must be aware of the SLAs in place governing specific systems. Any change or disruption of service will have SLA-based consequences.

■ Retired—The retired phase is where systems are removed from the CM framework and retired from IT service. Once a system is in the retired state there is not much for the IT organization to do. Preparation to bring a system to a retired state will require some work. The communications plan must be followed. The CM CIs need to be removed from the configuration management database (CMDB). The corporate data destruction policy needs to be followed when removing a system from live service. Backups should be performed if the system is being retired for a hardware upgrade.

Measurements

The measurement of IT is an area that is often overlooked. It must be focused on much more by IT departments because it is the way to prove IT efficiency and return on investment (ROI). Measurement is an area that when rushed through results in a few massaged log files that provide few positive results. There are various programs and methods for presenting measurement data. These are designed so that the information is presented in a way that is more pertinent to the management consuming the output. It is best to present the measurement data so that they are easily translatable into business functions and decisions. The automated systems that are used by the CM process need to be mined for measurement data. These items should include CIs, log information, program output and reports, and other program metrics that affect CM.

Configuration Items

Configurations items are the metrics output for CM. CIs need to be identified and then mined for feedback and input to the metrics program. CIs that should be considered are shown in Table 7.1.

Table 7.1   Configuration Items

Item	Description
Item name	The name that the CI goes by
Item number	The unique identification number assigned to this specific CI
Model number	Any device or computer will have a model number
Serial number	Any device or computer will have a serial number
Version number	All software will have a version number
Location	In larger organizations, the physical location is important; this could include country, state, city, building address, office number.
Item owner	Who is the person directly responsible for the item?
License	Most software requires a license number
Warranty expiration	Software and hardware will have a warranty expiration date
Current status	What is the CI state?
Build date	Date the item was built
Accepting date	Date the item was accepted into the environment
Parent CIs	CIs that are parent to this CI
Child CIs	CIs that are child to this CI
Other relationships	Any other CI relationships that exist
Change control	Any changes that have happened
Support information	Any support information
Documentation	Any support documentation
In progress	Any changes that are in progress

Measurement Points to Key Performance Indicators

The information that is gathered needs to be translated into key performance indicators (KPIs) that will mean something to the organization's management. In the CM world that means looking at CIs, log information, and CM interview output. This translation process is one of the more difficult things to do because it is not an exact science. This leaves the whole measurement process open to criticism because it is subjective and can be skewed by the person doing the translation. Even with this downside to the measurement process, using various best practices can add legitimacy to the measurement process. The process of KPI selection must be done by understanding what is important to management. Examples of converting measurement output to KPIs are shown in Table 7.2.

Table 7.2   Measures to KPI Conversion

CIs, log, and interview output	Key performance indicators
CI status	CM program status
CI warranty expiration date	System warranty status
User satisfaction poll	User satisfaction
CI relationships	CM complexity
Support status	Support state
Administrative polls	IT system health
Management polls	IT organizational health
Log information	Top issues
Log information	System security state
Compliance report	CM effectiveness
Support volume	Support costs
Support logs	SLA compliance
Compliance report	Regulatory compliance

The list in Table 7.2 is just a small sampling of what can be used for KPI information. This is an area that is open to interpretation by each company. Each company will need to do some research to understand which KPIs will be most important for their organization. The KPIs should be measurable and consistent, and should be able to support the strategies and vision of an organization. When working to calculate ROI, a precise audit needs to be performed to build credible numbers.

Scorecard Output

The balanced scorecard is a form of data presentation that many IT organizations use to present their information. The balanced scorecard was developed in the early 1990s by Robert Kaplan and David Norton. The balanced scorecard is a measurement system that is focused on using KPIs to support management objectives. The balanced scorecard framework is shown in Figure 7.3.

The balanced scorecard framework can be used for measuring many different strategies. CM metrics can easily be placed into this format for use by the management team. The benefit of using the balanced scorecard is that its effectiveness does not rely on specific monetary values, but instead is focused on proving vision and strategy execution. In Figure 7.3 the four pillars of the balanced scorecard are financial, customer, internal process, and employee learning and growth.

Each of these pillar areas must be filled out per strategic objectives. Using this framework one can show progress in management-driven strategies. By translating your output into KPIs that meet strategic objectives one can then place that information in the balanced scorecard framework. The filled-out scorecard can then be presented to management.

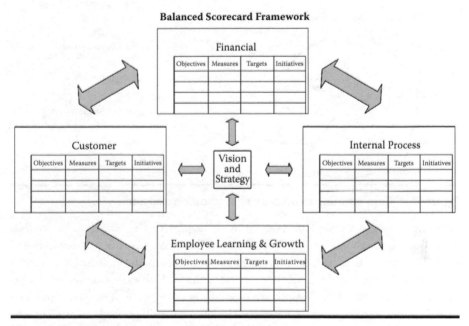

Figure 7.3   The balanced scorecard framework.

Program Effectiveness and Improvement

The program scorecard must be continually reviewed so that input information is always pertinent to the organization. Only information that maps to the scorecard should be translated into KPI information. Even the metrics program needs to be reviewed for program improvement. The output of the scorecard needs to be reviewed by management for effectiveness. The scorecard needs to reflect the strategic direction of IT and the organization. Many different types of status information can be used, and understanding where the information will be most effective is critical to status accounting. Log information and technical specifics should be used in troubleshooting issues when systems break down. Some of the log information may also be valuable if translated into KPIs for management review. The use of every metric component must be well thought out so that they are used in a way that provides the most value to the organization.

Verification

Compliance Checks

Compliance monitoring is an important piece of the CM verification process (Figure 7.4). By checking compliance, the CM process is validated. When there are

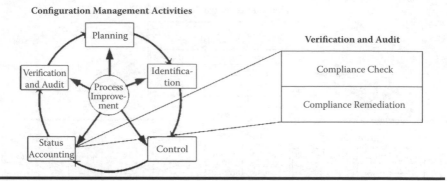

Figure 7.4 Configuration management verification and audit.

compliance issues the CM program must be a part of the remediation process, regardless of the source of noncompliance. When a system is out of compliance, CM tools can be used to bring a system back into compliance. When a system is out of compliance and the CMDB is incorrect, the CMDB can be corrected so that future issues do not arise. Compliance monitoring systems check resources to make sure they meet a configuration baseline. The baseline configuration must be in-line with the organization's compliance policy. Compliance is required in many different scenarios, but all of the various scenarios must be mandated.

Reasons for compliance include:

- Regulatory compliance
    Sarbanes-Oxley Act—The Sarbanes-Oxley Act of 2002 (SOX) was passed in response to the corporate accounting issues that arose from some high profile company failures. SOX was passed to boost public confidence in corporate accounting practices. The act mandates that organizations take responsibility for internal controls. This includes an audit of all internal controls. From an IT perspective it requires IT and IT security to ensure that the financial reporting structure is secure. Many organizations are adopting the Committee of Sponsoring Organizations of the Treadway Commission (COSO) standard to define control of financial systems. The COSO framework requires that the IT organization provide the following framework components:
    - Control environment—The control environment sets the tone for an organization, influencing the control consciousness of its people. It is the foundation for all other components of internal control, providing discipline and structure. Control environment factors include the integrity, ethical values, management operating style, and delegation of authority systems, as well as the processes for managing and developing people in the organization.

- Risk assessment—Every entity faces a variety of risks from external and internal sources that must be assessed. A precondition to risk assessment is establishment of objectives, and thus risk assessment is the identification and analysis of relevant risks in the achievement of assigned objectives. Risk assessment is a prerequisite for determining how risks should be managed.

- Control activities—Control activities are the policies and procedures that help ensure management directives are carried out. They help ensure that necessary actions are taken to address risks in achieving the organization's objectives. Control activities occur throughout the organization, at all levels and in all functions. They include a range of activities as diverse as approval, authorization, verification, reconciliation, review of operating performance, security of assets, and segregation of duties.

- Information and communication—Information systems play a key role in internal control systems because they produce reports, including operational, financial, and compliance-related information, that make it possible to manage the business. In a broader sense, effective communication must ensure that information flows down, across, and up in the organization. Effective communication should also be ensured with external parties, such as customers, suppliers, regulators, and shareholders.

- Monitoring—Internal control systems need to be monitored, a process that assesses the quality of the system's performance over time. This is accomplished through ongoing monitoring activities or separate evaluations. Internal control deficiencies detected through these monitoring activities should be reported upstream and corrective actions should be taken to ensure continuous improvement of the system.

Federal Information Security Management Act of 2002—The Federal Information Security Management Act (FISMA) is a law that is specific to information security. It mandates that government agencies be audited yearly for information security compliance. This act also affects all federal contractors. The following items are audited:

- Develop a hardware and software inventory
- Develop a Federal Information Processing Standards (FIPS) 199 security categorization
- Determination of system boundaries
- Determination and categorization of information types
- Develop a set of certification and accreditation (C&A) documents
- Performing risk assessments
- Accreditation of the system
- Continuous monitoring
- Plan of action and milestones

■ Corporate policy compliance—Corporate policy is mandated by the company. This can be made compulsory and enforced automatically. CM baseline compliance must be a part of the corporate policies that are checked.
■ Standard compliance—Adherence to industry standards provides great benefits to the organization. It proves an IT organization has done its due diligence and will help in any audit, internal or external. Standards make it easy for auditors to determine the various processes and procedures in place. Standards that are respected in the industry include CobiT, COSO, International Organization for Standardization (ISO), Information Technology Infrastructure Library (ITIL), Capability Maturity Model (CMM), and Octave.

Constraints Around Compliance Checks

An organization's compliance policies must contain constraints that the organization would like enforced. These compliance objectives must be well thought out. They must be focused on ensuring that the above compliance check objectives are completed. There need to be additional constraints set on the compliance checks. This should include:

■ Timeline for critical patches (1 day, 1 week)
■ Timeline for other patches
■ Antivirus update versions (n, n + 1, etc.)
■ When scans will occur
■ Scan frequency

Compliance Reporting

A change of status of an end user's compliance must be reported directly to the end user. This information also needs to be a part of the IT department's reporting structure. An optional step may be to report the denial of access to the end user's manager. Compliance reporting can be simple or very complex, depending on the organization's maturity. The most mature organizations will want the data presented in a clean and actionable format. Some organizations present their compliance information in a CobiT-formatted table, others use just simple graphs.

Compliance Remediation

Compliance remediation is about enforcing the compliance policy that has been set by IT management. The policy needs to identify specific actions that will be taken when a system is found to be out of compliance. The system management tools that exist can also be used to bring systems that are out of compliance back into compliance. The remediation steps can be tiered so that if a system cannot be resolved by one method it can be moved to the next level. There are many things that can be done when a system is found to be noncompliant:

- Automatically remediate—Most system management tools can automatically remediate systems that are discovered to be out of compliance. The only negative of these types of systems is they usually require a client, so the end user can circumvent the process by uninstalling the client.
- Quarantine—Some of the compliance systems can check for compliance and place noncompliant systems in a quarantine network. The quarantine network may also be used as a place for systems to "get healthy." When systems become compliant they can be checked to determine if they should be allowed back into the production network.
- Terminate network connectivity—Some products can terminate the network connectivity of systems that are noncompliant. Some systems will not terminate connections automatically; for those, the administrator has to monitor for noncompliance reports and manually disconnect the noncompliant host.
- Terminate user account—If a user continues to be noncompliant it may get to the point where terminating both the device and user access is required. When this happens the process must be well documented and accounted for in the CMDB.

Conclusion

The status and verification stage of CM is very important to the success of the CM program. Without it there would be no way to prove to management that the program is successful. Beyond proving success, using the balanced scorecard approach to present metrics can help an IT department show how their CM program is aligned with corporate strategy. It can also be used to show that the IT department is executing on their goals year after year. Metrics can also be used to identify areas that must be improved. The verification process also prepares an organization for compliance audits. By having an ongoing compliance program, an organization will always be ready to prove it is compliant with regulations, industry standards, and its own policies.

Chapter 8

Deployment Processes

The deployment process includes many of the configuration management (CM) tasks and programs. Deployment is a process that is repeated over and over as new software and hardware is introduced to the infrastructure to address business needs. The deployment process is very straightforward, but the details and how an organization actually implements them are complex. Many organizations neglect to follow the process and have issues with deployment because of the omission of critical steps. But dismissing certain steps as too costly or ineffective will later prove to be a poor decision. The steps exist to ensure that there is accountability and supportability in the deployment process. The deployment process is shown in Figure 8.1.

Selection Process

The selection process is the first step in the deployment process. The selection process is critical. The one thing an information technology (IT) department cannot afford to do is spend time and resources on projects that are not required or are ill-conceived. The selection process is about choosing partners and products to deliver a specific solution. Careful attention to budget is critical. IT departments have been carefully monitored from a budget standpoint for the past 7 years. In the current operating environment it is critical to ensure that the best value is delivered in solution deployment. The selection process is shown in Figure 8.2.

Needs Assessment

Needs assessment is an assessment of the needs of the business and its various business units. This review of technical deliverables must include the business owners.

135

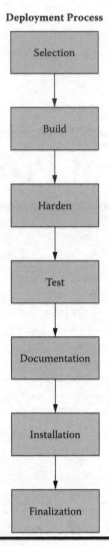

Deployment Process

Figure 8.1 The deployment process.

The requirements start with the business owners making requests to the IT management for various services. The requests should not be specific, but should be focused on how an IT service will improve operational efficiency or quality. The IT staff will worry about the technical and product details. A needs review can occur near the end of the year before the following year's budget is solidified. This will give the IT department time to prioritize new projects and the budgets required for

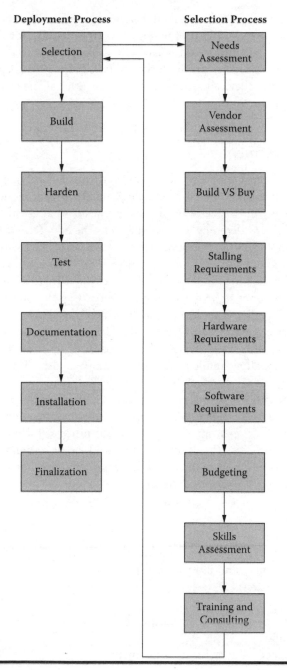

Figure 8.2   The selection process.

each project. The IT department should try to discover what initiated the request. Many times end users will hear of new services from friends or colleagues. The IT department should be aware of the latest IT developments in their industry segment. They need to understand both the positive and negative aspects of industry segment systems so they can articulate the complexities of any changes introduced into their current environment.

Vendor Assessment

Once there has been a review of the new projects the IT department will be adopting, a review of current vendor technology needs to be conducted. In mature businesses there will be line of business applications that are already in use that will need to be considered by any new project. The adoption of commercial off-the-shelf technology will greatly reduce the costs associated with installing and maintaining a set of software-based services. The other option is to build your own software, which in almost all cases is more expensive than using off-the-shelf software. Many times there are multiple vendors that provide a specific type of software functionality. The details may be different from vendor to vendor, but usually the basic services provided are similar and are grouped together into a specific category of software service. When assessing a vendor's software, the IT department must allow ample time, usually many months, if possible, to review features and make a well-researched decision. With many months for review, an IT department can set up lab environments and see which solution best meets their needs in both functionality and cost. In larger organizations there may even be a requirement to open up a project to a bid process, including a request for proposal (RFP) process. This is one way for an IT organization to review specific offerings and weigh their merit based on various factors. Some of the factors a company may use to assess a vendor's offering include:

- Cost
- Vendor's reputation
- Vendor's record on delivering solutions
- Organizational familiarity with a specific vendor's technology
- End user requests
- Usability
- Performance in a proof of concept lab
- Supportability
- Changes needed to existing infrastructure
- Help desk needs

Every system introduction needs to be reviewed individually against the selection factors. The weight of each selection factor will be different depending on the organization doing the review. Each IT department needs to determine what selection factors are most critical to their organization.

Build versus Buy

When reviewing solutions, there may be a lack of vendor products to do the job. In that case, if there is enough demand an IT organization may need to create the solution from scratch. When building your own solution you accept an additional set of issues. Building your own software solution is in almost all cases more expensive then using off-the-shelf software. An organization should only build their own software when a suitable solution does not exist or the current offerings do not meet their specialized needs. This will need to be assessed individually for each scenario. In most cases an IT organization will save money if they can purchase a solution. Even when some of the components are purchased and a subset of the solution is developed in house, there are still savings to be had.

Anything that is built must be supported. The support costs of internally built software are often poorly accounted for. In addition to the support costs, many times "homegrown" software is reliant on a few or even one individual in an organization; we have seen solutions fall apart because the "smart guy" decides to leave the company. The same can also apply to complicated packaged applications when there are only a few employees that understand how to operate a specific piece of software.

Even with all of the pitfalls of internally created applications, sometimes it is necessary to create homegrown solutions to meet a need. When an organization decides to create their own applications, proper processes need to be followed for sound development practices. Once the software is built, training and support must be a part of the process. Essentially any internally developed application should be treated as if it is a packaged product, with the delivering party (IT) being obligated to provide all of the services that are available for packaged software.

That brings us to an area that is somewhere between purchased software and homegrown software: open source software. If an organization has a highly skilled staff, open source software may be the way to go because you can obtain many pieces of software that can be modified per the open source agreement that the writers have placed on the package. The downside to using open source software is that IT staff will need to support it or someone IT pays will have to when anything goes wrong. This is where an IT organization will need to be honest with itself about the skill of its personnel with software development and its ability to support software and possibly make changes to the software so it works for the organization.

Staffing Requirements

When reviewing an IT solution, the staffing requirements need to be considered. A constant review of the IT staff skill set must be performed so that IT management can make changes and shift staff based on operational needs. When bringing on new services, there may be the need to bring in new staff or repurpose staff based on need. Wherever the staff comes from, when the system is new there will be some ramp-up time involved. When the staffing operational function is outsourced there may even be a need for additional time to bring the service online. The additional time and resources must be considered to ensure that a new service is initiated correctly.

Hardware Requirements

With new services being brought online, there will be the need for new hardware to drive the services. The resource requirements will be clearly listed in any vendor documentation. Based on the calculations provided in vendor documentation, an IT department can plan and budget for the needed hardware to support a specific service in their infrastructure. In the hardware estimate, IT managers need to plan for growth in both the service and the organization. This way there will be no shortcomings that will degrade the service. Slow service will always hinder a service's popularity with end users. Unpopular services are killed outright or through diminished funding. It is up to the IT staff to make sure that new services meet the end users' expectations, and one of the easiest ways to ensure a quality service is to make sure new applications run quickly.

Software Requirements

Software requirements can be very easy or complicated, depending on the organization and how it works, and what policies they have in place. All software must meet request for comments (RFC) requirements and be compliant with current organizational and security policies. Organizational policies can be very complicated, depending on the organization and what specifically is required for the software to be installed. Some of the things that may need to be considered when selecting software are:

- Hardware requirements
- Database needs
- Application servers
- Web servers
- Development environments
- Development languages
- Communication protocols
- Authentication methods
- Authorization methods
- Changes to the existing environment
- Directory needs

- Network requirements
- Additional software requirements

Budgeting

It is very important to get the budgeting correct. Sure there are times when projects go over, but making a habit of going over budget will shorten one's career in IT management. The best way to get the budget correct is to make sure that all of the aspects of a project are considered. Missing project components and then having to pull together funds later from some other source will ensure that the project as a whole is less effective. One way to ensure an adequate budget is to pad the budget, but overpadding will expose the fact that the scope of the project is not understood. The best way to get a budget correct is to meticulously cover all aspects of the deployment process and fund all of the steps in the process, including an exception for a margin of error.

Skills Assessment

All IT departments should have regular skills assessments to understand the abilities of their personnel. This assessment can then be used to ensure the correct skill sets exist in the organization when new projects are brought on. If there is a lack of a specific skill, the group can either have someone trained in the skill or the department can hire a new employee with the needed skills to cover the new project.

Training, Consulting, or Both

There are many ways to bring new skills into an organization. Employees can be trained in new skills. Consultants can be brought in to take care of the job. Or consultants can be brought in to run a specific program until the staff is adequately trained to run the service. Tasks can also be outsourced. Each decision has consequences. Larger companies with a focus on permanence must focus on training or hiring new staff. This way the skills will propagate throughout the organization and remain in the corporate culture. A combined approach of using training and consultants can be effective, whereby full-time staff learn by observing the consultants who are familiar with a new system.

Solution Architecture Build Process

The solution build process is where the technical gurus of the company get to show their stuff. Building a solution requires various groups within the IT organization—operational staff, networking staff, development staff, and IT management—to

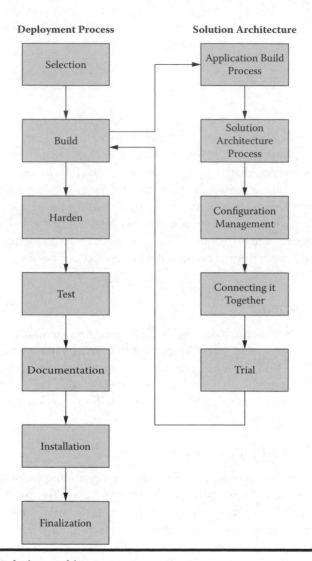

Figure 8.3   Solution architecture.

work together to put together a complete solution. Some of the steps in the process may be omitted depending on the solution that needs to be built. Certain solutions may require no software coding and rely on existing software solutions. The solution build process is shown in Figure 8.3.

Application Build Process

If there is coding required for a specific solution, this must begin first because it will probably be the task that requires the most time. Other pieces of the process can start in parallel to speed the overall solution build process in addition to supporting the development process. There are many books about the software development process. In this text we will not go into any detail about the build process because this book is more focused on broader IT management. The development required to bring a solution live can vary greatly depending on how much new code the solution requires. There are many off-the-shelf products that require little development. The only issue with off-the-shelf software is that many times it is not specific enough to meet the needs of an organization. Line of business (LOB) applications are very customizable. When using various LOB applications, organizations may need to develop various components of the application with either known programming languages or in some cases proprietary programming or scripting languages. In some instances there will need to be some "glue" code to connect various applications together.

Solution Architecture

The solution architecture is when all the pieces of the solution process are put together. This can include applications and glue code built in house as well as purchased software. The overall solution build includes cross IT organization collaboration to make sure that all of the correct groups are involved in the solution build process.

Configuration Management

When the solution is completely built, the configurations must be added to the configuration management database (CMDB). Previous chapters have discussed this process in depth.

Connecting It Together

When building a solution, there are times when the various components are built and configured by different groups within the IT department. There is a point when the various groups need to put all of the pieces together. This must take place in a test lab or trial area within the live production environment.

Trial

During the service deployment, a subset of trusted end users will need to be entered into a trial group. This group must include the IT staff that will support the new application. A trial should happen once the system is up and running in the production environment. It can even be open to limited trial while the new service is in the lab environment. The trial can be used to gather information on the end user experience. This way IT can improve the process and meet minimum user expectations before going live. The worst thing an IT group can do is go with a big line of business application release only to find that end users will not use the application.

Hardening Process

The hardening process must always happen before an application is released into the production environment. Hardening a system does not mean that it will then be "hack" proof, but it will ensure at least a minimum level of security is reached. By hardening a system, an IT security department does its due diligence in protecting corporate systems. The steps in the hardening process are shown in Figure 8.4.

Threat Modeling

Threat modeling is a method for discovering possible threats a piece of software or system may encounter. By going through the process of threat modeling a service manager can then put in place the countermeasures and controls to stop known threats. The threat model identifies threats to the system; it is not focused on mitigating risks. That comes later in the hardening process. There are entire books dedicated to threat modeling, so we will not go into great detail here.

Access Points

Threat modeling is a way of looking at your system through the eyes of the attacker. The first thing an attacker will look for is a way to get into your system. A networked entry point is always most desirable. The threat model must note all possible entry points. The entry points list should include every possible way an attacker can access a system, including:

- Login screens
- Communication ports
- Physical ports (USB, serial, etc.)
- Network application access
- Remote access protocols

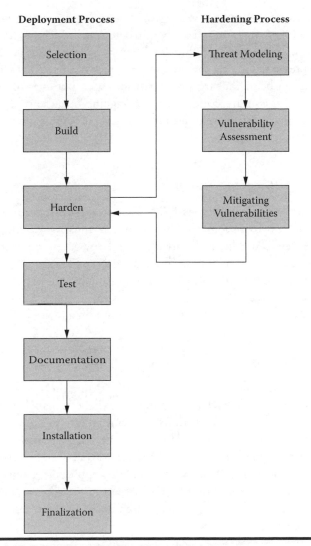

Figure 8.4   The hardening process.

Asset Targets

Understanding one's information assets is very important and a review performed yearly as a separate task from normal threat modeling will increase visibility. The value of various assets varies greatly from organization to organization. The determined value of informational assets will set the tone and budget for the information security group. The value of information will be different within various industries. Once the valuable information assets are identified an organization can use that information to decide how an attacker would go about accessing that information.

High-value information and key systems are targets for malicious attacks. An interesting exercise for an organization to try is to determine which systems would affect the company most if they were offline for 1 day. Some organizations are not so reliant on computer systems, and those companies may not have to worry about their information assets being the target of a malicious user. But for most organizations, their computer systems are critical to their ongoing operations. The determined value will help an organization understand the level of resources it needs to protect its information.

Access and Authorization Levels

The access people and applications have to other applications must be managed and limited. Access to various computing objects must be carefully monitored. Monitoring access can help catch intruders, and any access from unknown locations or excessive access should raise concern with the IT security group. There are applications that watch for these exact scenarios. Organizations that are vulnerable to network-based attacks will benefit from putting in place an application that monitors network activity and acts on spikes in certain activities.

Application Model

Each application that goes through the threat modeling process must be reviewed separately. All systems will have specific scenarios that can manifest vulnerabilities. When reviewing an application, various scenarios need to be created that will mirror what the threat modeling team thinks will be ways in which intruders could possibly attack the application. The various scenarios need to be listed and ranked by severity and probability. Dependencies on other applications must be noted and the communication channels must be understood in the application model. A list of all of the possible threat points needs to be noted in the threat model for use throughout the process.

Threat Understanding

Once all of the threat scenarios have been identified, the threats need to be listed and analyzed for severity and probability. A review of threats needs to take into consideration the environment the threat will occur in and how the organizational environment works. In all environments there is the possibility of human error, which raises the possibility of threats. These scenarios need to be considered with the probability of them happening. An employee may be coerced into giving up a password, but the probability of an attacker doing so at a bank is probably higher than at an auto parts reseller. All aspects of the threat need to be understood to make sure that after the threat is identified it can be properly addressed with mitigating measures.

Vulnerability Assessment

The vulnerability assessment is much different than threat modeling. Threat modeling is where possible threats are identified, while a vulnerability assessment is where attempts are made to breach a system with known attack techniques. There are two ways that one can conduct vulnerability assessments: automated vulnerability assessments and penetration test teams (human teams that attack systems). Automated systems are nice for periodic vulnerability checks, but for a more in-depth review of system vulnerability it is best to use a penetration test team.

Automated Assessments

There are many variations of automated vulnerability detection systems, including intrusion detection systems (IDS), network intrusion detection systems (NIDS), intrusion prevention systems (IPS), and host-based intrusion detection systems (HIDS). There are many vendors that sell systems that will search for system vulnerabilities. Larger organizations will have one or more types of assessment technology. These technologies are run against any new system that will be introduced into the production environment. This makes the person who runs the system scans aware of new systems and allows the new service managers to detect any large security vulnerabilities.

Penetration Test

Once the automated tests are done, the next step is to have professionals try to hack into your system. Large organizations usually have an internal team that does penetration testing. There are also consultants that specialize in penetration testing. If the system is critical, it is advisable to have both internal and external penetration test teams attack a system before it goes live. There are even groups that are teaching individuals to be certified ethical hackers. The EC-Council has a set of courses and exams. This is a good program, but as with any certification program, you need to look at the individual beyond the certification and make sure they have the skills to do the job you require. When hiring an external entity to do a penetration test, make sure you have a written contract in place. The contract must note all of the attack vectors that are in bounds and what things are off limits to the contractor.

Mitigating Vulnerabilities

Finally, vulnerabilities that have been identified need to be addressed. The vulnerabilities from both the vulnerability assessment and threat modeling are listed and ranked according to probability and severity. Risks can be dealt with in several ways: mitigate the risk, insure the risk, or accept the risk.

For new applications, many times mitigating the risk is as easy as a configuration change. These types of changes must be made immediately and added to the CM system so they become a part of the normal configuration environment. The next level of changes may include changes to a subsystem or may require add-ons to the original software. This level of change may require additional budget. The next type of vulnerability mitigation is to add additional systems to your current solution to perform specific security or hardening measures. These types of systems include firewalls, security protocols, access control systems, and encryption hardware and software.

If you cannot resolve a vulnerability, there are two other things that can happen. Insurance can be purchased to reduce or remove the risk from an organization and place the risk on the insurer. Or an organization can accept the risk and bear the burden itself. When an organization accepts a risk there must be a signoff process so that upper management is aware of and accepts the vulnerabilities.

Testing

For any IT organization, a test lab is an important part of the overall toolbox. The test lab is a place where they can try out things in an environment that is similar to the production environment. The test lab is a tool that can be used for verification of new initiatives and ideas.

Test Lab

The test lab needs to be a part of many different processes. A test lab needs to have a very strict protocol for usage and projects. Many organizations have a test lab in some form. Test labs need to have the same equipment that is used in the production environment. That is the only way the IT staff can prepare to take things live in the production environment. An IT department without a test lab is like a basketball team without a ball. There is no way for the team to prepare for a real game. They may be able to make an educated guess on how things work, but they will not know the specific mechanics. A test lab must have as much of the production environment as possible.

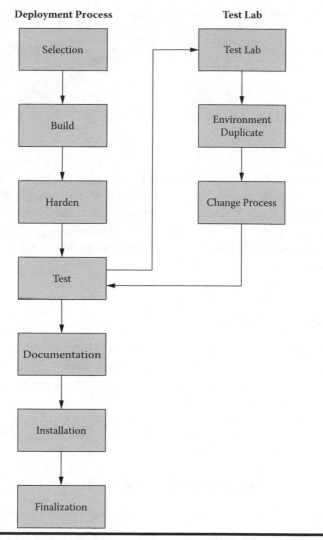

Deployment Process

Selection

Build

Harden

Test

Documentation

Installation

Finalization

Test Lab

Test Lab

Environment Duplicate

Change Process

Figure 8.5 The test lab.

Duplicate Environment

A test lab must be able to duplicate the environments that need to be tested. In some duplication efforts even exact wire types may be critical in troubleshooting complicated environments. Every component must be duplicated. In some instances there may be a budgetary need to reduce costs. One way to reduce costs in a test lab is the virtualization of system hardware. This is acceptable for software solutions, but when testing a networking environment, the lab must include networking hardware such as switches and routers, and as much of the live environment as possible. When changes need to be made to hardware-specific operating systems, the lab must provide the ability to make changes to those pieces of equipment.

Change Process

The test lab is an integral part of the change process. Any changes to the production environment must go through the test process in a duplicate environment. The test lab must duplicate the change and the environment the change is going to be placed in. Application compatibility issues can be caught by running all other applications on the platform being tested. Putting changes through this type of lab process allows the IT department to make the change with a level of confidence. The acceptance process must include a signoff by lab personnel that tested the change in the environment.

Documentation

The documentation for commercial applications is provided with the applications. The company will need to do some documentation work when there is a company-specific use for an application (Figure 8.6). Line of business applications are the most typical applications that will require an IT department to rework the application's documentation so it makes sense for the organization. Also, if an organization creates custom applications or add-ons, those will need documentation as well.

Software and Hardware Documentation

Documentation comes with the software and hardware that an organization purchases. Most end users do not even want to look at the hardware documentation. Some like to have a copy of the software application documentation. But most will look to the IT department to provide training on new applications.

Organization-Specific Documentation

More important is the documentation work that needs to be done on custom applications. The documentation needs to be specific so that an end user can follow step by step and perform the new tasks required of them.

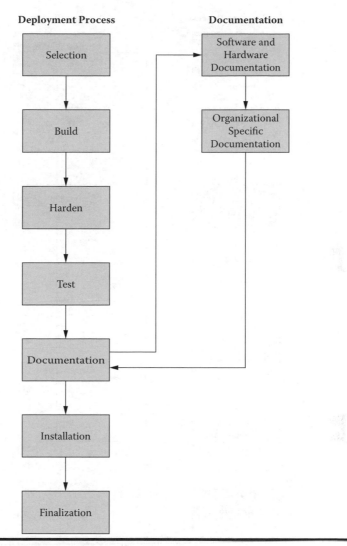

Figure 8.6   The documentation process.

Installation

Now that all of the preparation work has been done it is time to take the plans live and install the new service in the production environment (Figure 8.7). A few questions need to be answered: Where will the service be installed? How will it be installed? Who will do what tasks?

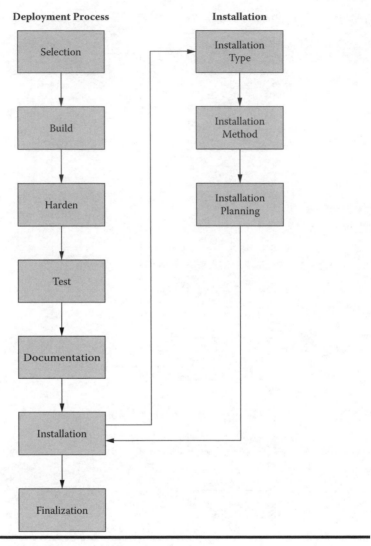

Figure 8.7 **The installation process.**

Installation Type

When deploying a system into the production environment, the target systems need to be identified. Server systems are easier than having to push systems out to the end users. In some cases software may need to be put on both servers and clients. Each type of install is very different, so planning needs to take place for the various types of installations. Hardware needs to be identified as targets for the software.

Installation Method

Software can be installed in several different automated ways— systems management software, OS-based software push, PXE boot-based software install—and if required software can be installed manually. There are multiple vendors that support each of these methods and it is up to the IT department to select the preferred solution. In the worst-case scenario, IT can install software manually.

Installation Planning

Planning for the installation will ensure that it goes smoothly and is finished in the scheduled time. Planning can identify the required staff for the various tasks. It can assign a timeline to all of the tasks so that project planners can be aware of any issues with the installation process.

Finalization

The finalization of a deployment is about making sure the installation is ready to be taken live in the production environment (Figure 8.8). There are a several tasks that must be completed to make sure the offering is ready to be supported by the IT department.

Installation and Operational Verification Process

With the installation complete, there will be a signoff process where someone other than the installer checks the configuration against what is logged in the CMDB. This is a secondary check to make sure there is nothing that was missed during the installation. After the system is handed over to a service management team, a check must be performed on the operational components to make sure that the operations team is capable of handling the day-to-day management of the system.

Check Installation

The installation must be verified by someone that was not a part of the installation group. All of the configurations that have been entered into the CMDB must be verified as accurate. This verification will catch any misconfigurations. Once the installation is verified as accurate it can then be considered production ready, and from that point any changes to the configuration must go through the change management process. This way the level of accountability will be raised on the offering and it can be considered a trusted service.

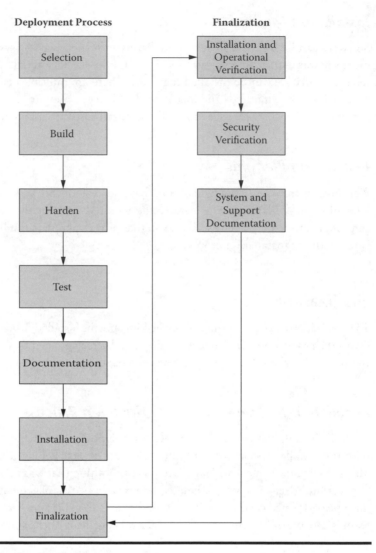

Figure 8.8 The finalization process.

Check Operations

The service is handed over to an operations group once the installation is verified. The operational components of a service must also be verified. This may require that some changes be made to the service operations team. Things to check for in an operational review are:

- Staff training
- Staff numbers

- Knowledge of service
- Understanding of documented procedures
- Incident response
- Business continuity

This is a short list of the things to verify. There are many others that are business and application specific.

Security Verification Process: Vulnerability Assessment

Security checks were performed during the system hardening process. This is a great way to find flaws in the architecture. The production system must be checked again once it is in place. Inevitably there will be some changes between the architecture phase and the systems that are placed in production; these differences may not even be noted anywhere. Because there is a human element to software deployment there is always the chance that there will be some missed system vulnerabilities.

Run Scans

The software-based scans must be run again against the system. In addition to a one-time scan that is heavily scrutinized, scans of all systems should be a regular occurrence in enterprise-level production IT environments. The first scan is used to identify a baseline of health. From this baseline it will be easier for the scans to identify changes in the system.

Internal Penetration Test

These tests were run once before, but it is important to perform penetration tests in the final phase as well. Internal penetration tests are performed by larger enterprise organizations that have the resources to have their own penetration test teams. These tests are also a great way to create a baseline of system health. The internal penetration test accentuates the intricacies of the system and is a great resource in case there is need for incident response.

External Penetration Test

External penetration tests are something that should be performed by all organizations, regardless of size, deploying a new large software service. This second set of penetration tests is critical to ensure things are ready to go. External testers have a different skill set than internal penetration testers and can discover new vulnerabilities. External testers are a great second check for people that may be too close to the project to see all of the flaws. One thing to make sure is that the organization's IT department must consider external testers a positive. All external consultants should be used as tools for organizational improvement. A hostile internal environment will only diminish the work of the external consultants by making it less effective. Consultants rely on correct input from the IT staff to make their conclusions. Any deception only hurts an IT organization by giving it a false sense of security.

Initial System and Support Documentation

System and support documentation is very important in the handover process of software deployment from the install/build team to the operations team. Even if the operations team is involved in the build, the two functions are very different. Even when a software deployment is successful, it does not mean the project overall is successful until the operational goals have been realized. This may happen over many years. Quality documentation is key to this success. Within IT organizations, change is normal. IT organizations seem to change faster than other departments; this is indicative of the way technology is changing. Good documentation can allow these changes to occur without causing a degradation in the quality of service.

Check the Support Process

A support process needs to be created and in place before a service is available to the end users. The support process, if correctly managed, will improve over time. It takes some time to work out all of the issues in new products and services. With time, issues appear and are eventually resolved. The process must support both change and improvement so that the support required over time is reduced.

Check the Documentation

The documentation must be checked for technical and operational accuracy. Problems will eventually come to light via the support process. A review of the documentation reduces the number of errors in the initial version. Revisions need to be made to the documentation so that at a certain point the service can be considered mature and only needs to change based on the broader environment the service is deployed in. The documentation should be targeted to specific users and must be simple and provide step-by-step solutions to various scenarios an end user may encounter. Administrator documentation can be more technically specific.

Gather End User Feedback

Many IT organizations work without soliciting end user feedback. The end user is your customer. End user feedback should be gathered frequently to make sure there is an acceptable level of confidence in the IT organization and their services. The end users should understand the issues the IT organization faces so that IT can be seen as an asset to the organization instead of a necessary evil. Training can go a long way in improving IT's organizational perception. When an IT organization is seen as doing a poor job it will become increasingly difficult to provide quality service.

Conclusion

The deployment process is a linear process that must be followed in specific order. This order is shown in Figure 8.9. The deployment process is risky for IT organizations to execute because failures will waste large amounts of the IT budget. The

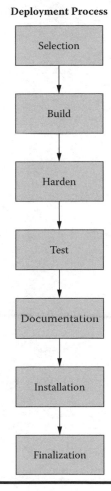

Deployment Process

Figure 8.9   The configuration management deployment process.

positive aspect of deployment is it provides a valued service to the organization to improve the business. The more successful an organization is at deploying new technology, the more successful the IT organization as a whole will be viewed. Careful adherence to a well-defined deployment process will help IT be successful in their overall goals.

Chapter 9

Operate and Maintain Processes

The operate and maintain phase of configuration management (CM) covers routine operations and support functions such as account provisioning, security management, and storage management, as well as hardware, firmware, and software changes, additions, and deletions. The operate and maintain phase also includes system monitoring and audit functions for performance, compliance, and incident management. These activities constitute the bulk of a system's lifecycle and the majority of the work performed by the information technology (IT) department. They are also the principle cause of system failures. Poor operations and support practices lead to misconfigurations, operator errors, and unauthorized changes. These three items are by far the most common causes of system failures, followed by software and hardware failures. While these may be the cause, they are really a symptom of a larger issue: the proper application of CM principles in the operate and maintain phase.

System operations and support have been described as the grunt work of IT; not glamorous, but absolutely essential to successful business operations. IT is such an integral part of most business processes that organizations simply cannot function without it. After the 1991 World Trade Center bombing, 80% of the businesses in the towers suffered irreversible losses, not from the destruction or loss of data, but from an inability to access the IT systems required to conduct business. Ultimately more than 60% of those businesses failed entirely. That was more than 15 years ago, and dependency has grown substantially since then. Unfortunately, in most cases, IT staffing, expertise, and budget have not grown proportionately. The result is constrained IT operations and support until they can no longer proactively manage systems. Instead, IT operations and support become a "firefighting" unit, only capable of reacting to the most critical issues of the moment. This has left a number of the items discussed in this chapter severely neglected. This has also contributed to the success of a number of widespread attacks (i.e., Code Red, Slammer, and Blaster) and data compromises, and ultimately led to the imposition of a number of new IT-related laws and regulations. While few IT professionals would be willing to call these events "godsends," they did lead to significant improvements in operations and support processes, including a number of new strategies and technologies that will be discussed here.

Proper operations and support staffing combined with good configuration and change management is absolutely essential to the viability and success of an organization. The lack of proper resources creates reactionary operations and support functions, reduced reliability, poor security, and increased costs. Good practices reduce costs, promote proactive services, and allow IT organizations to quickly adopt new technologies in support of changing business objectives.

This chapter is divided into sections covering the following operation and maintenance topics: routine service tasks, update tasks, baseline system measurements, remediation tasks, and system and support documentation. The final section covers system support processes and procedures.

Routine Service Tasks

The majority of operation and support resources are dedicated to everyday operational tasks, including account provisioning and maintenance, security management, storage management, and performance management. These tasks and how they are related to CM are covered in the sections below. While the topics are dealt with individually, it is important to remember that the combination of all of these task is what constitutes systems operations.

Account Provisioning and Maintenance

These tasks have come to be known as identity management (IDM). The term encompasses user provisioning, access, and password management. It also encompasses the concept of centralized credential management and usage across multiple disparate computing platforms and applications. As IT utilization has increased, so have the number of disparate systems, applications, and user roles, making IDM a compelling challenge for most IT organizations. At the same time, security concerns have increased the frequency of password changes, further increasing account management and incident support requirements.

The primary goals of IDM are to simplify provisioning and maintenance workflows, and reduce account management costs. The ultimate goal is to provide a single credential management point capable of transparently granting users access to IT resources regardless of their location or disposition. This is commonly known as single sign-on (SSO)—a system capable of authenticating and authorizing user access to systems and applications from a single user identity regardless of the underlying operating system or platform. While SSO is the goal, it is not a practical reality in most computing environments; however, major advances in IDM have been made in recent years, including meta-directory technologies. A meta-directory system pulls user identity information from multiple system stores (databases, directories, trusted computer bases, etc.) and integrates it into a single location where it can be synchronized and managed as a single entity. Some meta-directories also include workflow engines to facilitate user lifecycle management, including initial account provisioning, access changes related to position or status changes, and deletions for retirements and terminations. These systems are particularly effective when they can access human resource stores, gathering the user information directly and automatically to make the appropriate system access changes.

Typically account management is not tied to CM, with one notable exception: administration and ownership information is captured in the configuration management database (CMDB) for notification and system remediation purposes. When changes to user accounts occur, these changes also need to be reflected in the CMDB, otherwise there is a possibility that the appropriate personnel will not be notified of pending system changes or required remediations. Incorrect notification information will also keep issues from being properly managed.

There are a number of good IDM products available, including HP Openview IDM, Oracle Fusion, and Microsoft MIIS. The primary things to look for in these products are integration and extensibility: How many other directories/data stores is the system capable of interacting with? Can the functionality of the system be extended to include actions such as the direct updating of CMDB user fields? Tools that use a common database are also advantageous because they allow the use of enhanced reporting services and built-in data transfer and transformation services.

Like directory services, IDM will undoubtedly become a core IT service; the old methods of account provisioning and maintenance simply cannot scale in modern IT environments. Good IDM enhances the user experience, reduces security risks, and facilitates regulatory compliance. Poor IDM wastes valuable IT resources (i.e., highly trained staff consumed by routine administrative tasks) and put the operational integrity of the IT infrastructure at risk from unsecured tests, generic and unused accounts, and weak passwords.

One thing to avoid is customized user stores. Novice developers often find it easier to store user information in a database rather than using unfamiliar application programming interfaces (APIs) to pull information from the corporate IDM database or directory. Building customized user stores only exacerbates IDM problems by spreading user information across even more disparate locations. One task IT departments often overlook is the need to clean up the identity mess left behind once they have established a mature IDM strategy. When left active, old, obsolete, and unused accounts can be used as backdoors to bypass security controls and compromise data. Organizations need to form IDM policies and procedures defining how users will be created and where user identity information will be stored. IT developers should be aware of these identity stores and mandated to use them. When multiple stores exist, IDM policies must define what user attributes are in the core or central user store and what attributes are placed in secondary directories. The central or authoritative user store in most cases cannot be the sole location for all user information. Doing this would make user searches slow and ineffective. Core user attributes usually include:

- User name
- User ID
- User address
- User email address
- User phone number

Some of the identity attributes that can be found in secondary stores include:

- Tax identification information (e.g., Social Security number)
- Date of birth
- Medical insurance
- User interface preferences
- Application-specific access authorizations

In secondary stores, the user ID can be used as a synchronization key. This allows the real user name to be obfuscated behind a "core" alias if that is the desired outcome.

Security Management

Security management encompasses IT components at multiple levels within the infrastructure, including perimeter defenses, network and host security, and data protection. Security management tasks are often conducted by a number of different teams. For example, the operations teams may handle log consolidation and collation, the network team may handle the virtual private network (VPN), wireless, and router security, and the security team may handle firewall configurations. The exact distribution of these tasks will depend on organizational need. Ideally security management should be a security team function. This provides a separation of duties that increases the integrity and accuracy of security-related data. Allowing operations personnel to control and maintain security devices, logs, and audit trails makes it possible for a disgruntled or malicious employee to violate system security and destroy the evidence (logs) of a violation. At a minimum, the security team should be responsible for firewall configurations, public key infrastructure (PKI) management, security log consolidation, and compliance monitoring. Furthermore, the security team should always be copied on all security-related update notifications and alerts generated by antivirus and intrusion detection/prevention systems. Some companies assign all or a portion of IDM to the security team, especially when smart cards, tokens, or other security devices are involved.

There are several critical relationships between security management and CM. Maintaining current and accurate configuration information for all security-related devices is critical. Restoring an old configuration could result in security vulnerabilities. CMDB updates for security devices must be mandated as part of the change management process. Furthermore, changes to security devices must be verified as correct and complete. The number one cause of security device failure is misconfiguration. All changes to security controls and control devices must be confirmed, preferably by a third party (i.e., someone not directly involved in the configuration change). For Internet systems, some organizations prefer to use external penetration testing companies for this function. It is also important to securely store all security device configurations. If they are stored in the common CMDB, they need to be encrypted, otherwise, they should be stored on a file system with appropriate access controls and access auditing to ensure only security personnel have access. Backups of these files must be encrypted, especially if they will be stored off-site. Copies of the encryption keys should be maintained by the security team.

Current and accurate configuration information also facilitates security patch application. CMDB information can be used to identify the systems with vulnerable versions of an application or operating system. System criticality classifications in the CMDB can then be used to prioritize security update deployment. The same information also facilitates incident response by helping security and support personnel quickly identify vulnerable systems and risks so location information in the CMDB can be used to put controls in place to contain the incident. CMDB information can also be used to facilitate the rebuilding of compromised systems.

As attacks have increased, security management has become an increasingly more complex and difficult task that requires ever-increasing levels of expertise. Consequently many organizations have elected to outsource security management tasks, including firewall and intrusion detection/prevention monitoring and maintenance. The key to outsourcing these services is good oversight. At least one person within the organization should have the requisite security knowledge necessary to audit and verify the outsourcer's compliance with company security policies and requirements. Furthermore, all contracts and service level agreements (SLAs) must include security monitoring and reporting requirements.

Security controls and requirements are often at odds with operational objectives. Operations is focused on delivering services to end users. Given the choice between security and service, for them security requirements are undoubtedly second. To ensure good security management practices, it is best to separate operations and security management operations. When this is not possible, employ the "trust but verify" principle through consistent monitoring and audit logging.

Storage Management

Storage management has been given a number of different names over the years, including hierarchical storage management (HSM), data storage management (DSM), enterprise storage management (ESM), and most recently data protection management (DPM). All these designations incorporate the principles of on-line, near-line, and off-line storage management, including backup, archival, and disaster recovery. On-line and near-line management tasks include setting storage quotas, data replication, free space monitoring, space allocation, and deleted, temporary, and obsolete files cleanup. Off-line tasks include file backup, archiving, media management, off-site storage, and disaster recovery. Storage management also includes the analysis of storage requirements and utilization trends.

Storage management is another operation and maintenance task that has increased exponentially in recent years. At this writing the average Fortune 500 company is managing more than 200 terabytes of stored data. To put this is perspective, as little as 20 years ago this was the total storage capacity of all these organizations combined! Storage management technologies have improved considerably in recent years due in part to the plummeting cost of disk storage. In 1982 the per kilobyte cost of data storage was 15 cents, at this writing it is less that one-millionth of a cent. The availability of low-cost storage has in some ways reduced the cost of on-line storage management; for example, eliminating the need for quotas and allowing the intervals between cleanup tasks to be increased. Virtual disk management technologies have also reduced the time required to reallocate space between logical disk partitions. The opposite is true for off-line storage management, where the deluge of data has made backup, archiving, and recovery tasks incredibly challenging.

Fortunately low-cost disk storage also makes it possible to use replication and copy technologies to manage backups and archives. DPM is quickly replacing traditional tape backup technologies. DPM is a convergence of backup, archiving, and disaster recovery. DPM has also unified these activities, which in the past were treated as separate activities. The availability of inexpensive disk storage has made it possible to craft a comprehensive data protection solution with a single software offering. The primary advantages of DPM are reduced backup times, increased reliability, faster restores, on-line archiving, site-to-site replication, and continuous data protection (real-time data duplication). Another technology to consider when building a storage management strategy is encryption. In the past, the overhead associated with encryption was too great to make the bulk encryption of disk data practical. New technologies based on a simple idea—place the encryption device between the server and storage device—provide full-time, full-disk encryption capabilities. This is an excellent way to secure on-line data and ensure the confidentiality and integrity of backups stored off-site.

The relationship between storage management and CM is straightforward. Changes to on-line disk storage allocations and capacity need to be reflected in the CMDB. Changes to backup, archiving, and disaster recovery systems and agents must also be properly updated in the CMDB. Updates must be controlled through change management and the changes reflected in the CMDB. Since off-line and DPM data are critical to disaster recovery and incident management, CMDB updates should be mandated as part of the change management process for these systems. Changes to these systems should also be verified to protect against potential data loss should the change cause backup processes to fail.

Storage management is essential to system operations and the restoration of business functionality in system failure and disaster scenarios. Good storage management practices reduce downtime, protect data, and ensure business continuity. Leveraging DPM disk-based backup reduces backup and restore times and lowers off-line storage management costs by consolidating backup, archiving, and disaster recovery tasks into a single solution.

Performance Management

Performance management is the set of system monitoring processes an organization uses to ensure systems are meeting business operation demands. Performance is typically measured against an established set of baselines. Performance management tasks include monitoring system central processing unit (CPU) load, memory utilization, network utilization, disk capacity, and so forth. Performance management has been a central component of system operation and support for many years and is highly automated. Consequently the impact of performance management on operations and support staff has been relatively minor despite increases in the number of managed systems. Most systems have integrated performance management capabilities; the most common being the Simple Network Management Protocol (SNMP). These capabilities also include alerting and notification functions. These services are typically linked to a central console that is used to graph and display performance statistics and generate alerts when system performance fails to meet established thresholds.

Performance management service and agent configurations are kept in the CMDB. Changes to these services need to be controlled through change management and updated configuration parameters reflected in the CMDB. If these services are used for security-related monitoring, CMDB updates should be mandated as part of the change management process.

Performance management is particularly important for newly deployed systems, because major system bugs are usually identified in the first 90 days of operation.

Good performance monitoring allows the IT organization to proactively identify and resolve potential system bottlenecks and impending failures, thus reducing downtime and associated productivity losses.

Update Tasks

Often referred to as change, add, and delete tasks, updates are a regular part of system operations and support. Activities include additions, changes, and deletions to system hardware, firmware, software, and applications. Although the number of managed systems has increased, the hardware operation and maintenance burden has remained relatively constant primarily because of increased hardware reliability and hardware maintenance outsourcing. The opposite is true for software. Software change, add, and delete requirements have been growing at a tremendous pace. This section introduces software update management, the primary topic for the second half of this book.

Operating System and Application Updates

One of the largest components in the operate and maintain arena is operating system (OS) and application updates. Updating or patching systems is a common maintenance task that has been elevated in importance by security concerns. Today, update and patch management programs have both operations (maintenance) and security (risk management) elements. The security element is the result of a sharp reduction in the "time to exploit." Time to exploit is the difference in time between the announcement of a vulnerability and the appearance of the associated exploit code. The Nimba worm's time to exploit was nearly a year, but the time has been decreasing rapidly. The Blaster worm appeared a mere 26 days after the patch was released. By the end of 2004 the Symantec Internet Security Report had fixed the average time to exploit for the last half of 2004 at less than 6 days.

Simply stated, a patch is an update to a piece of software (throughout the remainder of this book the terms patch and update are used interchangeably). When a patch involves repairing a security vulnerability in a system, it also becomes a critical part of the risk management function. A vulnerability is a flaw in the system which, if exploited, can lead to system compromise, putting critical data resources at risk of disclosure, theft, modification, or destruction. Therefore patching a system to prevent it from being exploited is clearly a risk management function.

Patch/Update Challenges

Time to exploit is undoubtedly the biggest challenge for operations and support personnel tasked with maintaining secure systems. A 6-day turnaround is barely enough time to get an update installed in the next available change window, never mind testing, packaging, and deployment requirements. Other factors, including change management requirements, missing vendor notifications or files, periodic business service requirements (e.g., quarterly financial reports), lack of sufficient privilege or system access, and insufficient time or resources, can significantly influence update installation timelines.

Nonetheless, failing to resolve system and application flaws can have devastating effects on IT infrastructure integrity and business operations. Self-propagating worms and viruses can quickly overwhelm available network bandwidth and compromise multiple systems, requiring rebuilds and restores before normal operations can be restored. Such events not only lead to massive downtime and productivity losses, but recovery costs can be substantial. For example, an organization with an unknown number of compromised systems may need to hire a "red team" to assess and identify infected systems. Red teams consist of security experts skilled in the detection of root kits, Trojans, backdoors, and other types of exploits. They do not come cheap; a team of five people can cost in excess of $50,000 per week. There are also potential downstream costs from compromises, including notification costs for the personally identifiable information (PII) disclosure (e.g., Social Security, credit card, or bank account numbers) as well as regulatory fines, legal costs, and erosion of the organization's customer base.

In addition to the potentially adverse effects of failing to update systems, there are potential compatibility and performance impacts associated with the introduction of updates into the existing computing environment. Adding new software, hardware, or firmware to the current install base must be managed with caution. The key to success is proper evaluation, prioritization, and testing. In modern IT infrastructures there are many dependencies between systems; thorough testing ensures critical impacts are avoided. Therein lies the dilemma: How is it possible to quickly deploy and thoroughly test at the same time? The following sections introduce the Information Technology Infrastructure Library (ITIL) processes used to receive, verify, evaluate, test, and deploy software updates, including how to establish a deployment timeline and prioritize updates to meet today's update management challenges.

Overview of ITIL: Patch Management Quadrants and Tasks

The ITIL update/patch management process is divided into four quadrants: assess, identify, evaluate, and plan and deploy (Figure 9.1). There are a number of tasks associated with each quadrant; these are covered in detail in Chapters 10 through 15, including industry best practices and lessons learned. The purpose of this section is to introduce the reader to the goals/purpose of each quadrant.

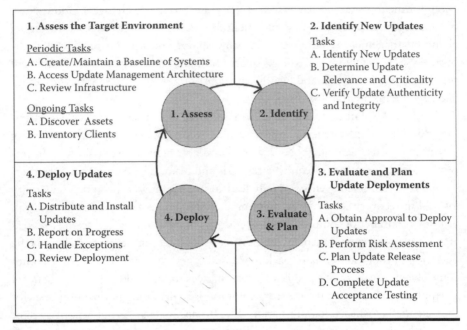

Figure 9.1   ITIL update management process.

Quadrant 1: Assess

The purpose of this quadrant is to evaluate the environment that updates will be deployed in to ensure the update process is current, has adequate capability, and is applicable to all active systems. Quadrant 1 has two types of tasks: those that are conducted periodically and those that are done on an ongoing or regular basis. Periodic tasks include evaluating new requirements and updating system baselines. A baseline is the minimum required settings for a system. Baselines establish what must be done to keep systems up to date and are the basis for compliance measurement and reporting. New internal security or functionality requirements as well as vendor releases often require revisions to system baselines. For example, the release of a vendor service pack or patch bundle often means that patches and updates will no longer be supplied for an old version of the software. This means the OS version baseline must be updated to ensure systems can be updated with critical patches in the future. It is also necessary to evaluate the architecture and infrastructure components from time-to-time to ensure they are adequate. As companies grow, diversify, and expand geographically their technology requirements change. For example, remote offices and portable systems introduce significant challenges into the patching process. So do operations in multiple time zones and those crossing bandwidth-restricted links. The update architecture and infrastructure components must change to accommodate this growth. If they don't, it may be impossible to deliver and deploy patches that ensure system security and operational integrity.

An architecture based on the deployment of patches on a quarterly basis does not work in a 6-day time-to-exploit environment, nor does an infrastructure designed to deliver patches on a 100 megabit Ethernet work effectively on systems connected on 56 kilobit dial-in connection. This is why it is an absolute necessity to periodically review these elements of an update/patch management program.

Change is a certainty in the IT world; new systems are introduced, malfunctioning systems are rebuilt, and old systems are retired, and in many instances these systems are not company owned or managed systems. These are vendor or contractor PCs, third-party service provider systems (e.g., voice mail, Voice over Internet Protocol [VoIP], etc.) or employee-owned smart phones, personal digital assistants (PDAs), and laptops that are not actively managed by IT operations or support. However, this does not exempt them from patch management requirements. When these systems are attached to the internal network they represent a substantial risk to company resources if they do not conform to company baseline requirements. Therefore it is necessary to have an ongoing assessment process to keep system inventories up to date and to discover new (previously unknown) systems on the network. It is not possible to secure or maintain what you do not know about, so these ongoing assessment tasks are crucial to the success of IT security and operations.

Quadrant 2: Identify

The purpose of the identify quadrant is to ensure that IT and security personnel are aware of new vendor patch/update releases. Security vulnerabilities can show up in any number of IT products, including operating systems, services, utilities, and applications. Having current information about these updates is a daunting task, considering that the average IT shop supports more than 300 such entities. If this number seems high, consider this: it is not unusual to find enterprises supporting 6–10 versions of the Unix OS in addition to 6–10 versions of Windows and two or three versions of the Mac OS. Add a couple of difference versions of office and messaging applications (i.e., Word, Excel, Project, Visio, Outlook, Endora, Instant Messenger, etc.), two or three versions of Web browsers and browser plug-ins, plus various versions of common utilities like antivirus, WinZip, and QuickTime along with your standard business applications and it is not difficult to achieve these numbers. The number of vendors and the various ways in which these vendors supply update information only complicates the matter. Larger vendors such as Microsoft and Hewlett-Packard have proactive notification systems, but smaller vendors may only post update information on a public Web site. Identifying and querying vendor update information (intelligence gathering) is only one aspect of the identify quadrant.

After an update has been identified, it is necessary to determine how critical the patch is and whether or not it is applicable to the current install base. This requires an accurate inventory of system, utility, and application software, including current versions as well as any previously installed hot fixes or updates. The final task in the identify quadrant is the procurement and verification of the update code from the manufacturer or trusted agent.

Quadrant 3: Evaluate and Plan

The purpose of the evaluate and plan quadrant is to ready updates for deployment. Tasks include determining the deployment timelines based on the risks the software flaw poses to IT assets. A security flaw that gives administrator access to high-value systems will have a short deployment timeline, whereas a flaw with no significant security or reliability issues would have a long deployment timeline. Once the deployment timeline has been determined, the deployment can be submitted for change management approval and patch release engineering can be done. Release engineering involves the creation of patch deployment packages. For example, companies that use Microsoft SMS as their primary deployment tool would create Microsoft installer (MSI) packages. Other deployment methods may require the creation of custom scripts or packages for other third-party installation tools. Once a package is created it must be tested to verify it works properly on the various types of systems on which it will be deployed. All installation packages should include an uninstall (rollback) option. If the installer does not support uninstall then a second installation package must be created to roll back the install in the event of patch or system failure. Testing must also be conducted to ensure this package works properly. In conjunction with the automated methods, manual steps for installing and uninstalling the patch must also be documented to support any one-off or unmanaged systems that require manual patching. When the planning and engineering portions are completed the information must be communicated to the system administrators and owners so they can begin acceptance testing to identify and resolve any potential system-specific compatibility or performance issues.

Quadrant 4: Deploy

The deploy quadrant installs the updates and verifies the installation was successful. Tasks in this quadrant include scheduling deployments through the change management process, automated or manual patch installation, and the verification of proper patch installation and system operation. It is inevitable that some patch incompatibilities will arise from time to time, so another important task in this quadrant is exception handling. When testing or deployment activities result in installation failures, incompatibilities, or adverse system impacts, there must be a well-defined process for reporting problems and getting fixes or workarounds in a timely manner. If problems cannot be resolved within the required deployment timeframes there must be a clear procedure for requesting, evaluating, and granting exceptions. Another key activity in the deploy quadrant is reporting. Regular reporting shows deployment progress against required timelines and also serves as a risk reduction record for security-related updates. Two types of reports are needed: a detailed horizontal report to system and application owners to keep them informed on their patching status, and a summary vertical report to give senior managers an overview of update process.

There is one final activity in this quadrant that should not be overlooked: the deployment review. Each deployment should be reviewed, issues and problems identified, and steps taken to improve the process and prevent reoccurrences.

The relationship between CM and update tasks is an obvious one. Changes, additions, and deletions to system hardware, firmware, and software must be properly recorded through the change management program and the CMDB updated to reflect the results of these operations. While challenging, change, add, and delete tasks can be managed and automated in a way that maintains system reliability, mediates system risks, and minimizes the impact of change on user productivity and business operations.

Baseline System Measurement

No matter how good your processes are, you still must be able to demonstrate/prove they are effective. Baseline measurement is a monitoring function designed to collect usage, performance, security, configuration, and audit information for comparison to established requirements and to track system operational characteristics over time. Performance and reliability monitoring are long-standing operations tasks with well-defined metrics and thresholds; usage and baseline compliance measurements are not. This has a lot to do with how operations effectiveness is commonly measured (i.e., uptime, response time, trouble calls, etc.). The focus of operations has been on reliability and performance. That focus is beginning to change as a result of the impacts security incidents have had on companies, as well as emerging regulatory requirements.

On the software side of the equation, baseline measurement has two specific tasks: audit log management and baseline security/configuration compliance. The audit log management process defines how audit log information is collected, consolidated, and processed. This includes defining the audit metrics at the device and processing levels. Device metrics identify what items will be audited (e.g., privileged access attempts) and what data will be collected (e.g., failed and successful attempts). Baseline compliance management is an auditing function designed to evaluate system compliance with internal policies, standards, and procedures. It should not be confused with legal or regulatory compliance, which monitors adherence to external laws, regulations, contractual agreements, and so forth.

Baseline compliance management is typically conducted by the organization's security or internal auditing team with the assistance of system operations and support. The overall goal of baseline compliance measurement is to determine the effectiveness of existing controls. Controls, whether technical or procedural, are only valuable if they work correctly. Controls are implemented to reduce risk; companies must have ways to measure the effectiveness of their controls to ensure they are working properly and meeting risk reduction expectations. Baseline compliance management solutions provide a consistent repeatable way to measure control performance against established baselines, report on risk reduction, and demonstrate return on investment.

Measurement is often overlooked by IT departments, but good measurement practices can be invaluable. Bill Hewlett, the cofounder of Hewlett-Packard, said it best, "You cannot manage what you cannot measure." Measurement can be used to demonstrate operational effectiveness and return on investment and to justify new IT projects and spending. It must be an integral part of IT operate and maintain functionality.

Remediation Tasks

No matter how proficient an organization's operate and maintain functions are, systems are going to fail or fall out of compliance from time to time and require remediation. Remediation may require component replacement or updates to existing components or component configurations. For hardware components, repair tasks involve the identification and replacement of failed components, including the procurement of replacement parts. In the past, components were repaired, but this is seldom the case today; replacing components is usually faster and less costly. For software components, the opposite is usually true. Transitioning between software products is usually too time consuming to make replacement a viable option. Applying updates or workarounds is the more common remediation method.

Misconfiguration and unauthorized changes are the most common causes of system malfunctions and failures. The CMDB contains the sanctioned system configuration. Comparing the existing system configuration against the CMDB is a quick way to identity what has been changed. In many instances remediation is simply a matter of reversing these changes and restoring the system to its proper operating configuration. In other instances the system may require a vendor hot fix or update. Remediation would then follow the processes outlined in the "Update Tasks" section above, which includes recording update changes in the CMDB. Workarounds are the other remediation option. When workarounds alter system configurations, these changes must be recorded in the CMDB as well.

When systems break or fail there must be procedures in place to quickly identify and resolve the problem. This is equally true when systems fall out of compliance (i.e., fail baseline security checks). Clear remediation procedures, including problem escalation, for all operation and maintenance staff are absolutely essential to ensure operational integrity throughout the IT infrastructure.

System and Support Documentation

One of the key points of this book that is emphasized over and over again is the need for everyone involved in IT operations and support to clearly understand what is expected of them (i.e., what tasks they are responsible for and the timelines available to complete those tasks). The best way to convey this information to stakeholders is through consistent precise documentation. Unfortunately documentation has not been a strong point in IT operations in the past. However, emerging regulatory requirements, such as the Sarbanes-Oxley Act of 2002 (SOX), are forcing IT organizations to improve their documentation practices. The difficult question is, What should be documented?

From a CM standpoint, systems are documented in the CMDB and can be reported on in the form best suited to the stakeholders' requirements using report generation applications. Similarly, performance and baseline compliance results are available from measurement stores. However, these stores only contain "what" information (what systems exists, what is configured, what is compliant, etc.). Effective operations and support also require procedures and guidelines for "how" (how to deploy, configure, operate, troubleshoot, etc.). Part of the operate and maintain task is to keep the "how" documentation in synch with the "what." When widespread changes are made to system configurations, operations, support, and help desk documentation must be reviewed and updated. Outdated documentation can lead to operations and support errors that compromise security, impact user productivity, and reduce business operational efficiency. It is highly recommended that IT organizations maintain technical writing resources on staff and integrate documentation update and review processes into their operate and maintain functionality.

System Support

The final section is this chapter briefly reviews a number of additional support processes related to the operate and maintain function. Some are covered in greater detail in other chapters.

Incident Management

Incident management consists of the processes and procedures used to verify, control (contain), and resolve system security violations. In some instances, incident management may also include the collection and preservation of evidence related to an incident. Incident management is facilitated by CMDB information. The CMDB is the authoritative source of system configuration information and can be used to detect and verify the presence of unauthorized system changes, including unauthorized services or software, disabled security controls, and altered auditing mechanisms. For example, the process list in Table 9.1 contains what appears to

Table 9.1   PsList 1.21 – Process Information Lister

PsList 1.21 – Process Information Lister
Copyright © 1999–2002 Mark Russinovich
Sysinternals – www.sysinternals.com
Process information for STACK-TST:

Name	Pid	Pri	Thd	Hnd	Mem	User time	Kernel time	Elapsed time
Idle	0	0	1	0	28	0:00:00.000	26:43:02.187	0:00:00.000
System	4	8	58	315	236	0:00:00.000	0:25:28.031	0:00:00.000
smss	484	11	3	21	388	0:00:00.015	0:00:00.015	27:36:27.033
csrss	904	13	12	478	4300	0:00:01.984	0:00:14.281	27:36:25.486
winlogon	928	13	20	651	4476	0:00:00.968	0:00:00.703	27:36:24.939
services	972	9	15	290	4284	0:00:01.156	0:00:02.359	27:36:24.846
lsass	984	9	20	360	1444	0:00:09.093	0:00:02.218	27:36:24.830
svchost	1152	8	19	208	4964	0:00:00.203	0:00:00.078	27:36:24.642
svchost	1208	8	10	320	4280	0:00:00.234	0:00:00.296	27:36:24.408
spoolsv	1680	8	13	144	6344	0:00:00.093	0:00:00.109	27:36:23.799
Lexspool	376	8	2	116	2732	0:00:16.593	0:00:32.046	27:36:23.408
svchost	508	8	7	134	4376	0:00:00.125	0:00:00.093	27:36:23.080
wdfmgr	576	8	4	65	1696	0:00:00.015	0:00:00.015	27:36:22.971
alg	1616	8	5	109	3524	0:00:00.015	0:00:00.000	27:36:21.861
explorer	868	8	16	581	24324	0:00:29.546	0:00:37.140	27:36:06.721
rundll32	1952	8	3	102	5176	0:00:00.828	0:00:00.421	27:36:04.986
IEXPLORE	2688	8	6	390	2316	0:00:01.250	0:00:02.859	3:02:21.718
cmd	548	8	1	32	2588	0:00:00.015	0:00:00.015	0:01:58.078
pslist	1628	13	2	72	1608	0:00:00.015	0:00:00.015	0:00:00.000

be a Lexmark spooler application. However, the CMDB did not contain a Lexmark printer or print driver for this system. Based on this information, the system administrator further investigated the Lexspool process and determined it was a renamed copy of Netcat configured for backdoor command shell access.

The CMDB can also be used to identify critical systems and network segments so containment efforts can be focused on protecting those resources. If the attack targets specific systems, software, or revisions, the CMDB can be used to identify those systems as well.

One aspect of incident management can seriously impact change management. Often the urgency of attack remediation causes a lot of changes to be made to systems outside of the change management process. While this is perfectly understandable, procedures must be in place to ensure these changes are recorded and the CMDB updated appropriately once the incident is under control. It is best practice for all incident management personnel to maintain a log of all their activities and findings throughout the incident. If diligently applied, these logs are excellent sources of system change information. Verifying properly updated change information should always be an agenda item for postmortem incident reviews.

Problem Management

Problem management covers non-security-related system issues. Like incident management, it consists of the processes and procedures for verifying, containing, and resolving system malfunctions and failures. Problem management is facilitated by CMDB information. The CMDB is the authoritative source of system configuration information and can be used to detect and verify the presence of unauthorized system changes. The CMDB can also be used to identify other systems that may be susceptible to this problem based on system hardware, software, and revisions.

When problems impact critical systems or large numbers of systems, problem management can have the same urgency concerns as incident management. When changes are made to systems outside of the change management process, there must be procedures in place to ensure those changes are recorded and the CMDB updated appropriately. Problem management (unlike incident management, which can involve legal and law enforcement activities) has no written log requirements. However, this is still the best practice and the best way to ensure changes are tracked and properly documented once the problem has been resolved. Problem management reviews should always include an agenda item to confirm all changes are properly recorded and the CMDB updated.

Change Management

Change management is defined as the process used to plan, initiate, realize, and record changes to production systems. Change and CM are tightly integrated processes. CM relies on change management to ensure updates and changes to system configurations do not adversely impact business operations and productivity. Change management depends on the accuracy of configuration data to properly evaluate these potential impacts. Change management is covered in detail in Chapter 13.

Release Management

Release management consists of the processes and procedures used to deploy changes into an IT environment. The goal of the release management process is to ensure that approved changes are successfully deployed into production with the least possible disruption to user productivity and business operations.

Like change management, release management is tightly integrated with CM. The results of release management are what drive changes to the CMDB. Successful deployments trigger CMDB changes. Release management practices are discussed extensively in Chapter 14.

Help Desk

Efficient and effective end user support is essential for the realization of business objectives. Organizations must have a viable way to resolve issues impacting user productivity and business operations. Most help or service desk functions are tiered. Tier one personnel handle the majority of routine end user issues, escalating issues they cannot resolve to tier two. Depending on the size and complexity of the organization, additional internal support tiers may be available for problem escalation, including escalations to vendors. Help desk personnel can leverage CMDB information to acquire system configuration information, including installed software and revisions and recent system changes, to help them diagnosis end user problems. In most cases help desk personnel should have no need to update CMDB information. Qualified support engineers should schedule and execute significant changes to system configurations and then record CMDB changes. Ideally this update will include an update to the help desk knowledge base to simplify the resolution of similar incidents in the future.

Conclusion

Operation and maintenance tasks represent the core functionality of most IT organizations. IT staff will spend about 80% of their time performing operations and support functions. As reliance on IT systems for critical business operations has increased, so has the load on operations and support personnel. Not only have availability requirements increased, but security exploits have driven update requirements into very short timelines. The situation is further exacerbated by the exponential growth of on-line data storage, increased regulation, cross-platform IDM, and geographically dispersed computing environments. While requirements have increased substantially, IT staffing has not. All of these factors combined make the automation of IT operate and maintain functions an absolute necessity, and that begins with an accurate, up-to-date asset inventory and CMDB.

Chapter 10

Patch/Update Management: Assess Tasks

Patch/update management consists of four distinct activities: assess, identify, evaluate and plan, and deploy. Each activity consists of a number of individual tasks. Figure 10.1 shows the update management process as four quadrants. This chapter covers the tasks in the assess quadrant.

The tasks in the assess quadrant are divided into two groups: ongoing tasks and periodic tasks. As the names imply, ongoing tasks are continuous and periodic tasks are conducted at appropriate intervals. Periodic tasks are also fundamental components that must be completed when setting up a patch/update management program, so both aspects of these components are presented.

Setup and Periodic Assessment Tasks

There are four tasks that must be accomplished when setting up an update management function; these tasks must be performed periodically thereafter to maintain the effectiveness and efficiency of the update process. These include maintaining a good baseline of system information and requirements, identifying and subscribing to update information sources, and ensuring the update architecture and infrastructure are sufficient. The review periods will vary depending on company requirements and growth. Companies that are growing rapidly will need to assess

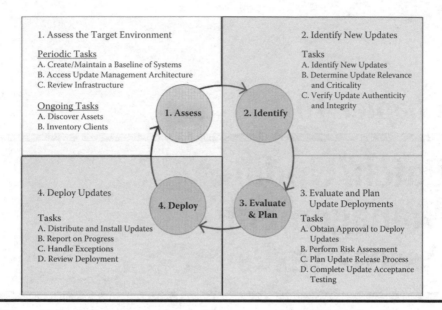

Figure 10.1 Update management process.

more often, especially if there are major changes to information technology (IT) management or infrastructure (e.g., changes as a result of a company merger or acquisition). Architecture and infrastructure reviews should be conducted annually; system baselines should be conducted on a quarterly basis.

System Baselining

Update/patch management is a subset of configuration management (CM), so several tasks are simply extensions of standard CM tasks. For example, update management requires a current and accurate inventory of systems. An IT asset inventory is a standard CM process. It is covered in detail in Chapter 4 and thus there is no need to repeat it here. Instead, this section will concentrate on the information required for update operations. The key pieces of information required for update operations include:

■ Location and identification information
■ Hardware and software model or version information
■ Notification information
■ Deployment information
■ Verification and tracking information

The extent of the data gathered will vary depending on the tools and methods a company uses for CM. Some tools may gather and maintain the information as part of their standard operations, others may require custom scripting. Automation is really the key to efficient collection and management of update information; whenever possible, take advantage of existing system automation capabilities to enhance these tasks. It is also important to note that baseline information will vary depending on the role of the system and the potential impact changes could have on productivity and business continuity. Business critical server and host systems or those with large populations of users require additional update information to manage and minimize potentially adverse impacts. Single or limited use systems such as workstations and laptops have fewer required changes. Since these systems are commonly managed by different support groups, Table 10.3 is included at the end of this section to note these differences.

The following sections contain examples of some of the data elements that might be collected under each of the five areas listed above. They contain the most common elements, not all of which may be relevant to your operations, and there may be elements your operations require that are not covered.

System Identification/Locator Information

These data elements are used to uniquely identify a system and determine its location. These are standard configuration management database (CMDB) data elements such as asset inventory number, system name, and network address (see Chapter 4 for detailed information regarding these elements).

System-Level Versioning Information

System-level versioning information is used to determine the applicability of an update to a system. Different hardware platforms, operating systems, and configurations often require different versions of an update or different deployment techniques. Most of this information is part of the standard CMDB, including operating system (OS) and OS version, installed applications and application versions, hardware make and model, etc. (see Chapter 4 for detailed information regarding these elements). One element of the versioning information that is important to the update process is the historical list of installed updates. This information is necessary to determine the sequencing and applicability of updates; some updates have prerequisite updates, others may have been superseded by previously installed updates. Make sure this information is being captured in the CMDB.

Notification Information

Notification information is used to inform the people involved in the update process of new updates, installation timelines, and remediation actions. Notifications can include system administrators or support groups, system/application owners, users, and any other parties that may be affected by a system update or change. The system owner is usually captured as part of the standard CMDB, and in some instances this may be sufficient for notification in small environments. Larger or more complex environments will need additional data elements to manage update scheduling, deployments, and verification tasks, including:

- Administrator contact—The person or group responsible for the installation of updates on the system. In most companies this is the system administrator or support team responsible for rolling out updates.
- Secondary administrator contact—The person or group should be contacted if the primary administrator contact is not available. When the primary administrator contact is a group, this information usually is not required.
- Owner contact—The person that is accountable for the update status of the system. This person is the escalation point when system updates or remediation actions are not accomplished within established timeframes. Most often this is the manager of the administrator contact or the owner of the line of business application running on the system.
- Line of business administrator contact—The person or group responsible for the installation of updates on the line of business application or applications installed on the system. This parameter is only needed when administrative functions for the system and applications are segregated. In most companies the operations or support group has responsibility for the system and its installed applications.
- Line of business secondary administrator contact—The person or group that is contacted if the primary line of business administrator contact is not available.
- User contact group—The name of the mail or other message distribution list used to notify system users of upcoming changes to the system and how those changes will affect system availability.
- Dependency contacts—One or more persons or groups that may need to be notified before any change to the system can be deployed. Many systems provide critical pieces of information to other systems or need to be operational through critical reporting periods. The criticality of these dependencies is not always obvious to operations or support personnel. The dependency contacts element provides a way to manage these dependencies to avoid inadvertent impacts on business and system processes.

Deployment Information

The information elements in this section track system-specific information affecting the deployment of updates. This includes administrative parameters such as system status, change approval, change window, and reporting requirements, as well as technological parameters such as platform configurations, deployment type, and deployment method. Data elements for deployment include:

- System status—A high-level indicator of the system's ability to accept updates. Computer systems are in a constant state of change; systems are frequently built, rebuilt, renamed, or retired. Third-party systems, test devices, and one-off systems are often exempt from standard deployments. System status provides a simple way to determine whether or not any updates should be deployed to the system. Common status values are shown in Table 10.1.
- Status expiration—The date the current status expires; mostly used to track exemptions. Some exemptions are blanket—they never expire—while others are issued for specific periods of time. This parameter can be used to track these exemptions and return the system to default status at the end of the exemption period.
- Platform configuration—A list of any platform-specific configuration or installation parameters that could affect the way updates are deployed to the system; for example, clustering, load balancing, port restrictions, host-based firewalls, intrusion detection/prevention system, etc.
- Deployment type—A high-level parameter that defines the methodology used to update this system. Common deployment types are shown in Table 10.2.
- Change window—A timeframe or list of timeframes when updates can be installed on the system and the system restarted if necessary.
- Change restrictions—A list of specific timeframes when the system cannot be patched. These restrictions are usually due to regulatory requirements, where the liability for missing reporting deadlines is substantial but can include other company-specific requirements. Change restrictions override change windows so a system that could normally be updated every Sunday morning is skipped during critical reporting periods.
- Primary deployment method—The name of the standard application or tool used to update the system (e.g., SMS, Big Fix, WSUS, Altiris, etc.).
- Primary deployment version—The version of the application or tool being used to deploy updates. When third-party tools are used to deploy vendor patches it is necessary to track the version of the tool to ensure compatibility between the tool and the vendor-released update package.
- Primary deployment format—The format of the patch package (e.g., MSI, Slipstream, EXE, etc.). Most vendors put patches in a standard format that is native to the operating system or applications, but this is not always the case. The target system for the patch must be able to support the format of the patch

deployment package or the installation will fail. This parameter can be used to flag any unsupported deployment formats.

■ Secondary deployment method—The backup deployment method is used to deploy the update if the primary method fails. If the primary method is SMS, but the management agent has not been installed or has been disabled, this parameter specifies a secondary delivery methodology.

■ Deployment vehicle—The media that will be used to deploy updates to this device. This is primarily a throttling parameter. If the system is located on a wide area network (WAN), virtual private network (VPN), or dial-in connection, the deployment method may need to be altered to support the reduced bandwidth. For example, the Background Intelligent Transfer Service (BITS) protocol may be invoked to deliver patches to VPN or dial-in connected systems. If the system is not connected to the network at all, then the deployment vehicle may be a CD or DVD that is sent to the administrator of this off-line system.

Verification and Tracking Information

The final set of data elements is essentially for record keeping. They are used to track the success of deployments and changes to the CMDB. One of these elements

Table 10.1   System Status Values

Status value	Description
Active/default	System is in active use on the network
Restricted	System is in active use but on a restricted bandwidth connection such as a remote or home office using frame relay, DSL, or dial-in
Inactive/dead	The system is in the IT asset inventory or CMDB but is no longer actively used
Exempt	System is exempt from standard operations and support update processes

Table 10.2   Update Deployment Types

Deployment type	Description
Manual	Updates are applied manually to the system by support
Deliver	Updates are copied to the system but the installation is manually initiated by support personnel
Install	Updates are copied to the system and installed using the parameters set by the deployment tool
Restricted	Updates are copied to the system and installed using bandwidth-sensitive technologies

is the last deployment verification, that is, the date and time the installation of the last deployed update was verified as successfully installed. This is really a quick check parameter that makes it possible to easily generate a status report of systems that have not deployed the latest update. Also included in this set of information are the standard CMDB tracking fields: last update, last updated by, and record creation date. Table 10.3 shows the differences in how these data elements apply to workstation and server systems.

To summarize, this section on system baselining defined a number of key information elements that need to be periodically tracked and updated for patch/update deployment purposes. It is by no means comprehensive; each organization

Table 10.3   Workstation and Server Data Differences

Data element	Application
System identification/locator information	All systems
System-level versioning information	All systems
Administrator contact	All systems
Secondary administrator contact	Server systems
Owner contact	Server systems
	Workstation owner contact usually the primary user or the workstation support group
Line of business administrator contact	Application server systems
Dependency contacts	Server systems
System status	All systems
Status expiration	All systems not in the default status
Platform configuration	Server systems
Deployment type	Server systems as appropriate Install for workstations
Change window	Server systems
Change restrictions	Server systems Workstations involved in critical evolutions
Primary deployment method	All systems
Primary deployment version	All systems
Primary deployment format	All systems
Secondary deployment method	All systems
Deployment vehicle	All systems
Last deployment verification	All systems
Last update, last updated by, and record creation date	All systems

must determine which of these data elements are applicable to their update management program and what other elements may need to be added. It is recommended that system baseline information be updated at least quarterly, or more frequently if possible. When practical, automation should be used to gather system baseline information and cross-reference techniques used to verify the accuracy of the information.

Requirements Baselining

Requirements are the second set of system baselines that must be captured. Determining security baselines is covered in detail in Chapter 16 (Baseline Compliance Management Processes), so this section is a simple overview. Requirements baselining consists of a review of all applicable system policies, standards, best practices, etc. to determine how these requirements will be enforced on each type or classification of system. Some requirements may be enforced through system administration (manual), some through network services such as Active Directory group policy objects (GPOs), and others through vendor applications such as Cisco Works. The objective is to identify the requirements that will be enforced through the update process. The obvious one is critical patches, but other requirements, including security settings, required software, or disallowed software, can also be enforced using update management.

The information gathered during this phase will help define the primary and secondary deployment methods, packaging formats, and delivery/install vehicles used to deploy these updates. This information helps define the program's initial architecture and infrastructure requirements and drives the review of these components. Besides document reviews there are two other activities that can help with the requirements baselining effort. Reviewing help desk and support logs can point to recurring issues that technically may not be requirements, but nonetheless need to be addressed. A good vulnerability scan of systems can also identify additional security issues that need to be addressed.

Subscription Baselining

The next task is to identify and evaluate sources of update information. The first step is to list all the hardware and software vendors captured during the system baselining task and determine the range of model numbers and software versions currently deployed. Once this is established, the source(s) of each vendor's update information must be determined. Potential sources include Web site uniform resource locators (URLs), newsletters, personal contacts, etc. The sources are then saved in the vendor table in the CMDB. It is important to double-check original equipment manufacturer (OEM) items to determine if the OEM or the licensee is responsible for providing updates. For example, video chip manufacturers may provide drivers for their chip sets, but the manufacturer of the video card or motherboard using the chips is usually responsible for distributing updates for those drivers.

Whenever possible, try to identify alternate sources for update information as well. Several organizations and security portals such as the Computer Emergency Response Team (CERT) (http://www.cert.org), Computer Incident Advisory Capability (CIAC) (http://www.ciac.org), and Bugtraq (http://www.securityfocus.com) track vulnerabilities and associated fixes. If you have a large number of vendors and limited resources you may want to consider outsourcing this task to a subscription service. These services provide detailed and timely notifications on security vulnerabilities and fixes from thousands of resources worldwide that can be customized to your particular IT environment. Another advantage of these services is that they have a host of security threat and incident information that can be used to help justify security and system maintenance spending. Google maintains a good list of subscription and update information sources at http://directory.google.com/Top/Computers/Security/Advisories_and_Patches.

Next, it will be necessary to determine how often these sources should be checked for new update information. There are two methods vendors use to distribute update information: publish and notify. Published information is passive notification; it requires you to actively monitor the vendor's published sources for update information. Notify is active notification; the vendor sends update information to people or groups within the organization via mail, email, text message, page, etc. Notify is the preferred method for receiving update information. For vendors that do not provide proactive notification, it may still be possible to create scripts or use utilities such as Web crawlers or text-based browsers to gather update information and generate notifications. Lynx (http://lynx.isc.org) is an example of a utility than can be scheduled to periodically extract update information published on a Web site. Lynx is an open source text-based browser with command line scripting capabilities; it can access Web pages, search for new or updated information, and generate emails, text messages, or pager notifications. Proactive notification is the best way to receive information on updates, especially critical updates, but it should not be the sole source of update information; other sources should also be checked regularly.

The final elements of the subscription task are establishing who will be responsible for maintaining the subscription, who will receive notifications, and who can subscribe to these information sources. Responsibility for subscriptions will vary depending on the organization. Line of business application owners are usually responsible for updates to their applications, otherwise the responsibility for updates is usually split between support groups and security. Subscriptions should always be set up to notify multiple people to ensure coverage when personnel are on vacation, sick leave, and so on. Mailing lists and groups can be leveraged for this purpose. The information security group must be copied on all security-related updates and should be copied on all notifications in case there are any potential security impacts that are not readily apparent. Notification processing needs to be a 24 hours a day,

7 days a week (24/7) activity. Attackers often leverage the absence of personnel on holidays and weekends to improve the proliferation and success of their attacks. Consequently 24/7 proactive notification to key personnel is essential. Whenever possible, use notification services that will send proactive alerts for critical situations. Once the subscriptions, notification services, and alerts have been set up, they should be tested to ensure they are working as expected; especially the notifications that you have scripted. Periodic testing must also be conducted to ensure vendor notifications are still being received and changes to published information sources have not affected script or utility operations.

There will be some instances when update information needs to be gathered manually; that is, someone will need to speak to a vendor representative or read something sent to them in the mail (e.g., a newsletter, flyer, etc.). Whatever the source, the first time a new update is identified it should be entered into a log and then verified for authenticity. The log entry provides a metric for measuring response and tracking timelines for evaluation, testing, and deployment. Verifying the authenticity of the notification avoids unnecessary processing for hoaxes.

Subscriptions are an essential part of the update process. It is impossible to maintain the security and reliability of systems without timely information on newly discovered vulnerabilities and fixes. It is important to establish a formal process for receiving, verifying, and processing new update notifications 24/7. Whenever possible, establish multiple reliable sources for update information and disperse notifications to multiple people to ensure a timely response. Automate as much of the subscription process as possible and use proactive notification techniques. Manual notification methods should only be used when no other alternative is available.

Architecture Review

The update architecture must be reviewed periodically to ensure it is meeting its objectives. Organizational polices and standards dictate the baseline update requirements. The update architecture is the framework for implementing those requirements. The architecture defines the management, operational, and technological aspects of a system. It consists of a series of building blocks and interfaces required to achieve the specified functionality for present and future requirements. These building blocks include the functional, organizational, facilities, operations, and maintenance elements necessary to provide the coverage, functionality, capability, scalability, manageability, reliability, and measurability of the update system. Before looking at the individual building blocks, let's consider the goals for each of the elements listed above:

■ Coverage—The IT landscape is constantly being changed and updated to support new business initiatives and requirements. The coverage goal is to provide an architecture that is flexible and robust enough to incorporate the new systems, processes, and technology necessary to ensure they can be updated. For example, when a new system requires a different deployment technique, can the Deployment Vehicle field in the CMDB be updated to support this requirement? This is equally true of devices being removed from the management system. As machines are retired, can subscriptions, testing, and deployment be modified to exclude these systems?

■ Functionality—Along with coverage, it is necessary to ensure the existing update management systems have adequate functionality to support updating these new systems. The functionality goal is to ensure new requirements are identified so appropriate procedures and infrastructure changes can be made to support them. For example, the introduction of a new OS into the patch management process may require an update to the patch management application or the agent installed on the clients.

■ Capacity—An architecture review also looks at capacity; that is, the ability of the system to service all covered systems within the required timeframes. An update management system may have adequate functionality and coverage, but additional functional requirements and increases in the number of machines covered can overwhelm system resources. For example, it is not unusual to find an update management system originally designed to only deploy patches being used for discovery tasks, compliance monitoring, and hardware and software inventory. Periodic capacity reviews ensure adequate processing, memory, and storage capacity is available to support current service demands.

■ Scalability—In concert with the capacity review, it is important to look at the scalability of the existing architecture. Scalability is the ability to expand capacity. A scalability review looks at the existing system processes and supporting technologies to determine whether or not they can be scaled to meet projected increases in system functionality. Consolidation and standardization are two common scenarios that require scalability reviews because these efforts often take update management processes and technology designed to support a single department and expand it to encompass multiple departments or the entire enterprise. While a centralized management system servicing local area network (LAN) attached machines may be able to efficiently support a large department, it may not be able to scale to support WAN, VPN, or dial-in attached machines. Under these bandwidth restrictions, a distributed management system may be required.

■ Manageability—The ability to manage update processes and technology efficiently across multiple departments and physical locations is an important aspect of a successful update management program. A manageability review looks at what level of effort is required to gather, process, measure, and report on update management information. Reviews will vary depending on the management model (centralized, distributed, mixed), but should always include people, processes, and technology practices. A manageability review should look at the staffing levels and skills required to efficiently manage the program, as well as the skills and tools needed to effectively operate program technologies.

■ Reliability—Sometimes referred to as availability, reliability defines the operational expectations for the update management system. It can be associated with the redundant or resilient properties of the hardware platform the system runs on, as well as the dependability of the software (lack of bugs/crashes, ongoing development, etc.). While the availability/reliability requirements for an update management system are not as critical as many other production systems, they must ensure that the system can consistently meet existing service level agreements (SLAs) and expectations.

■ Measurability—Finally, a way to prove the architecture elements are meeting functional and operational expectations must be established. Measurability defines the metrics that will be used for each architectural element. It does not define the techniques for gathering the information, only the expected results. Table 10.4 contains an example of these metrics. The infrastructure components must provide a way to measure these elements (e.g., collecting uptime statistics on the update management system to measure system availability).

Table 10.4   Service Level Expectations

Architectural element	Function or operational expectation
Coverage	100% company owned systems, 100% contracted/lease systems
	100% personally owned systems used for VPN (quarantine and notify only)
Functionality	100% approved operating systems and supported applications
	100% company supported locations including home offices
	100% company supported connections including LAN, WAN, wireless, VPN, and dial-up
Capacity	*Deployment*
	100% of server/host systems patched within established timeframes
	100% of directly connected workstations within established timeframes
	70% of remote access workstations within established timeframes, 98% within timeframe × 2
	Reporting
	100% of all directly connected systems daily
	100% of all remote access workstations weekly
Availability/ reliability	100% of deployments completed within established timeframes
	<0.1% of deployment failure due to update hardware or software failures

Functional Building Blocks

The functional building block of the update management framework consists of the tasks and supporting elements required to identify, acquire, validate, test, deploy, and verify updates. Figure 10.2 depicts these elements.

Organizational Building Blocks

The architecture defines in broad terms the organizational aspects of the update management program, including:

- Operation—Who will operate the program? Update functions can be done internally, but many companies will opt to outsource some or all of their update management program as part of a larger server or desktop management contract.
- Accountability—Who will ultimately be responsible for the execution of the program? Some companies view updates as an operations function, others assign responsibility to the security department, and for outsourced programs, some companies make contract management accountable for the vendor's update performance.
- Organizational model—What aspects of the program will be centralized and which will be dispersed? This is particularly important for larger organizations with multiple divisions. Dedicated centralized functions can improve efficiency by eliminating duplication of effort, automating tasks, and reducing errors. Centralization makes perfect sense for some update management functions; for example, rating the criticality of a patch is something that can

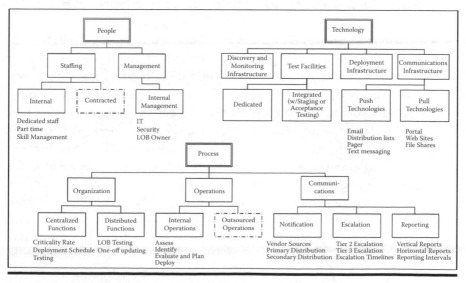

Figure 10.2   Update management architecture.

(and should) be done at the enterprise level. This is not to suggest that criticality ratings should be determined without input from divisional security and operations personnel, only that criticality ratings should be consistent across the entire enterprise and should therefore be set by a centralized authority.

> Testing is another good example. Given the nature and skill requirements for software testing, centralized patch testing for standard configurations is the logical choice. However, centralized testing does not work well for specialized configurations or custom line of business applications; the testing for these systems needs to be dispersed to the personnel that have the knowledge required to properly test update compatibility.

■ Operations model—What program tasks will have dedicated staff and which will rely on part-time participation? Some update management tasks such as testing require specialized skills and benefit from a dedicated staff. A staff dedicated to a specific set of tasks is more efficient, can provide better coverage, and produces fewer errors and rework. By comparison, when update tasks are ancillary duties, they are often viewed as "extra work" and given lower priority or executed quickly to "get them out of the way." This leads to errors and rework that reduces the overall effectiveness of the program.

■ Skills management—How will critical skills be tracked to ensure constant coverage and proper execution of update tasks? Update management is crucial to consistent reliable IT operations. Therefore it is necessary to ensure personnel have the necessary training and cross-training so update management tasks can be executed within required timeframes and with a high degree of proficiency.

■ Communications model—How will update information and results be communicated? Update management is a critical process that requires a fair amount of cross-functional cooperation. Line of business application owners, system administrators, network operations, systems support, security, help desk, departmental coordinators, and end users all require accurate and timely update information to ensure updates are properly deployed and maintained. The model must also identify management communications for escalation and reporting purposes. The communications model identifies these communication channels and defines the nature of each communication. For example, some communications will be active (they will push information to people) and others will be passive (people will pull information). Where appropriate, the communication model should also specify backup (primary and secondary) communications channels. In other words, if email is the primary method and it is inoperable, what is the backup method of notification?

Facility Building Blocks

This portion of the architecture defines the physical facilities that will be required to support the program, including:

- Testing facility—Proper update management requires an isolated facility for receiving, testing, and packaging vendor updates that mirrors the production environment. Many organizations have a staging facility for testing and training purposes that can be used for update compatibility, packaging, and deployment testing.

- Deployment infrastructure—Update management requires technologies and methods for deploying updates to systems. The deployment infrastructure acknowledges that different deployment vehicles and formats are required to accomplish update delivery and installation tasks on different types and classes of systems and identifies the primary and secondary methods needed to accomplish these tasks. For example, some updates require image transfers (read-only memory [ROM] updates), others require simple file transfers, and others require the execution of code at the system or application level.

- Scanning/monitor infrastructure—Once an update has been deployed it is necessary to verify and maintain its functionality. The goal at the architectural level is to identify the different monitoring methods required to accomplish update verification and maintenance tasks on different types of systems and to identify potential methods for accomplishing these tasks. This includes primary and secondary methods when appropriate. For example, a monitoring method that requires an agent on the target system will require a secondary method of monitoring for systems with a missing or malfunctioning agent.

- Communications infrastructure—Many update management tasks rely on clear and timely communications with internal and external parties. Therefore, at the architectural level, it is necessary to identify the different communications facilities required to gather, verify, and distribute update information, including messages, alerts, binaries, and executables. The communications infrastructure acknowledges that different channels may be necessary to facilitate these communications and identifies the various methods that will be required. For example, a SharePoint portal can be used for message and executable distribution using content change alerts and file repositories. Primary and secondary methods should be identified where appropriate.

Other facilities associated with update management include system build facilities, discovery/monitoring facilities, and asset inventory. These facilities are covered in detail in Chapter 6.

Infrastructure Review

The update infrastructure also requires periodic review to ensure it is meeting operational and functional expectations. Infrastructure takes the architectural building blocks and creates actionable solutions that implement the program requirements at a global level, that is, the solutions apply to the enterprise as a whole rather than specific groups or technologies. For example, a network infrastructure provides connectivity solutions to the organization as a whole rather than point solutions for one division.

Infrastructure consists of the people, processes, and technologies necessary to meet specific program goals (requirements). While architecture defines the operational and functional expectation, infrastructure is the vehicle for meeting those expectations. For update management there are three primary infrastructure components to consider: test, deployment, and monitoring/discovery. Each must be evaluated to ensure they are meeting coverage, functionality, capacity, and availability/reliability requirements for existing systems and will be able to meet those requirements for the foreseeable future.

Test Infrastructure

The test infrastructure includes the people, processes, and technology required to test the compatibility, performance, and deployment of updates. Compatibility tests ensure the update does not break any required system functionality, while performance testing ensures the update does not negatively impact system operational capacity. Deployment testing verifies that the update package itself deploys properly and can be rolled back if the patch causes a system to malfunction or fail. The main elements that need to be evaluated are coverage, functionality, capacity, and reliability. Coverage includes determining if all the systems and system configurations have defined test criteria and test plans, as well as the skilled personnel necessary to conduct the testing. Functionality determines if the necessary facilities are in place to conduct all the required test scenarios, including the necessary test equipment, test environment, and automation (i.e., scripts, applications, etc.). Capacity examines whether or not the existing level of personnel and facilities are sufficient to complete the required testing within the required timeframes. Reliability determines if the testing process is producing consistent results. The purpose of testing is to reduce the probability that an update deployment will negatively impact the operation of IT systems. Periodic evaluation of the test infrastructure helps ensure this goal can be met in a consistent and sustainable manner.

Deployment Infrastructure

The deployment infrastructure includes the people, processes, and technology required to deliver, install, and verify updates to systems. The main goal of the evaluation is to determine if the existing deployment infrastructure has sufficient capacity, functionality, and reliability to meet existing and future deployment requirements and timelines. Coverage is not usually an issue; it is assumed that if a vendor provides an update it also provides a means to install it, so technically all systems are covered. However, in some instances this coverage may require time-consuming manual operations that work against capacity requirements. Capacity determines if the existing staffing levels and delivery mechanisms are sufficient to consistently deploy updates to all covered systems. Poor compliance levels are often indicative of poor deployment capacity. A deployment infrastructure evaluation should also take into consideration functionality; can they store all the required information and do they have the necessary deployment vehicles and verification capabilities? Often this functionality is spread across multiple systems, so it is also important to consider the manageability of these systems as capacity requirements increase. Finally, the deployment infrastructure review should evaluate the reliability of these mechanisms and their ability to consistently deliver updates to covered systems within established timeframes. A periodic deployment infrastructure review ensures that existing people, processes, and technologies are consistently meeting deployment requirements. The review also provides the information needed for proactive planning to meet future requirements.

Monitoring/Discovery Infrastructure

The monitoring and discovery infrastructure includes the people, processes, and technologies required to identify, locate, and measure systems against established update baselines. While they are combined here, in some organizations these may be two separate infrastructures. Nonetheless, the goals of the review will be essentially the same: do these mechanisms have sufficient coverage, capacity, functionality, and reliability to meet existing and future monitoring and discovery requirements. Coverage includes the ability to locate the devices attached to a network segment throughout the entire network; extract sufficient information from the system to determine what, if any, baselines apply to the device; and determine if the device meets those baselines. Capacity examines whether or not existing mechanisms can accomplish these three tasks within reasonable timeframes. For example, can the monitoring system measure all systems for compliance within deployment timelines? If the deployment timeline is 4 days, then the monitoring system should have the capability to measure all systems within a 2-day timeframe (see Chapter 16 for further discussion on monitoring timelines and techniques). Functionality determines if the discovery mechanism is thorough enough and whether or not the necessary information can be gathered and measurements made once a system has been located. Reliability looks at the accuracy of the mechanism performing these functions. These functions are usually accomplished with multiple tools and utilities, so it is important when reviewing this infrastructure to consider the manageability of these systems as well. The purpose of monitoring and discovery is to reduce or eliminate noncompliant systems attached to the network. Periodic review helps ensure that the existing people, processes, and technologies are meeting that goal and also helps identify and plan for enhancements that will be needed to meet future requirements.

Communications Infrastructure

One other component that should be periodically reviewed for its effectiveness is the communications infrastructure. Clear and timely communications are crucial to the update management process. Stakeholders must be made aware of new updates and deployment timelines, regularly informed of their compliance status, and provided with good feedback and escalation paths. Communications can take a number of different forms, including push technologies such as mailing lists and pull technologies such as portals. Each must be evaluated to ensure it provides the necessary coverage, functionality, capacity, and reliability. Coverage ensures that everyone involved in the process receives the information they need. Functionality ensures that information is in a consistent and usable format. Capacity ensures it is delivered or available so everyone can accomplish their assigned tasks within the required timeframes. Reliability examines the distribution mechanisms to determine if they are achieving consistent results. The only way to ensure that people can accomplish their required tasks within established timeframes is to provide them with the information they need to accomplish those tasks. A periodic review of the communications infrastructure helps ensure those mechanisms are consistently and reliably delivering that information.

Program Optimization Review

The final periodic review is program optimization, the process of examining established program metrics and outcomes to ensure the existing program is achieving the desired results and to identify areas that can be improved to reduce costs and increase overall program effectiveness and efficiency. This type of review looks at two key elements: the metrics used to measure program performance and the actual performance of the program itself. The intent of this review is (1) to determine whether or not sufficient performance information is being gathered, and (2) to identify and prioritize actions to improve future results. For example, an optimization review would evaluate the performance reported to date and identify any changes or additional information that may be required. It would also assess deployment failures, rollbacks, etc., to identify root causes. Finally, it would review the feedback and suggestions stakeholders and participants have provided. Continuous improvement is an important aspect of program management that should not be overlooked. It ensures the program can demonstrate value and return on investment to the organization through performance metrics, while reducing the impact of the program on the people involved through optimization.

Ongoing Tasks

There are three assessment tasks that must be executed on a continuous (ongoing) basis: IT asset discovery, asset inventory, and compliance monitoring. Asset inventory is covered in detail in Chapter 6 (Configuration Management Control), so this section will only address the discovery and monitoring tasks.

Information Technology Asset Discovery

It is impossible to secure what you do not know about, so it is important to maintain an accurate inventory of what is attached to the network. This is not a trivial task; not every system attached to the network will go through the standard build and inventory process. Vendor and contractor systems, test and development systems, and third-party or personally owned systems are often attached to the network without the knowledge or consent of operations. These unknown or "rogue" systems represent a substantial threat to the stability and security of the internal network on two fronts. First, vendor, contractor, and personally owned portable systems that have been compromised while attached to public/ external networks can introduce malicious code (i.e., worms, viruses, etc.) when they are attached to the internal network (this is a common source of infection in many organizations). Second, rogue systems attached to the internal network can be used to increase the success and impact of an attack. This is possible because rouge systems are not part of the standard patch rotation or compliance monitoring process and therefore are likely to have unpatched vulnerabilities or other security weaknesses such as weak passwords, unsecured services, etc. The IT asset discovery process is designed to locate and identify these systems so they can be remediated before they pose any serious threat to internal resources. The discovery process also provides greater visibility into the actual environment being managed and adds essential system information to the IT asset inventory and other system management services.

Dealing with unknown/rogue systems requires two distinct processes: discovery and remediation. This section covers several ways to identify rogue systems attached to the network. It is followed by a section on remediation—bringing these systems into the known system space or removing them from the network.

Discovery methods fall into two basic categories: passive discovery and active discovery. Active methods provide real-time or near-real-time detection of new devices; passive discovery methods periodically scan the network to detect new devices.

Passive Discovery Methods

Internet Protocol Scanning

Internet Protocol (IP) scanning is one of the most commonly used discovery methods. An IP scanner is an application that attempts to access and identify systems connected to the network based on a range of IP addresses. The scanner attempts to communicate with the target IP address by initiating Transmission Control Protocol (TCP) or User Datagram Protocol (UDP) handshakes to common service ports. Depending on the services or software that are running, the target machine will generate a response. Based on these responses, the scanner can deduce the presence of the device and potentially the system name, OS version, and system role (e.g., router, Web server, database management system [DBMS], etc.). These results can then be compared to CMDB records to determine whether or not this is a known or rogue device.

Internet Protocol scanners are fairly simple to use, reasonably accurate, and have good performance attributes. Also, there are a large number of IP scanners available, so it should not be difficult to find one that suits your particular needs. Because IP scanners generate relatively small amounts of network traffic they can be used effectively on low-bandwidth connections, including dial-up. This efficiency also makes it possible to scan a large number of addresses in a relatively short period of time. This improves their effectiveness by permitting them to be run more often.

Internet Protocol scanners also have their limitations. Scans are only conducted on a periodic basis, so only those systems that are online when the scan is conducted will be detected. Remote or portable systems that only access the network for short periods may never be detected. Periodic scanning also means a rogue device can be on the network distributing worms or other malware for a significant period of time before being detected. The greater the interval between scans, the more significant these issues become. IP scanners are not selective; they report on every device that responds within the specified address range. Therefore it may be necessary to filter the results to eliminate some devices before comparing them to CMDB records.

Network devices such as firewalls and routers using IP filters, as well as similar host-based security measures, can significantly reduce the effectiveness of IP scanners by masking or limiting the responses needed to properly identify a device. Network services such as proxy Ping, Dynamic Host Configuration Protocol (DHCP), and dynamic Domain Name System (DNS) can also skew results by reporting nonexistent systems or making systems appear under multiple IP addresses or name records.

Simple Network Management Protocol Scanning

Simple Network Management Protocol (SNMP) scanners are similar to IP scanners in that they can be configured to scan a range of IP address or specific targets. All the devices attached to the network are configured to respond to a standard SNMP system group query. This read-only query is mandatory for all SNMP implementations and should return the following information:

- System name—The administratively assigned name of this device; usually the fully qualified domain name (FQDN).
- System description—A textual description of the device, including the system's hardware type, software operating system, and networking software.
- System contact—A textual description of the person or group responsible for managing this device, including information on how to contact this person (i.e., phone number, email, etc.).
- System location—The physical location of this device (e.g., telephone closet, 3rd floor, Bldg. 4).
- System uptime—The amount of time, in hundreds of seconds, since the last system restart.

Simple Network Management Protocol scanning has several advantages. SNMP queries have very little impact on network bandwidth or targeted systems so they can be used to scan a large number of systems across all types of connections. Network devices such as firewalls and routers can be easily configured to allow SNMP operations across network segments without significantly increasing risk. The queries are read-only and return most of the key management data required. Queries can also be tuned to specific types of systems using different community strings, eliminating the need to filter results to remove unwanted responses.

On the downside, SNMP queries cannot distinguish between a nonexistent node and an active node that does not have SNMP enabled; both will fail to respond. This means SNMP scans need to incorporate other methods such as Ping or reverse DNS lookup to validate results. Since SNMP uses UDP, results can be adversely impacted by network bandwidth availability. The usefulness of the returned data may also vary. The text fields have no specific format, so it may be difficult to accurately parse the data elements (i.e., OS type, version, etc.), and the amount of contact and location information returned depends entirely on what was entered in those fields when the SNMP agent was configured.

Network Service Query

Network services that dynamically register systems can also be used for discovery purposes. For example, the database of a DHCP service contains system names and media access control (MAC) and IP addresses. Periodically querying the DHCP service for a list of active devices and comparing the results to the CMDB will reveal rogue systems. This is equally true of naming systems such as dynamic DNS and Windows Internet Name Service (WINS); periodically comparing registered system names to CMDB entries will expose unknown devices. Systems also dynamically register their MAC and IP addresses in router Address Resolution Protocol (ARP) tables, so comparing ARP data to CMDB entries is an effective way to find rogues.

One big advantage in using the service query method is that it requires no new or custom tools. These services are already present on the network and systems automatically register with them. The key to the effectiveness of this method is to set the query interval short enough to capture the data before the service ages out (drops) the information. A good rule of thumb is to set the interval to one-half the aging value. For example, a DHCP system that expires leases every 24 hours can be queried as little as twice a day, but an ARP service that drops inactive nodes in 40 minutes must be queried every 20 minutes.

There are several issues with using network services data for discovery purposes. The data are only collected on a periodic basis, so only those systems that are registered when the data are collected will be found. If the interval between queries is too long, records will age out and some systems will not be detected. Periodic scanning also means a rogue device can be on the network for some period of time before it is detected. Depending on the service, the results may need to be filtered because they contain all types of devices (i.e., ARP) or augmented because they only contain a subset of devices (i.e., WINS). Another important thing to remember: systems are not required to use these services (e.g., systems with static IPs do not register with DHCP). This will also affect the accuracy of the results.

Finally, it is important to understand that these services are not designed for this kind of use. Extracting data can be difficult and could potentially cause the service to malfunction. ARP is the exception. Router ARP tables can be queried using SNMP, but ARP is not a centralized database. It is necessary to query all the distribution routers to collect all the required data.

Network Probe

The final passive discovery method uses network probes to collect node information. A probe is a device that monitors network traffic and gathers data about the devices sending or receiving packets. Remote monitoring is an Internet Engineering Task Force (IETF) standard monitoring specification designed to provide network administrators with diagnostic, planning, and performance information. Several commercial and freeware probes have been designed to specifically address security issues such as unauthorized network devices for wired and wireless environments. (e.g., Etherboy, NDG Software; AirMagnet Distributed, AirMagnet Products).

Probes are very efficient. They use minimal network bandwidth by only generating traffic in response to report queries. Probes gather information about systems over time and can usually determine the system name, OS, and version with reasonable accuracy. Depending on the implementation, probes can filter and consolidate data and automatically forward it to a central collection console.

However, probes have limited effectiveness because they can only see systems that generate traffic on the segment they are connected to. It is not practical to place probes on every segment, but placing them on commonly used segments, such as the Internet feed or network backbone, will improve their effectiveness. Nonetheless, a rogue system that never generates traffic on probe-monitored segments can remain on the network and never be detected. The accuracy of probe results can also be reduced if high traffic volumes exceed the probe's processing capabilities, causing it to drop packets.

Summary

Passive discovery methods can be reasonably effective at finding unknown or rogue systems. They are fairly simple to use, reasonably accurate, and very efficient. There are a large number of passive scanners available, so it is not difficult to find one suited to your particular requirements, and they will work in most environments without any infrastructure changes. However, scans conducted on a periodic basis can only detect devices that are online during the scanning period, consequently systems that access the network for short periods may not be detected. Periodic scanning makes it possible for infected devices to be connected to the network for a significant period of time before being detected. Finally, scanning applications are not particularly selective; they report on every device that responds within the specified address range, making it necessary to filter the results.

Active Discovery Methods

Active discovery methods have the advantage of providing real-time or near-real-time detection of new devices. Active discovery uses network devices and services to identify devices connected to the network.

Network Service Monitoring

The network service query technique in the passive monitoring section above can be enhanced to provide proactive real-time notifications by setting up a process to monitor changes in the service data files. For example, if changes to the DHCP database are monitored, as soon as a device registers with DHCP, the management system is notified of the change and can take action to identify the new system. For systems that are unknown, further actions can be taken to gather additional inventory information.

This solution has the same advantages as the network service query method, with the added advantage of providing near-real-time detection of new or rogue devices. However, an infected system may still have sufficient active access to the network to spread the infection. It is also important to remember that, like the query method, the results may need to be filtered to specific devices and the accuracy of the results depends on the systems using the services being monitored. The fact that this is a custom solution is also a disadvantage from a maintenance and service perspective. The volume of changes may also influence the effectiveness of results if it overwhelms the process.

Network Probe Simple Network Management Protocol Traps

Some network probes can be configured to generate SNMP traps when they detect a new node. This is a standard capability of remote monitoring probes. When the trap is received, the network management system can initiate a process to identify the system, gather additional inventory information, or take remediation action.

This method has the advantage of supplying near-real-time detection, but an infected system will still have active access to the network and could spread the infection. This method has the same limitations as the passive network probe solution; it can only monitor for new nodes on a single segment. If a rogue system is not connected to a monitored segment, it will never be detected. The accuracy of a probe can also be reduced by high traffic volumes that exceed the probe's processing capabilities or interfere with SNMP trap deliveries.

IEEE 802.1X

The IEEE 802.1X standard defines port-based network access control for Ethernet networks. This port-based network access control uses the physical characteristics of the switched LAN infrastructure to authenticate devices attached to a LAN port. Access to the port can be denied if the authentication process fails. Although this standard is primarily used for wireless (802.11) networks, many vendors also support it on wired Ethernet LANs.

The IEEE 802.1X standard defines four major components: the port access entity (PAE), the supplicant, the authenticator, and the authentication server. A PAE is a LAN port that supports the IEEE 802.1X protocol. A PAE can adopt the role of the authenticator, the supplicant, or both. A supplicant is a PAE that is attempting to access services on the network, typically an end user device such as a laptop, workstation, or personal digital assistant (PDA). An authenticator is a PAE that enforces authentication before granting the supplicant network access. For wireless connections, the authenticator is the logical LAN port on a wireless access point; on a wired network it is a physical port on an Ethernet switch.

The authentication server is used to verify the credentials of the supplicant. The authenticator collects credentials from the supplicant and passes them to the authentication server for verification. The authentication server can be a component of the authenticator device, but more often it is a separate device such as a Remote Authentication Dial-In User Service (RADIUS) server. Figure 10.3 shows these components for a wireless LAN network.

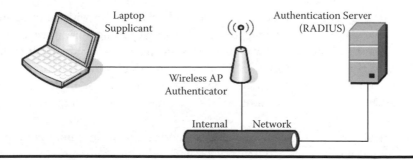

Figure 10.3   Wireless 802.1X components.

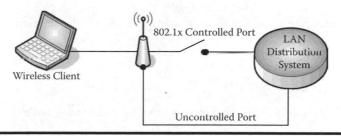

Figure 10.4   Controlled and uncontrolled ports for IEEE 802.1X.

An authenticator has two types of ports. It uses an uncontrolled port to communicate with LAN devices and exchange data with the authentication server. It uses a controlled port to communicate with supplicants. Before authentication, no network traffic is forwarded between the supplicant (client) and the network. This has the advantage of preventing an infected device from spreading that infection on the network. Figure 10.4 shows the two types of ports in a wireless configuration.

Once the client is authenticated, the controlled port is switched on so the client can send Ethernet frames to the network. In a wireless network, multiple clients can be connected to the logical ports on an access point; on a wired network only one client is connected to a physical port on the Ethernet switch.

The 802.1X mechanism supports multiple authentication methods via the Extensible Authentication Protocol (EAP). These include PEAP-MSCHAPv2, digital certificates (EAP-TLS), and two-factor authentication using tokens. For each of these authentication methods, a RADIUS server is used to verify credentials and provide the "EAP Successful" message to the authenticator.

The major advantage of 802.1X is that it works in real time and will keep unauthorized/rogue systems off the network entirely. This prevents the spread of worms and viruses from infected rogue systems. Some of the major drawbacks include:

■ The entire infrastructure must support 802.1X, including compatible switches, wireless access points, and clients.

- The 802.1X protocol does not prevent a known system with an infection or vulnerability from attaching to the network and putting other systems at risk.
- Unauthenticated devices can piggyback on an authenticated port. If multiple devices are connected via a hub or switch to a single 802.1X port on a distribution switch, only one device needs to authenticate for all devices to gain access to the network (most 802.1X switches can be configured to disallow this behavior).
- The 802.1X protocol does not provide notification or inventory information for unknown systems; systems that fail to authenticate are simply not allowed on the network. Monitoring RADIUS accounting and EAP message logs can provide some information regarding these devices, but this is not real time and may not be sufficient to effectively identify and remediate unmanaged systems.

Internet Protocol Security

Internet Protocol Security (IPSec) provides the logical equivalent of 802.1X. Instead of preventing the physical connection of a device to the network, it prevents logical connections between systems. Where 802.1X relies on switches and access points to apply physical controls, IPSec makes the systems themselves the control points. IPSec has two protection mechanisms: the authentication header (AH) and the encapsulated security payload (ESP). The AH is used for authentication and the ESP is used for encryption and integrity. IPSec uses security associations (SAs) to establish connections between systems. Two systems with a common SA can authenticate one another and set up a data connection. SAs can also be set up dynamically using the Internet Key Exchange (IKE) protocol, which includes the mutual authentication of devices making the connection using certificates, Kerberos, and other mechanisms.

Since unknown or rogue systems do not have the required SAs or access to the required authentication mechanisms, they cannot connect to systems requiring IPSec connections. IPSec does not prevent unmanaged systems from being physically connected to the network, but it does deny them logical access to other systems, thus preventing the exploitation of vulnerabilities or the spreading of malicious code. IPSec is supported on most operating systems and requires no major infrastructure upgrades to implement. IPSec is also supported on many network control devices such as routers, switches, and VPN servers. This allows for a number of expanded control scenarios, including using IPSec VPN connections on internal segments (e.g., using VPN connections to attach wireless clients to the wired network). However, configuring an infrastructure to use IPSec can be challenging.

One big disadvantage to IPSec is the lack of tools for managing IPSec connections across vendor platforms. This means many connections must be manually configured and maintained. Manual configurations usually require fixed IP addresses which can interfere with dynamically allocated IP schemes (i.e., DHCP). Systems with common OSs fair better; for example, Windows-based systems can use GPOs to centrally manage IPSec settings and Kerberos to perform dynamic authentications. This makes the practical deployment of IPSec fairly straightforward. Coverage is another issue; while most host devices (i.e., servers) can be configured to only accept IPSec connections, end user systems (i.e., workstations and laptops) must be configured to allow non-IPSec connections to Web sites, Instant Messenger (IM) servers, etc. This can make them susceptible to compromise from infected rogue devices. Finally, IPSec does not provide notification or inventory information for unknown systems. Systems that fail authentication are simply not allowed to connect to an IPSec-protected resource. Monitoring IPSec and system authentication logs can provide some information regarding unknown devices, but this is not real time and may not be sufficient to effectively identify and remediate an unmanaged system.

Health Check Mechanisms

Several companies are producing "health check" mechanisms that help administrators enforce compliance with security and configuration policies before granting network access. These mechanisms were first introduced on remote access connections. After a system connected to the remote access server (RAS) it was denied network access while the VPN or connection agent performed the necessary health checks. This capability has been expanded to include wired and wireless connections. Health check mechanisms are not security controls per se, but can help prevent the introduction of malicious code and unmanaged systems to the network. Health check mechanisms consist of three components: a client agent, a policy service, and an enforcement agent. When a system is first connected to the network, the enforcement agent requests the health status of the device from the client agent. Any system without the agent will obviously fail, otherwise the enforcement agent will compare the returned health status to the appropriate policy on the policy service. If the system passes the health check, it is granted access to the network; if not, network access is blocked or the device is referred to a remediation process.

Remediation referral is a major advantage on two fronts: first, it allows system issues to be proactively addressed and automatically resolved, and second, it allows (depending on the capabilities of the mechanism) remediation to perform just about any action. Developers and administrators can create solutions for validating any number of requirements and provide the needed remediation, including system identification and inventory, staff notification, update deployment, and system quarantine. Furthermore, these mechanisms work in real time so malicious activity is proactively prevented.

Health check mechanisms do have their disadvantages. They are not designed to secure a network from malicious users, they are designed to help administrators maintain the health of the computers on the network, which in turn helps maintain the network's overall integrity. Just because a system complies with all the defined health policies does not mean it is not infected with malicious code, it only means that the infection is not covered by existing policies. The ability of a system to gain network access also depends on the enforcement mechanism. For example, if the enforcement mechanism uses DHCP, it is relatively easy to bypass enforcement using a fixed IP address. On the other hand, if 802.1X is used for enforcement, it would be very difficult to bypass.

Hotel Model

The previous solutions are transparent to the user, that is, they do not require user interaction for the system to be granted access to the network. However, user interaction is a viable alternative. Sometimes called the "hotel model" because of its use in hotel guest rooms, this solution requires the user to open a browser and access a Web site for authentication and a health check before being allowed to access the entire network. The process might look like this:

1. Ports on the access switch are configured with a default configuration that restricts node access to a limited number of resources such as the DHCP server and a health check Web site.
2. When a system is first attached to the port it is issued an IP address, but can only access the health check Web site.
3. The user opens a Web browser (this could be automated by placing it in the Startup folder) that is redirected to the health check Web server.
4. The health check is performed and the results forwarded to a control system (e.g., a network management system).
5. If the health check is successful, the management system removes the access restrictions from the port, granting the system access to the network. If the system does not pass, the browser is redirected to a remediation Web site.

This process is a one-time event; it only takes place when the node is first connected to the network. The user will not be required to reauthenticate or redo the health check unless the system has been powered down or physically disconnected from the port. Only these two events will cause the port to be reset to the default configuration and force the user to go through the browser authentication and health check process again.

There are a number of advantages to this solution. First, it applies equally to all workstations (company or third party) attaching to the network. Second, it can perform user authentication and health check functions and provide detailed logs of these transactions. This provides maximum security because it prevents the node from sending any packets on the internal network until it has passed these checks. The hotel model also reduces administration and support requirements—

administration because third-party systems are not required to be joined to the domain nor are third-party users required to have domain accounts to access the internal network. Support is reduced because remediation does not require direct help desk/support involvement. If a system fails to pass a health check, remediation actions can be automatically initiated by the checking mechanism or the user can be redirected to a remediation site to download an antivirus signature, install patches, etc. Finally, the solution is flexible. It can be customized to accommodate all types of patch and baseline security checks, authentication methods, and health check schemes.

The principle disadvantage is its lack of transparency. The hotel model requires users to perform one or more additional actions, such as opening the browser and entering user credentials to gain network access. This may increase the number of support calls until users are accustomed to this procedure. This impact can be reduced through user education, automating the execution of the browser during user login, and using integrated authentication methods to eliminate the secondary entry of user credentials. The system also has a degree of hardware dependency. It requires access components that support this configuration (i.e., port-based access control list [ACL], port reset, etc.) as well as sufficient health check Web servers to process attaching nodes. While several companies have created appliances that implement the hotel model, if they do not provide the features needed for a particular environment, the final limitation of this method may be the cost of creating and maintaining the custom code required to meet those needs.

Summary

Active discovery methods can accurately identify unknown or rogue systems in real or near real time. They are more complex to operate, but produce better overall results. There are fewer active discovery tools, but they tend to be more selective, so results do not require extensive filtering. However, active tools may require customization to effectively address some specific requirements. Also, some active methods such as 802.1X can require substantial infrastructure changes. Nonetheless, active discovery methods do prevent infected devices from accessing the network for any substantial period of time, and this alone may be well worth the investment.

Unknown System Remediation

Finding unknown systems is only half the process. Once found, these systems must be identified, located, and integrated into the management process or removed from the network. The IP address is usually sufficient to narrow a system's location to a specific area and to notify the support or security personnel responsible for that area. The area personnel must take the steps necessary to mitigate the risks these systems represent. These steps can include joining the system to the domain, installing required software and updates, configuring required system policies, disabling generic user accounts, etc.

Location Procedures

Finding the location of a rogue node can be challenging, so it is a good idea to build a set of procedures that can provide consistent results. Most discovery processes will only provide you with the node name, IP address, and MAC address, and that's not much to go on. Sometimes the node name can give clues to the location of a device (e.g., LAB2SQL5 could indicate that the node is located in Lab 2). The IP address will also give you a general area (building, floor, or section) where the node is connected. Narrowing it down to a specific physical location is a little more complicated and usually involves network operations and support. Before going into further detail, one very viable option for identifying rouge nodes is to disconnect them, block further access to the network, and wait for someone to call the support desk for help. In many instances this is much easier than physically locating the device. Physically locating a device depends a lot on how it is connected to the network.

There are three basic types of connections: wired, wireless, and virtual/remote. To find a device connected to a wired Ethernet network, the process looks like this:

1. Using the IP address, identify the network devices the node could be attached to. Most IP address ranges only span a limited number of devices, such as all the switches in a single building.
2. Survey these devices for the MAC address of the target device to identify the port the device is connected to.
3. Trace the cable connected to this port through the patch system to a physical outlet in the service area (office, cubical, conference room, etc.).
4. Find the node or nodes connected to this outlet and identify the rogue.

This procedure works fairly consistently for wired devices. It does, however, involve a fair amount of work on the network operations side to query the network devices and locate the port, and on the network support side to visit the wiring closet and hand trace the port connection to a wall jack. This technique does not work at all for wireless and virtual/remote connections.

Remote connections are easy to trace to a port because they go through a network access device such a VPN server or modem bank. Assuming RADIUS is being used to authenticate these devices, a quick look at the RADIUS logs will show which network access device and port this device is attached to, and in some instances the log will contain the user ID of the person logging in. On dial-in connections, the log may also contain caller ID information. Sometimes this information is helpful in tracing the physical location of the device. However, when pass-through authentication is used, the RADIUS logs are not going to provide a lot of information about the physical location of the device or who owns it, which is the ultimate goal of the location procedure. It may be possible to correlate some of the RADIUS log information, such as caller ID, VPN source address, or log times, with other sources of information, such as authentication logs, to identify the owner or location of the device, but this simply adds an additional layer of difficulty to the task.

Wireless is even more challenging because there is no physical connection; the node can be anywhere within the service range of the access point, including above or below it. If 802.1X or Wi-Fi Protected Access (WPA) is being used to secure wireless access, then the RADIUS logs may provide some clues as to the owner, but certainly not the location. In most cases, blocking the node and waiting for the support call is the simplest way to identify the node.

Remediation Procedures

To be effective, remediation procedures must be well defined and have established timelines. Table 10.5 presents an example of how this process might work for a system requiring remediation for high-risk vulnerabilities.

The timeframe for system remediation is based on two factors: the risks associated with the system, and company policies and standards governing risk remediation. For example, a system running a worm executable (e.g., msblaster.exe) would require immediate remediation, whereas a system missing a medium-risk security patch might have a 2 week timeframe.

Table 10.5   Remediation Procedure

	Action	*Timeframe*
1	Establish system owner/administrator	Within 4 hours of discovery
2	Determine management requirements (third party, lab/test, one-off, unmanageable)	Within 1 business day
3a	If unmanageable, remove from network	As soon as possible
3b	Enter system into CMDB	Within 1 business day
4	Determine remediation requirements	Within 1 business day
5	Develop remediation plan	Within 1 business day
6	Test remediation solutions for system compatibility	Within 5 business days
7	Deploy remediation solutions	Within 7 business days
8	Verify system compliance	As soon as possible

The actual remediation actions will vary depending on the requirements, operating system, and system management services the company uses for remediation. Some possible remediation actions could include:

■ Join the computer to the domain—Joining the computer to the domain allows security GPOs to be applied to remediate some vulnerabilities; for example, a GPO could turn on the personal firewall and configure it to block all but essential services. A software deployment GPO could be used to install system management agents (e.g., SMS) on the system. Once installed, these agents could contact system management services to have required software and updates installed. Just adding the computer to the domain would be sufficient for the system management service to begin remediation procedures if the service uses domain or organizational unit memberships to identify the systems it services.

■ Inform system management services—It may be possible to pass the node name or address to the system management service or add it to the service's node list, which would in turn cause the system management service to remediate the system. This is the approach used by health check mechanisms. When a system requires remediation the health check service sends the node information to the remediation service. For example, if the system's antivirus signature file is out of date, the health check service notifies the antivirus vendor's console and the node is updated.

■ Move the system to a restricted/controlled network segment—When the network device will support it, the node can be assigned to a restricted or quarantined network segment. This restricted segment might provide limited services to the user, such as Web-based mail and Internet or demilitarized zone (DMZ) access. It might also contain fix-up services to remediate the security issues with the device so it can be granted full access. This approach is used with some remote access systems such as the Microsoft RRAS server. When the client attaches to the server it is put on a quarantined network and a script is run to check the node for compliance to company policies and requirements. Systems that pass the checks are granted full access, those that do not remain on the quarantined network or are disconnected.

■ Manually apply updates and settings—When automated remediation is not possible, the required updates and settings can be applied to the node manually. This doesn't necessarily mean the support person needs to physically visit the device. Manual simply means someone must perform some action specific to the node in order to remediate it. Actions could include initiating a remote console or terminal server session, running a script remotely, sending the user an auto-executing CD, and so forth.

Conclusion

This chapter has covered several aspects of update management setup and assessment, including periodic and ongoing activities. The activities required to create and maintain an effective and efficient update management program include establishing a baseline of systems, establishing subscription services, creating a communications plan, developing an update management architecture, and building the supporting infrastructure. Ongoing tasks include IT asset inventory maintenance, asset discovery, and rogue/unknown system remediation. In the next chapter we will discuss how these tasks feed into the identify tasks in quadrant 2 of the update management process.

Chapter 11

Patch/Update Management: Identify Tasks

The identify quadrant of the update management function involves a number of tasks related to receiving and authenticating update information, determining the technology stream, and establishing the group or groups that will be responsible for handling the remainder of the identify tasks (Figure 11.1). These include determining the current or future applicability of the update to the computing environment, the creation of release notes, and the downloading, validation, and testing of the update.

It is important to understand that there are two distinct types of updates. The first type is a patch or hot fix. This is usually an update that is issued to resolve a single problem. The second type of update is a patch bundle or service pack. These contain multiple or cumulative updates. The main differences between the two are size, functionality, and deployment time. Patches and hot fixes are typically small, issued to resolve significant security or system stability problems, and need to be installed quickly. Patches and hot fixes do not add functionality to the system. Patch bundles and service patches are usually version upgrades to the operating system (OS) or line of business application. They are usually large in size because they contain all previously released patches or hot fixes as well as minor bug fixes and some additional functionality. Their deployment is not usually critical unless the new functionality or one of the bug fixes is critical to your computing environment. Since patch bundles and service packs make massive changes to the system,

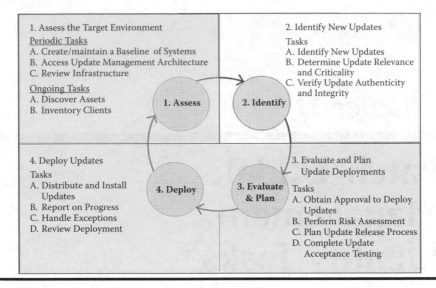

Figure 11.1   Update management identify quadrant.

they require additional testing to ensure compatibility, and the larger size of these updates usually requires additional deployment planning.

Identify New Updates

Once the subscription task becomes operational, it should start supplying notifications about new updates. These notifications will take two forms: proactive vendor contacts, emails, or alerts, and passive posts to Web pages, bulletins, etc. Whatever the source of the information, there must be a consistent procedure for the timely reception and processing of notifications. Attacks can be launched at any time and attackers commonly use weekends and holidays (when systems are less likely to be monitored) to increase the success of their attacks. This means notification monitoring must be a 24/7 operation to ensure the security and stability of an organization's systems.

Since updates are spread across multiple technologies, coordinating a consistent response can be challenging. Assuming the subscription service has been setup properly, notifications should be delivered to the appropriate technology group or groups by default. It is the responsibility of each technology group to ensure that the notifications are processed within established timelines. In other words, there must always be a person with the appropriate knowledge available to receive and evaluate notifications.

The first step in the acknowledgment process is to log the notification to a centralized logging system. It is only necessary to record the first occurrence of the notification, unless subsequent versions of the notification have substantial changes or updates. All personnel that receive an update notification should check the logging system to see if a record of the update notification exists, and if it does not, create it. This record establishes the starting point (date and time) of the processing timeline.

Next, the notification needs to be screened to determine if it is valid or has any security relevance. There is always a possibility that proactive notifications (those sent by email, pager, or text message) are hoaxes, so they must be validated as genuine vendor announcements to avoid unnecessary processing. There are several ways this can be done. If the notification came by email, the email headers can be reviewed to determine if the source of the notification is the vendor's mail system. The following header code segment shows this notification, purportedly sent from the Microsoft Security Response Center, is a hoax sent by berg@ servicenode.com.

```
Return-Path: <berg@mail.servicenode.com>
Received: from [24.113.32.74] (HELO wavebroadband.net)
 by wavebroadband.net (CommuniGate Pro SMTP 4.2.8)
 with ESMTP id 52184568 for w.stack@wavebroadband.com;
 Tue, 28 Nov 2006 18:26:02 -0800
Received: from [67.37.169.176] (HELO mail.servicenode.com)
 by wavebroadband.net (CommuniGate Pro SMTP 4.2.8)
 with ESMTP id 120581854 for w.stack@wavebroadband.com;
 Tue, 28 Nov 2006 18:26:01 -0800
Received: by mail.servicenode.com (Postfix, from userid 1029)
 id A372A10BB684; Tue, 28 Nov 2006 20:27:40 -0600 (CST)
To: w.stack@wavebroadband.com
Subject: Alert: Zero Day Exploit Update - IMMEDIATE ACTION
REQUIRED!
From: Microsoft Security Response Center <msrc@microsoft.com>
Content-Type: text/html
Message-Id: <20061129022740.A372A10BB684@mail.servicenode.com>
Date: Tue, 28 Nov 2006 20:27:40 -0600 (CST)
```

The reviewer can also confirm the notification by contacting a vendor source or visiting the vendor's Web site to review posted information about the update. Some vendors digitally sign their notifications to prove authenticity. If the notification is valid, a copy of the notification should be sent to the information security group to be evaluated for potential security relevance.

When an invalid notification is received, the notification record in the centralized logging system should be updated to reflect the invalid status so everyone will be aware of the situation and not take any further action. Information about the invalid notification should also be fed back to the group responsible for that notification subscription and to the security team for further investigation. Notifications that prove invalid should raise concerns about the quality of the information coming from that particular source. Reliable sources should be screening information for hoaxes before passing it on.

It is important that this screening process have very well-defined execution timelines (Figure 11.2). For example, notifications should be validated and security relevance established within hours of being received. When these timelines are not met, there should be well-defined escalation procedures to get the process back on track.

Once the screening process is completed, an "update council" meeting consisting of subject matter experts from the stakeholder teams should be convened. Updates often apply across multiple operational and support organizations, so it is prudent to get the assessment of each of these organizations when developing a processing strategy. This is especially true for security-related updates. The goal of the update council meeting is to determine the relevance and severity of the update and develop a response that minimizes the risks to the organization's business processes and computing resources. The severity determination outlined here varies slightly from the Information Technology Infrastructure Library (ITIL) process, which only requires an escalation (emergency update) determination during this phase. Determining the overall severity and establishing specific processing timelines at this point in the process is just as effective and actually provides for more efficient processing of the update tasks moving forward.

The processing strategy must include the assignment of a technology group (or groups) responsible for conducting acceptance testing, generating release notes, and preparing for the initial distribution of the patch to all stakeholders. This assignment is usually based on the technology stream the update applies to. Table 11.1 contains examples of some technology streams and associated support groups.

Note: The information security group must retain overall responsibility for the processing of all security-related updates, although the actual technical aspects may be handled by the individual technology support groups. This is necessary to ensure compliance with establish security requirements.

The update council model provides an excellent way to get a quick in-depth analysis of the requirements and potential impacts of a newly released update and facilitates the assignment of the remaining identify tasks. Convening an update council from multiple groups, especially for companies that span multiple time zones, can be a difficult, if not impossible, task. As an alternative, companies may choose to use the "lead team" approach instead. In the lead team model, a single entity is assigned responsibility for processing updates. A lead team consists of people from one or more technology streams, and, for security-related updates, must contain a member from the information security group. When needed, the group can supplement its ranks by soliciting assistance from any of the stakeholder groups.

Whether an organization uses the update council or lead team model, good leadership and good facilitation are critical to the success of the initial relevance,

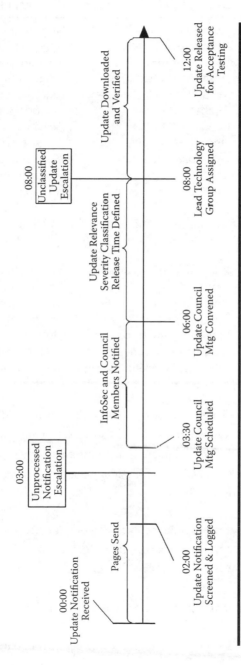

Figure 11.2 Update notification processing timeline.

Table 11.1 Sample Technology Streams

Technology stream	Description	Support group
Infrastructure servers	Domain controls, DNS, DHCP, LDAP, NMS	Network planning and engineering
End user services	File and print servers, printers, plotters, Fax	Network planning and engineering
Database servers	MS SQL, Oracle, Sybase, Siebel	Database administration and support group
Messaging servers	Exchange, SMTP, POP3, Instant Messaging	Exchange planning and engineering group
Voice servers	PBX, VoIP, voice mail	Voice and telephony engineering
Application servers	Financials, PeopleSoft, SAP	LOB application support group
Web servers	IIS, Apache, DMZ, and hosted systems	Web engineering and support, vendor management group
Networking infrastructure	Routers, switches, load balancers, etc.	Network planning and engineering
Workstations	Desktop, laptops, engineering stations	Desktop planning and engineering group
Mobile devices	Blueberry, Smartphone, pagers, cell phones	Mobility engineering and support group
Security	Any security-related update	Information security group

severity, and response determinations. The overall goal is to identify issues and make the necessary determinations quickly so update processing can continue. Having a specific agenda for the update council meeting with a specific set of items that must be addressed is invaluable. The following topics are a good example of what should be covered:

- Relevance—Does this update apply to any of our systems?
- Severity—What adverse impacts could we experience?
- Classification—What severity classification and deployment timelines should be established?
- Release—What, if any, prerequisites, sequencing, processing, or other release issues are there?
- Technology—What technology group will perform update verification and acceptance testing?
- Notification—What notification procedures will be used?

Sending information about the updates that will be covered to the attendees in advance is also valuable. Make sure someone is assigned to record the issues and determinations the group makes and distribute those notes afterward to all the stakeholders. Finally, the group must have leadership (management representation) capable of pushing through decisions when impasses arise.

The questions above highlight the principle tasks the update council or lead team must accomplish to complete the identify process, including determining the relevance of the update, preparing release notes, acquiring and verifying the binaries, and distributing the update to stakeholders. Now let's look at each of these in more detail.

Relevance

A large number of software updates are issued every day from a variety of sources and not every update is going to apply to your organization's installed computing base. It is the job of the update council to determine if the update is relevant to any of the existing systems in their computing environment. Having a good information technology (IT) software inventory is invaluable to this process. A good software inventory makes it possible to quickly establish which versions of the software enumerated in the vendor's notification are present in your environment. The alternative is to request this information from the system administrators, but this introduces a delay in the evaluation process that may not be acceptable, especially for critical security updates. When considering relevance, it may also be beneficial to look at a couple of other factors, including existing IT projects. If your organization is in the process of upgrading and the update is not critical, there is little reason to deploy it. Another possibility is an update that applies to an unused subcomponent of the system or one that provides functionality that is not supported, for example, an update to the Portable Operating System Interface (POSIX) subsystem or the installation of the Malicious Software Detection utility. Either of these situations would make it unnecessary to deploy the update. Once relevance has been established processing can continue.

If a patch is not applicable to the organization then it can be disregarded and the centralized log updated to reflect this status. It also makes sense to notify the group responsible for the subscription process to see if it is possible to modify the subscription to eliminate these irrelevant notifications. We usually think of irrelevant in the context of the past, in other words, software or versions that we no longer use, but this is not always the case. It is possible for an update to be irrelevant because the organization has not yet adopted the version of the software to which the update applies. Therefore it is important to maintain a record of this update so the organization will have access to this information should system changes make the update relevant in the future.

Severity

If the update is relevant, the next determination that must be made is severity. This involves identifying the risks associated with the deployment or nondeployment of this update and, based on those risks, establishing a severity classification. The organization's update deployment policy should contain the definitions, evaluation criteria, and execution timelines for each severity classification the organization has established. As mentioned previously, this step varies slightly from the standard ITIL process, which only requires an escalation (emergency update) determination during this phase.

Many organizations skip this process and simply use the vendor's severity rating. This is a mistake. Vendors rate their updates using criterion that may not be applicable to your organization. For example, Table 11.2 contains the criteria that Microsoft uses to rate their updates.

Note that Microsoft's definition of critical is a vulnerability that can become an automated attack, such as a worm or virus. Combined with the average time to exploit information, it can indicate how soon systems may be subject to attack but not how much impact that attack will have. In contrast, a patch that would keep a critical system from crashing regularly might warrant a critical rating in your organization but only a low rating to the vendor because it is not exploitable. Failing to perform a reasonable risk assessment on an update also makes it impossible to prioritize deployments or deploy updates in stages.

Risks

Organizations must weigh both the operational risks (loss of system integrity or stability) and the security risks when determining the proper course of action. The update council approach facilitates this by getting all the key players together to make this decision. It is up to the council to balance the operational and security risks when determining update severity. Risk is based on two primary factors:

Table 11.2　Microsoft Update Severity Rating Criteria

Rating	Definition
Critical	A vulnerability whose exploitation could allow the propagation of an Internet worm without user action
Important	A vulnerability whose exploitation could result in compromise of the confidentiality, integrity, or availability of users' data, or of the integrity or availability of processing resources
Moderate	Exploitability is mitigated to a significant degree by factors such as default configuration, auditing, or difficulty of exploitation
Low	A vulnerability whose exploitation is extremely difficult or whose impact is minimal

impact and likelihood. The more critical a system is, the greater the impact will be if the system fails or is compromised. System criticality is evaluated as part of the IT asset inventory process. It is based on a number of different factors, including what is stored on the system, how much revenue the system generates, how many people use the system, and so on. Likelihood is a function of system exposure based on factors such as system version, location, and the presence of existing controls. Examples of factors that reduce exposure include updates that only apply to a small number of systems with a particular version of the software, systems located on isolated segments, and systems behind firewalls or routers that block traffic on the exploitable port. The council must weigh these against other potential impacts the deployment may have on system operations, including the impact the deployment will have on network bandwidth, reboot issues, compatibility problems, and so forth, and come up with the appropriate severity classification. While the vendor's rating may provide some insight into the risks associated with the update, it should not be the only factor considered when classifying severity.

Classification

Severity classification is based on policy. The organization's update deployment policy should contain the definitions and evaluation criteria for each class, as well as the required implementation timelines. For additional information on update deployment policy components and suggested timelines see Chapter 15.

There is one special circumstance that warrants additional discussion: emergency updates. Certain situations may dictate the immediate deployment of an update. Zero-day exploits are a good example. In a zero-day situation, vulnerable systems are subject to compromise before or at the time of a patch release and therefore must be patched as soon as possible. Other reasons for escalation can include repetitive system failures impacting production or revenue targets, personnel safety, contractual obligations, and regulatory requirements. The above reasons are reactive, but companies may also choose to escalate an update for proactive reasons, for example, pushing out an update to protect systems against a newly reported virus or to deal with issues that have not manifested themselves locally but have been reported by other organizations.

Escalating an update to emergency status implies a risk potential that warrants the immediate deployment of an update, but an immediate deployment (one that bypasses proper testing and evaluation) can be risky. Therefore it is important to carefully weigh the risks and mitigation factors before escalating a patch installation to emergency status. For example, if a zero-day exploit could potentially compromise 50% of your system and the deployment of an untested patch is likely to cause performance issues on 10% of your systems, the latter action is the more sensible, provided the zero-day threat cannot be mitigated with other measures (e.g., putting a rule in the firewall that blocks the ports used by the exploit). On the other hand, if the exploit only applies to a small number of systems, escalated deployment may represent a greater risk to your environment and probably is not warranted.

If this is not an emergency update, normal processing can continue. The update council assigns a specific technology group (lead group) to complete the remaining identify tasks, beginning with the prerequisite and precedence requirements.

Release Notes

Many updates have specific dependencies that must be addressed before they can be installed. These can include specific OS version levels, installer versions, or previously installed updates. Failure to assess these requirements before beginning the evaluation and testing task can lead to extended testing times and missed deployment deadlines. If multiple updates are being processed for simultaneous installation, it is equally important to evaluate any potential issues with the sequence of the patch installs.

Note: Service pack and patch bundles are the most common examples of prerequisites that can cause major deployment issues. For example, Microsoft only produces updates for the current release and previous release service pack; systems that are more than two service packs behind must have the prerequisite service pack upgrade before they can receive the update. This can be problematic because service packs make a large number of changes to systems and consequently require fairly extensive compatibility testing. And service packs are usually quite large, making them difficult to deploy, especially across limited bandwidth connections. This is why it is important to establish deployment timelines for all updates. While service packs and patch bundles may not be critical updates at the time they are released, they become critical if they end up being a prerequisite for a critical patch. Establishing clear deployment timelines for service packs and patch bundles will avoid this situation and the potential risks associated with it, including system failures from service pack deployments as well as system exposures from critical patch deployment delays.

The prerequisites and sequencing information become part of the release notes the lead group prepares for the initial stakeholder notifications. Stakeholders will require this information for their deployment decisions, change management requests, timeline reconciliation, cost estimates, etc.

Download and Verify

The next step in the process is for the lead group to acquire the update and verify its authenticity, including the author of the update, the version(s), and the integrity of the binaries. The purpose of this step is to ensure the update is genuine and unaltered. Attackers have been known to take updates, alter them, then send them out with forged "update" notifications.

Not all updates require downloading files. Some updates may be simple registry, system, or application configuration changes, in which case the changes can simply be noted in the release documentation once the authenticity of the update information has been verified. When file downloads are required, the files should be downloaded to a quarantine file.

Quarantine

Quarantine is an environment that is isolated from the standard IT infrastructure. The primary purpose of quarantine is to prevent any potential virus or malware contained in the update from adversely impacting the production environment. The quarantine process is simple: the various versions of the files are verified for authenticity and integrity and then the operational characteristics of the patch are verified.

The process used to verify update files varies depending on how the vendor packages its updates. The two most common processes are signature and checksum. Some vendors digitally sign the individual binaries, others sign the entire distribution package. In either case it allows the authenticity and integrity of the files to be verified by comparing the signature in the download to the vendor's publicly issued X.509 certificate or posted signature. The screen shot in Figure 11.3 illustrates this verification for a Microsoft security patch.

Alternatively, the vendor may choose to generate one or more hash values for the individual files or the update package as a whole then publishes these hash values in a readily accessible place (e.g., their Web site). Apple Computer publishes SHA1 hashes on their Web site for all OS X updates (see http://www.apple.com/support/downloads). Once the update is downloaded, a checksum tool can be used to generate hash values for the downloaded files (or package). The resulting hash values should match the vendor's published values. If the values do not match, the problem must be reconciled before proceeding any further. The reason for the failure could be innocuous (the vendor made a change to the update and you have an older version) or the code could have been maliciously altered to include an exploit.

Other things to review during the verification process include proper file version numbers, dates, and sizes. These should be consistent with the information published in the vendor's notification. Any inconsistencies should be investigated and reconciled before the patch is released. If for any reason the update files cannot be verified then the update should be discarded and the source of the update notification or download notified. For subscription notifications, the group responsible for the subscription should also be notified so they can investigate the issue to determine what went wrong.

Figure 11.3   Digital signature verification.

Acceptance Testing

Once the update has been verified as genuine, the functionality of the update package needs to be tested for each of the applicable systems. The purpose of this test is to ensure the update's features function properly before distributing it to system owners for compatibility testing. Acceptance testing should take place on a minimally configured system (e.g., a standard workstation or server with a current set of updates). Each standard update feature should be tested for each version of the software currently supported by the organization.

Typical functionality verified by this task includes:

- Successful installation of the update
- Proper detection of versions
- Installation of the proper version(s) of the files
- Installation of all required files to the proper location(s)
- Correct changes to all configuration files and registry settings

If the update includes an uninstall option, this should also be tested to ensure it properly reverses all the installation changes. Any optional functionality included with the update should also tested if the organization uses it. For example, if the organization uses the Microsoft Slipstream option to incorporate updates into their standard builds, Slipstream functionality should be part of the acceptance testing. Other update installer options include:

- Update repair—Identifies and reinstalls files that were corrupted or overwritten after the update was initially installed.
- Network deployment—Configures the update for deployment from a network storage device (i.e., a file share).
- UI level—Specifies the types of notification the user will receive during the update installation.
- Logging—Specifies the logging file name and location as well as the level of messages to log (e.g., status messages, errors, failures, etc.).
- Module registration—Updates or repairs configuration files or registry settings that were corrupted or overwritten after the update was initially installed.

If the update passes all the functional tests it is ready for initial release to stakeholders for compatibility and performance testing.

Handover to the Evaluate and Plan Phase

The final tasks the update council or lead team must perform to trigger the next update management phase are patch staging and notification. Staging involves packaging the update binaries and internal release notes and making them available to the various stakeholder groups. This can be done via direct distribution (e.g., attached to the notification email) or by posting them to an internal site such as a file share. Finally, an update release notification must be sent to all stakeholders to let them know the update is ready for evaluation and deployment planning on their platforms. This should be a proactive notification (sent to individual support teams and members) rather than a passive posting to the update portal. The update release notification signifies the beginning of the deployment timeline, therefore it is essential that all parties involved in the deployment be apprised of the update release so they can begin the evaluation and planning processes. The update release notification should always be posted to the internal update distribution portal as well.

Many organizations simply copy or make the vendor bulletin the primary element of the update release notification and let the stakeholders use that information to determine their next step. While this is acceptable, it is probably more effective to distribute only the information (i.e., portions of the vendor notification) that actually pertains to the organization. Precise information eliminates ambiguity and provides clearer direction to everyone involved.

Conclusion

The identify phase of the update management function is a short-duration process consisting of a small number of focused tasks designed to ensure that all applicable updates to an organization's computers and applications are identified, verified as genuine, checked for proper functionality, and distributed to key stakeholders with specific organizational requirements and release notes. The identify phase eliminates unnecessary work by ensuring updates are valid, applicable, and functional before they are released and helps focus evaluation and planning processes to specific organizational needs.

Chapter 12

Patch/Update Management: Evaluate and Plan Tasks

The identify phase of the update management function establishes the need to deploy the update, but it is still necessary to plan the deployment to minimize any potential impacts to business operations. This is the purpose of the evaluation and plan phase: to create the deployment packages, test them for proper operations and compatibility, schedule them for deployment, and obtain permission to deploy them (Figure 12.1). Tasks in this phase are focused around change management, release management, and acceptance testing.

Typically the activities in the evaluate and plan phase are carried out by the individual support groups for each technology stream. In other words, the desktop support group performs these tasks for desktop systems, line of business owners for their applications, and so on. However, this does not always have to be the case. Some tasks, such as compatibility testing, can be centralized to improve efficiency and reduce the workload on the individual support groups.

Evaluate and plan tasks should constitute about half of the overall deployment timeline. For example, if the timeline to have the update deployed is 7 days, evaluate and plan tasks should take 3 to 4 days to complete (Figure 12.2).

For critical and important updates, the time to complete all the tasks in this phase can be very short. Having well-defined procedures, automated processes, and good communications is critical to the success of these tasks. Emergency changes typically bypass this phase and move directly to deployment.

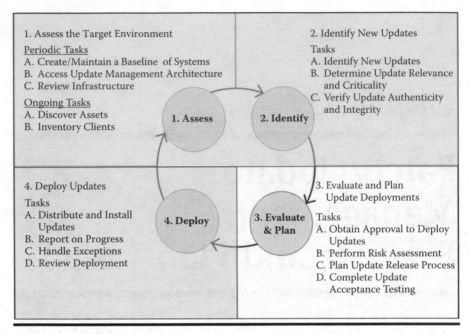

Figure 12.1   Update management evaluate and plan quadrant.

Change Management

All updates are changes to operating systems or application software and therefore are subject to the change management process. The goal of change management is to ensure changes to the technical and operational environment are performed in a consistent and reliable manner that minimizes impacts on business processes and productivity. A detailed description of the change management process is provided in Chapter 13. This section focuses on change management as it specifically relates to update deployment planning.

The primary goal of these change management activities is to obtain the necessary approval to deploy the update within the required timeline. It begins with the submission of a change request.

Request for Change

Submitting a request for change (RFC) application is one of the first tasks in the evaluate and plan phase. Submitting a change request this early in the process may seem odd, since some of the key change components (e.g., the rollback plan and risk factors) have yet to be determined. However, change requests take time to process through the change management system, so getting the process started early, especially for updates with short deployment timelines, is advantageous. It also gives other nontechnical groups, such as business operations, production, and human

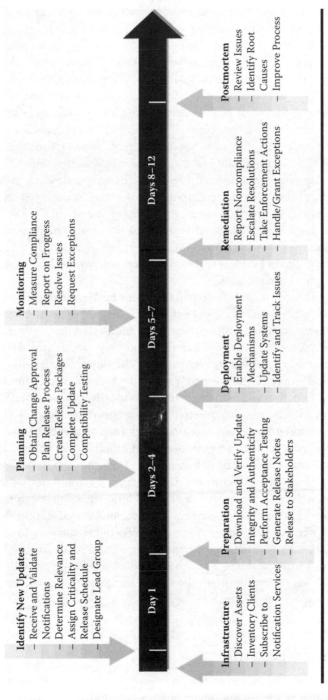

Identify New Updates
– Receive and Validate Notifications
– Determine Relevance
– Assign Criticality and Release Schedule
– Designate Lead Group

Planning
– Obtain Change Approval
– Plan Release Process
– Create Release Packages
– Complete Update Compatibility Testing

Monitoring
– Measure Compliance
– Report on Progress
– Resolve Issues
– Request Exceptions

Infrastructure
– Discover Assets
– Inventory Clients
– Subscribe to Notification Services

Preparation
– Download and Verify Update Integrity and Authenticity
– Perform Acceptance Testing
– Generate Release Notes
– Release to Stakeholders

Deployment
– Enable Deployment Mechanisms
– Update Systems
– Identify and Track Issues

Remediation
– Report Noncompliance
– Escalate Resolutions
– Take Enforcement Actions
– Handle/Grant Exceptions

Postmortem
– Review Issues
– Identify Root Causes
– Improve Process

Day 1   Days 2–4   Days 5–7   Days 8–12

Figure 12.2   Seven-day deployment timeline.

resources, an opportunity to evaluate the impact of the change on their processes. An example of this might be the business operations group reviewing the impact of a change scheduled during a critical reporting period. These factors can then be incorporated into the deployment plans.

There are several possible approaches to the change request task. The first approach is for the individual technology support groups to submit individual RFCs for each system they support. This can be tedious and results in a large number of requests that must be evaluated by the change advisory board. A better approach is to submit "bulk" or "blanket" change requests that cover entire classes of systems (e.g., one RFC for all file and print servers, one for all the Web servers, etc.). This significantly reduces the number of RFCs that must be processed. Bulk change requests can also specify multiple change windows to provide additional deployment flexibility; for example, "Change may be deployed on Saturday, Sunday, or Monday morning between the hours of 2 a.m. and 6 a.m. EST. All deployments must be completed and reported to the change management system on or before 6 a.m. August 8." This allows support groups to schedule deployments around specific group or business requirements, or to deploy updates in stages without submitting multiple requests.

Some organizations take this one step further by having the update council, lead team, or security group initiate a bulk RFC for all systems based on deployment timeline requirements. For example, the security group submits a bulk RFC for the installation of a security patch on all systems and only specifies the date and time the changes must be completed by. This provides visibility for the pending change to the nontechnical groups (business operations, human resources, etc.) involved in the change process and gives them an opportunity to identify any potential issues with the deployment. However, bulk requests like this can be counterproductive to change management because they do not contain enough information to ensure consistent and reliable deployment. They are best used as a notification mechanism and should be followed by bulk or individual system requests from the support groups.

Regardless of which group initiates the request, it is important that the change initiator provide as much information as possible so the request can be properly evaluated. This includes all the pertinent information derived during the identify phase, such as prerequisites, sequence requirements, and factors related to the severity classification, such as risks, deployment timelines, and so on. The goal is to head off any potential issues with the RFC that could unnecessarily delay deployment. Once the RFC has been submitted, the team can attend to the release planning, development, and testing tasks while the RFC is being processed.

Release Management

Release management is defined as the process of planning, testing, and executing changes. The goal of release management is to ensure that updates to production systems are deployed successfully with as little disruption to business processes as possible. The evaluate and plan phase encompasses the first two tasks of release management: planning and testing. These tasks include:

- Evaluating potential deployment risks
- Planning for the various deployment scenarios
- Determining deployment scheduling
- Developing the deployment procedures and packages
- Testing deployment procedures and packages
- Testing update performance and compatibility with the target systems

Evaluating Deployment Risks

Some initial risk evaluation was done to support the severity classification, but the focus of that evaluation was on the potential impact to overall business operations. The goal of the release risk evaluation is to facilitate the planning process by identifying potential impacts to computers or applications when the update is deployed. The process includes identifying the scope of the update (what systems it applies to), analyzing the changes the update makes to the system, and determining potential impacts to system performance and operation. The results of the evaluation drive the remaining planning and testing activities. For example, if the support team determines that the update makes no changes to critical system functionality, they may choose to deploy the update with minimal testing and no rollback procedure. On the other hand, if the update makes a number of changes to critical system components, the support team may decide to request a deployment exemption in order to perform exhaustive testing.

The risk evaluation is typically performed by one of the support team leads or managers with the input of subject matter experts (SMEs) for the targeted technologies. Most of the evaluation is based on vendor-supplied information, release notes from the initial evaluation, and historical experience. There are a couple of key pieces of information that can facilitate this evaluation. The first is a good inventory of system software, components, and configurations. This information helps the team identify and plan for any potential conflicts, prerequisites, or sequencing issues. The second is historical data from previous evaluations and deployments. Systems that have update problems tend to be repeat offenders; historical information helps pinpoint these systems so they can be targeted for additional testing and rollback planning. Previous experience also helps the planning team gauge user reactions (sensitivity, tolerance, etc.) to system changes.

For custom applications, having a list of the system components the application utilizes (Dynamic Link Library [DLL], services, protocols, etc.) can be invaluable. This makes it possible to quickly analyze whether or not an update changes anything related to the application so those areas can be targeted for additional testing. Chapter 17 contains information on the tools and technologies that can assist with system component mapping.

The evaluation must also consider potential impacts to users (downtime, reboots, etc.) as well as other deployment requirements, including sequencing for clustered systems, bandwidth availability, and other special needs. These factors may vary considerably depending on system usage. For example, an update failure or a reboot requirement on a server will affect multiple users, whereas the same factors on a workstation typically affect only one user. Another risk factor worth considering is rollback limitations. Some updates cannot be uninstalled, the system must be rebuilt. Since rebuilds take more time than a simple uninstall, deployments must be planned to accommodate this requirement.

Planning for the Various Deployment Scenarios

Once the evaluation has been completed, deployment planning can begin. The goal of the planning activity is to create deployment procedures and scheduling to deliver, install, and verify updates in an effective and efficient manner, and to create contingency procedures for dealing with installation issues or failures. The simplest way to approach these tasks is to look at the update as a series of installation scenarios. The primary differences in deployment requirements are usually based around three factors: location, connectivity, and availability, although your organization may have additional factors that must be considered.

Location

The location of a system can greatly affect the support team's ability to install and verify an update, and to deal with installation or update issues. Computer systems and applications that are colocated with support personnel represent the least complicated update scenario because support personnel have physical access to the machine. This means they can install and verify the update and repair or restore the system from the system console if necessary. The same luxury is not available for remotely located systems (e.g., a kiosk in a shopping mall), where significant support costs are involved either from contracted services or travel expenses for company personnel.

Remote system updates must be automated to the highest degree possible. Several vendors offer update management tools to assist with these tasks (see Chapter 17 for additional information). However, it is not wise to rely on a single installation or verification process when remote systems are involved. A secondary installation and verification method should be developed to ensure success should the primary deployment mechanism fail. This is particularly important for security or other priority updates with short deployment timeframes. Planning for remote system updates must always include contingency plans, including automated update rollback and

where they were interrupted rather than restarting the entire transfer the next time the system is connected. Detecting low bandwidth connections is key to the success of deployments on these connections. Some network access systems (NASs) and operating systems supply this information directly; alternatively Dynamic Host Configuration Protocol (DHCP) network address ranges assigned to VPN or dial-in DHCP connections can be used to detect low bandwidth connections.

It is important to note that none of these techniques are effective for deploying large updates such as service packs and patch bundles. Users are unlikely to stay connected for hours just to get an update installed. One technique for dealing with large updates is to repackage the update into smaller units. Multiple versions of a single update are often bundled into a single release package. Creating individual packages for each version can reduce packages to a manageable size. However, this requires the deployment mechanism to figure out which package to deploy. Also, be forewarned, repackaging updates is not a trivial task, it requires a fair amount of expertise to accomplish successfully. A good alternative (although somewhat labor intensive) is to distribute updates on CD, DVD, or other media via a courier, package, or postal delivery system. This is the most effective method for distributing very large updates like service packs that cannot be broken into smaller units. One advantage to this method is that step-by-step instructions can be included to assist the user with the installation. Some operating systems support an autostart option for CDs and DVDs; this can be leveraged to automate the installation. Several of the commercial update management systems have direct support for this type of distribution as well.

Availability

The final factor the planning process must take into consideration is availability. The availability of the system to be updated can be affected by its usage, surrounding controls, business criticality, and ownership. For example, servers are typically online 24 hours a day, desktops 8–10 hours a day, and portable systems less than 2 hours a day. Deployment planning must take into consideration these scenarios as well as availability issues around user absences for vacation, family leave, sabbatical, etc. Most of these issues can be resolved using startup, log-in, and scheduling techniques. Antivirus software is a good example: when automatic update is enabled, the antivirus agent checks for updates as part of the startup process and at scheduled intervals thereafter. Some remote access systems perform checks as part of their connection process. User logon scripts can also be used to check for missing updates.

Security and other management controls can also affect the availability of a system for patching. Scenarios where systems have personal (host-based) firewalls or are located on a segment controlled by a filtering router or firewall require additional planning. This is usually not an issue for "pull"-style update systems where the

system recover methods to deal with installation or update failures. For example, an update or system management tool such as SMS, Altiris, or PatchLink can be used as the primary installation and verification mechanism and a login script or other remote installation tool as the secondary mechanism. In its simplest form, the secondary mechanism can be a remote console or terminal connection that allows the support team to install the update manually.

Connectivity

The amount of bandwidth available to transfer the update to the system has an obvious impact on installation, especially when the updates are large. Streaming large updates to multiple machines simultaneously can have a huge impact on business operations, especially when the stream crosses relatively low bandwidth links. Home offices, traveling employees, and other virtual private network (VPN) or dial-in users frequently connect on low bandwidth connections. While these systems need to be updated, the connection speed poses significant challenges to the timely delivery of updates. Finally, systems with no connectivity, such as standalone kiosks, require the manual delivery of updates. While standalone systems have less risk associated with them, they still need to be updated, particularly if the updates are related to system performance or reliability.

To reduce bandwidth requirements for large-scale deployments, the deployment can be done in stages by distributing the update to a set number of systems each day or hour (for desktops) or within each maintenance window (for servers). Using multiple update distribution points will also reduce bandwidth requirements, especially for systems located across low bandwidth wide area network (WAN) connections such as those in remote office locations. Having a distribution point at the remote location means the update only needs to be copied across the WAN link once. However, distribution points complicate the installation process because procedures must be customized to point systems to the local distribution point. One technique that works well for this is including a routine in the installation package that detects the system's network address then associates that address with a local distribution point. Most commercial update management systems include distribution point capabilities.

Distributing updates to home office users, traveling employees, and others on very low bandwidth connections (i.e., VPN or dial-in) requires additional planning. Transfers across these connections often appear to the user as a system "lockup," so it is important to include a message and process meter in the update package to inform the user of the expected download time and download progress. Another technique that works extremely well for these connections is background transfers. This technique delivers the updates without "freezing" the user interface by making use of any bandwidth the user is not utilizing for other services. Background transfer protocols are also designed to deal with transfer interruptions, so transfers resume

Sending information about the updates that will be covered to the attendees in advance is also valuable. Make sure someone is assigned to record the issues and determinations the group makes and distribute those notes afterward to all the stakeholders. Finally, the group must have leadership (management representation) capable of pushing through decisions when impasses arise.

The questions above highlight the principle tasks the update council or lead team must accomplish to complete the identify process, including determining the relevance of the update, preparing release notes, acquiring and verifying the binaries, and distributing the update to stakeholders. Now let's look at each of these in more detail.

Relevance

A large number of software updates are issued every day from a variety of sources and not every update is going to apply to your organization's installed computing base. It is the job of the update council to determine if the update is relevant to any of the existing systems in their computing environment. Having a good information technology (IT) software inventory is invaluable to this process. A good software inventory makes it possible to quickly establish which versions of the software enumerated in the vendor's notification are present in your environment. The alternative is to request this information from the system administrators, but this introduces a delay in the evaluation process that may not be acceptable, especially for critical security updates. When considering relevance, it may also be beneficial to look at a couple of other factors, including existing IT projects. If your organization is in the process of upgrading and the update is not critical, there is little reason to deploy it. Another possibility is an update that applies to an unused subcomponent of the system or one that provides functionality that is not supported, for example, an update to the Portable Operating System Interface (POSIX) subsystem or the installation of the Malicious Software Detection utility. Either of these situations would make it unnecessary to deploy the update. Once relevance has been established processing can continue.

If a patch is not applicable to the organization then it can be disregarded and the centralized log updated to reflect this status. It also makes sense to notify the group responsible for the subscription process to see if it is possible to modify the subscription to eliminate these irrelevant notifications. We usually think of irrelevant in the context of the past, in other words, software or versions that we no longer use, but this is not always the case. It is possible for an update to be irrelevant because the organization has not yet adopted the version of the software to which the update applies. Therefore it is important to maintain a record of this update so the organization will have access to this information should system changes make the update relevant in the future.

Severity

If the update is relevant, the next determination that must be made is severity. This involves identifying the risks associated with the deployment or nondeployment of this update and, based on those risks, establishing a severity classification. The organization's update deployment policy should contain the definitions, evaluation criteria, and execution timelines for each severity classification the organization has established. As mentioned previously, this step varies slightly from the standard ITIL process, which only requires an escalation (emergency update) determination during this phase.

Many organizations skip this process and simply use the vendor's severity rating. This is a mistake. Vendors rate their updates using criterion that may not be applicable to your organization. For example, Table 11.2 contains the criteria that Microsoft uses to rate their updates.

Note that Microsoft's definition of critical is a vulnerability that can become an automated attack, such as a worm or virus. Combined with the average time to exploit information, it can indicate how soon systems may be subject to attack but not how much impact that attack will have. In contrast, a patch that would keep a critical system from crashing regularly might warrant a critical rating in your organization but only a low rating to the vendor because it is not exploitable. Failing to perform a reasonable risk assessment on an update also makes it impossible to prioritize deployments or deploy updates in stages.

Risks

Organizations must weigh both the operational risks (loss of system integrity or stability) and the security risks when determining the proper course of action. The update council approach facilitates this by getting all the key players together to make this decision. It is up to the council to balance the operational and security risks when determining update severity. Risk is based on two primary factors:

Table 11.2   Microsoft Update Severity Rating Criteria

Rating	Definition
Critical	A vulnerability whose exploitation could allow the propagation of an Internet worm without user action
Important	A vulnerability whose exploitation could result in compromise of the confidentiality, integrity, or availability of users' data, or of the integrity or availability of processing resources
Moderate	Exploitability is mitigated to a significant degree by factors such as default configuration, auditing, or difficulty of exploitation
Low	A vulnerability whose exploitation is extremely difficult or whose impact is minimal

impact and likelihood. The more critical a system is, the greater the impact will be if the system fails or is compromised. System criticality is evaluated as part of the IT asset inventory process. It is based on a number of different factors, including what is stored on the system, how much revenue the system generates, how many people use the system, and so on. Likelihood is a function of system exposure based on factors such as system version, location, and the presence of existing controls. Examples of factors that reduce exposure include updates that only apply to a small number of systems with a particular version of the software, systems located on isolated segments, and systems behind firewalls or routers that block traffic on the exploitable port. The council must weigh these against other potential impacts the deployment may have on system operations, including the impact the deployment will have on network bandwidth, reboot issues, compatibility problems, and so forth, and come up with the appropriate severity classification. While the vendor's rating may provide some insight into the risks associated with the update, it should not be the only factor considered when classifying severity.

Classification

Severity classification is based on policy. The organization's update deployment policy should contain the definitions and evaluation criteria for each class, as well as the required implementation timelines. For additional information on update deployment policy components and suggested timelines see Chapter 15.

There is one special circumstance that warrants additional discussion: emergency updates. Certain situations may dictate the immediate deployment of an update. Zero-day exploits are a good example. In a zero-day situation, vulnerable systems are subject to compromise before or at the time of a patch release and therefore must be patched as soon as possible. Other reasons for escalation can include repetitive system failures impacting production or revenue targets, personnel safety, contractual obligations, and regulatory requirements. The above reasons are reactive, but companies may also choose to escalate an update for proactive reasons, for example, pushing out an update to protect systems against a newly reported virus or to deal with issues that have not manifested themselves locally but have been reported by other organizations.

Escalating an update to emergency status implies a risk potential that warrants the immediate deployment of an update, but an immediate deployment (one that bypasses proper testing and evaluation) can be risky. Therefore it is important to carefully weigh the risks and mitigation factors before escalating a patch installation to emergency status. For example, if a zero-day exploit could potentially compromise 50% of your system and the deployment of an untested patch is likely to cause performance issues on 10% of your systems, the latter action is the more sensible, provided the zero-day threat cannot be mitigated with other measures (e.g., putting a rule in the firewall that blocks the ports used by the exploit). On

the other hand, if the exploit only applies to a small number of systems, escalated deployment may represent a greater risk to your environment and probably is not warranted.

If this is not an emergency update, normal processing can continue. The update council assigns a specific technology group (lead group) to complete the remaining identify tasks, beginning with the prerequisite and precedence requirements.

Release Notes

Many updates have specific dependencies that must be addressed before they can be installed. These can include specific OS version levels, installer versions, or previously installed updates. Failure to assess these requirements before beginning the evaluation and testing task can lead to extended testing times and missed deployment deadlines. If multiple updates are being processed for simultaneous installation, it is equally important to evaluate any potential issues with the sequence of the patch installs.

Note: Service pack and patch bundles are the most common examples of prerequisites that can cause major deployment issues. For example, Microsoft only produces updates for the current release and previous release service pack; systems that are more than two service packs behind must have the prerequisite service pack upgrade before they can receive the update. This can be problematic because service packs make a large number of changes to systems and consequently require fairly extensive compatibility testing. And service packs are usually quite large, making them difficult to deploy, especially across limited bandwidth connections. This is why it is important to establish deployment timelines for all updates. While service packs and patch bundles may not be critical updates at the time they are released, they become critical if they end up being a prerequisite for a critical patch. Establishing clear deployment timelines for service packs and patch bundles will avoid this situation and the potential risks associated with it, including system failures from service pack deployments as well as system exposures from critical patch deployment delays.

The prerequisites and sequencing information become part of the release notes the lead group prepares for the initial stakeholder notifications. Stakeholders will require this information for their deployment decisions, change management requests, timeline reconciliation, cost estimates, etc.

Download and Verify

The next step in the process is for the lead group to acquire the update and verify its authenticity, including the author of the update, the version(s), and the integrity of

the binaries. The purpose of this step is to ensure the update is genuine and unaltered. Attackers have been known to take updates, alter them, then send them out with forged "update" notifications.

Not all updates require downloading files. Some updates may be simple registry, system, or application configuration changes, in which case the changes can simply be noted in the release documentation once the authenticity of the update information has been verified. When file downloads are required, the files should be downloaded to a quarantine file.

Quarantine

Quarantine is an environment that is isolated from the standard IT infrastructure. The primary purpose of quarantine is to prevent any potential virus or malware contained in the update from adversely impacting the production environment. The quarantine process is simple: the various versions of the files are verified for authenticity and integrity and then the operational characteristics of the patch are verified.

The process used to verify update files varies depending on how the vendor packages its updates. The two most common processes are signature and checksum. Some vendors digitally sign the individual binaries, others sign the entire distribution package. In either case it allows the authenticity and integrity of the files to be verified by comparing the signature in the download to the vendor's publicly issued X.509 certificate or posted signature. The screen shot in Figure 11.3 illustrates this verification for a Microsoft security patch.

Alternatively, the vendor may choose to generate one or more hash values for the individual files or the update package as a whole then publishes these hash values in a readily accessible place (e.g., their Web site). Apple Computer publishes SHA1 hashes on their Web site for all OS X updates (see http://www.apple.com/support/downloads). Once the update is downloaded, a checksum tool can be used to generate hash values for the downloaded files (or package). The resulting hash values should match the vendor's published values. If the values do not match, the problem must be reconciled before proceeding any further. The reason for the failure could be innocuous (the vendor made a change to the update and you have an older version) or the code could have been maliciously altered to include an exploit.

Other things to review during the verification process include proper file version numbers, dates, and sizes. These should be consistent with the information published in the vendor's notification. Any inconsistencies should be investigated and reconciled before the patch is released. If for any reason the update files cannot be verified then the update should be discarded and the source of the update notification or download notified. For subscription notifications, the group responsible for the subscription should also be notified so they can investigate the issue to determine what went wrong.

Figure 11.3 **Digital signature verification.**

Acceptance Testing

Once the update has been verified as genuine, the functionality of the update package needs to be tested for each of the applicable systems. The purpose of this test is to ensure the update's features function properly before distributing it to system owners for compatibility testing. Acceptance testing should take place on a minimally configured system (e.g., a standard workstation or server with a current set of updates). Each standard update feature should be tested for each version of the software currently supported by the organization.

Typical functionality verified by this task includes:

- Successful installation of the update
- Proper detection of versions
- Installation of the proper version(s) of the files
- Installation of all required files to the proper location(s)
- Correct changes to all configuration files and registry settings

If the update includes an uninstall option, this should also be tested to ensure it properly reverses all the installation changes. Any optional functionality included

with the update should also tested if the organization uses it. For example, if the organization uses the Microsoft Slipstream option to incorporate updates into their standard builds, Slipstream functionality should be part of the acceptance testing. Other update installer options include:

- Update repair—Identifies and reinstalls files that were corrupted or overwritten after the update was initially installed.
- Network deployment—Configures the update for deployment from a network storage device (i.e., a file share).
- UI level—Specifies the types of notification the user will receive during the update installation.
- Logging—Specifies the logging file name and location as well as the level of messages to log (e.g., status messages, errors, failures, etc.).
- Module registration—Updates or repairs configuration files or registry settings that were corrupted or overwritten after the update was initially installed.

If the update passes all the functional tests it is ready for initial release to stakeholders for compatibility and performance testing.

Handover to the Evaluate and Plan Phase

The final tasks the update council or lead team must perform to trigger the next update management phase are patch staging and notification. Staging involves packaging the update binaries and internal release notes and making them available to the various stakeholder groups. This can be done via direct distribution (e.g., attached to the notification email) or by posting them to an internal site such as a file share. Finally, an update release notification must be sent to all stakeholders to let them know the update is ready for evaluation and deployment planning on their platforms. This should be a proactive notification (sent to individual support teams and members) rather than a passive posting to the update portal. The update release notification signifies the beginning of the deployment timeline, therefore it is essential that all parties involved in the deployment be apprised of the update release so they can begin the evaluation and planning processes. The update release notification should always be posted to the internal update distribution portal as well.

Many organizations simply copy or make the vendor bulletin the primary element of the update release notification and let the stakeholders use that information to determine their next step. While this is acceptable, it is probably more effective to distribute only the information (i.e., portions of the vendor notification) that actually pertains to the organization. Precise information eliminates ambiguity and provides clearer direction to everyone involved.

Conclusion

The identify phase of the update management function is a short-duration process consisting of a small number of focused tasks designed to ensure that all applicable updates to an organization's computers and applications are identified, verified as genuine, checked for proper functionality, and distributed to key stakeholders with specific organizational requirements and release notes. The identify phase eliminates unnecessary work by ensuring updates are valid, applicable, and functional before they are released and helps focus evaluation and planning processes to specific organizational needs.

Chapter 12

Patch/Update Management: Evaluate and Plan Tasks

The identify phase of the update management function establishes the need to deploy the update, but it is still necessary to plan the deployment to minimize any potential impacts to business operations. This is the purpose of the evaluation and plan phase: to create the deployment packages, test them for proper operations and compatibility, schedule them for deployment, and obtain permission to deploy them (Figure 12.1). Tasks in this phase are focused around change management, release management, and acceptance testing.

Typically the activities in the evaluate and plan phase are carried out by the individual support groups for each technology stream. In other words, the desktop support group performs these tasks for desktop systems, line of business owners for their applications, and so on. However, this does not always have to be the case. Some tasks, such as compatibility testing, can be centralized to improve efficiency and reduce the workload on the individual support groups.

Evaluate and plan tasks should constitute about half of the overall deployment timeline. For example, if the timeline to have the update deployed is 7 days, evaluate and plan tasks should take 3 to 4 days to complete (Figure 12.2).

For critical and important updates, the time to complete all the tasks in this phase can be very short. Having well-defined procedures, automated processes, and good communications is critical to the success of these tasks. Emergency changes typically bypass this phase and move directly to deployment.

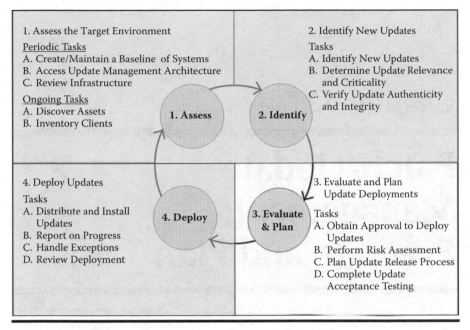

1. Assess the Target Environment

Periodic Tasks
A. Create/Maintain a Baseline of Systems
B. Access Update Management Architecture
C. Review Infrastructure

Ongoing Tasks
A. Discover Assets
B. Inventory Clients

2. Identify New Updates

Tasks
A. Identify New Updates
B. Determine Update Relevance
   and Criticality
C. Verify Update Authenticity
   and Integrity

4. Deploy Updates

Tasks
A. Distribute and Install
   Updates
B. Report on Progress
C. Handle Exceptions
D. Review Deployment

3. Evaluate and Plan
   Update Deployments

Tasks
A. Obtain Approval to Deploy
   Updates
B. Perform Risk Assessment
C. Plan Update Release Process
D. Complete Update
   Acceptance Testing

Figure 12.1   Update management evaluate and plan quadrant.

Change Management

All updates are changes to operating systems or application software and therefore are subject to the change management process. The goal of change management is to ensure changes to the technical and operational environment are performed in a consistent and reliable manner that minimizes impacts on business processes and productivity. A detailed description of the change management process is provided in Chapter 13. This section focuses on change management as it specifically relates to update deployment planning.

The primary goal of these change management activities is to obtain the necessary approval to deploy the update within the required timeline. It begins with the submission of a change request.

Request for Change

Submitting a request for change (RFC) application is one of the first tasks in the evaluate and plan phase. Submitting a change request this early in the process may seem odd, since some of the key change components (e.g., the rollback plan and risk factors) have yet to be determined. However, change requests take time to process through the change management system, so getting the process started early, especially for updates with short deployment timelines, is advantageous. It also gives other nontechnical groups, such as business operations, production, and human

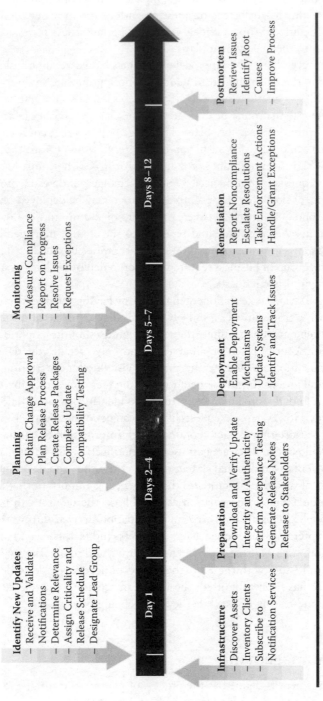

Identify New Updates
– Receive and Validate Notifications
– Determine Relevance
– Assign Criticality and Release Schedule
– Designate Lead Group

Planning
– Obtain Change Approval
– Plan Release Process
– Create Release Packages
– Complete Update Compatibility Testing

Monitoring
– Measure Compliance
– Report on Progress
– Resolve Issues
– Request Exceptions

Postmortem
– Review Issues
– Identify Root Causes
– Improve Process

Infrastructure
– Discover Assets
– Inventory Clients
– Subscribe to Notification Services

Preparation
– Download and Verify Update Integrity and Authenticity
– Perform Acceptance Testing
– Generate Release Notes
– Release to Stakeholders

Deployment
– Enable Deployment Mechanisms
– Update Systems
– Identify and Track Issues

Remediation
– Report Noncompliance
– Escalate Resolutions
– Take Enforcement Actions
– Handle/Grant Exceptions

Day 1   Days 2–4   Days 5–7   Days 8–12

Figure 12.2   Seven-day deployment timeline.

resources, an opportunity to evaluate the impact of the change on their processes. An example of this might be the business operations group reviewing the impact of a change scheduled during a critical reporting period. These factors can then be incorporated into the deployment plans.

There are several possible approaches to the change request task. The first approach is for the individual technology support groups to submit individual RFCs for each system they support. This can be tedious and results in a large number of requests that must be evaluated by the change advisory board. A better approach is to submit "bulk" or "blanket" change requests that cover entire classes of systems (e.g., one RFC for all file and print servers, one for all the Web servers, etc.). This significantly reduces the number of RFCs that must be processed. Bulk change requests can also specify multiple change windows to provide additional deployment flexibility; for example, "Change may be deployed on Saturday, Sunday, or Monday morning between the hours of 2 a.m. and 6 a.m. EST. All deployments must be completed and reported to the change management system on or before 6 a.m. August 8." This allows support groups to schedule deployments around specific group or business requirements, or to deploy updates in stages without submitting multiple requests.

Some organizations take this one step further by having the update council, lead team, or security group initiate a bulk RFC for all systems based on deployment timeline requirements. For example, the security group submits a bulk RFC for the installation of a security patch on all systems and only specifies the date and time the changes must be completed by. This provides visibility for the pending change to the nontechnical groups (business operations, human resources, etc.) involved in the change process and gives them an opportunity to identify any potential issues with the deployment. However, bulk requests like this can be counterproductive to change management because they do not contain enough information to ensure consistent and reliable deployment. They are best used as a notification mechanism and should be followed by bulk or individual system requests from the support groups.

Regardless of which group initiates the request, it is important that the change initiator provide as much information as possible so the request can be properly evaluated. This includes all the pertinent information derived during the identify phase, such as prerequisites, sequence requirements, and factors related to the severity classification, such as risks, deployment timelines, and so on. The goal is to head off any potential issues with the RFC that could unnecessarily delay deployment. Once the RFC has been submitted, the team can attend to the release planning, development, and testing tasks while the RFC is being processed.

Release Management

Release management is defined as the process of planning, testing, and executing changes. The goal of release management is to ensure that updates to production

systems are deployed successfully with as little disruption to business processes as possible. The evaluate and plan phase encompasses the first two tasks of release management: planning and testing. These tasks include:

- Evaluating potential deployment risks
- Planning for the various deployment scenarios
- Determining deployment scheduling
- Developing the deployment procedures and packages
- Testing deployment procedures and packages
- Testing update performance and compatibility with the target systems

Evaluating Deployment Risks

Some initial risk evaluation was done to support the severity classification, but the focus of that evaluation was on the potential impact to overall business operations. The goal of the release risk evaluation is to facilitate the planning process by identifying potential impacts to computers or applications when the update is deployed. The process includes identifying the scope of the update (what systems it applies to), analyzing the changes the update makes to the system, and determining potential impacts to system performance and operation. The results of the evaluation drive the remaining planning and testing activities. For example, if the support team determines that the update makes no changes to critical system functionality, they may choose to deploy the update with minimal testing and no rollback procedure. On the other hand, if the update makes a number of changes to critical system components, the support team may decide to request a deployment exemption in order to perform exhaustive testing.

The risk evaluation is typically performed by one of the support team leads or managers with the input of subject matter experts (SMEs) for the targeted technologies. Most of the evaluation is based on vendor-supplied information, release notes from the initial evaluation, and historical experience. There are a couple of key pieces of information that can facilitate this evaluation. The first is a good inventory of system software, components, and configurations. This information helps the team identify and plan for any potential conflicts, prerequisites, or sequencing issues. The second is historical data from previous evaluations and deployments. Systems that have update problems tend to be repeat offenders; historical information helps pinpoint these systems so they can be targeted for additional testing and rollback planning. Previous experience also helps the planning team gauge user reactions (sensitivity, tolerance, etc.) to system changes.

For custom applications, having a list of the system components the application utilizes (Dynamic Link Library [DLL], services, protocols, etc.) can be invaluable. This makes it possible to quickly analyze whether or not an update changes anything related to the application so those areas can be targeted for additional

testing. Chapter 17 contains information on the tools and technologies that can assist with system component mapping.

The evaluation must also consider potential impacts to users (downtime, reboots, etc.) as well as other deployment requirements, including sequencing for clustered systems, bandwidth availability, and other special needs. These factors may vary considerably depending on system usage. For example, an update failure or a reboot requirement on a server will affect multiple users, whereas the same factors on a workstation typically affect only one user. Another risk factor worth considering is rollback limitations. Some updates cannot be uninstalled, the system must be rebuilt. Since rebuilds take more time than a simple uninstall, deployments must be planned to accommodate this requirement.

Planning for the Various Deployment Scenarios

Once the evaluation has been completed, deployment planning can begin. The goal of the planning activity is to create deployment procedures and scheduling to deliver, install, and verify updates in an effective and efficient manner, and to create contingency procedures for dealing with installation issues or failures. The simplest way to approach these tasks is to look at the update as a series of installation scenarios. The primary differences in deployment requirements are usually based around three factors: location, connectivity, and availability, although your organization may have additional factors that must be considered.

Location

The location of a system can greatly affect the support team's ability to install and verify an update, and to deal with installation or update issues. Computer systems and applications that are colocated with support personnel represent the least complicated update scenario because support personnel have physical access to the machine. This means they can install and verify the update and repair or restore the system from the system console if necessary. The same luxury is not available for remotely located systems (e.g., a kiosk in a shopping mall), where significant support costs are involved either from contracted services or travel expenses for company personnel.

Remote system updates must be automated to the highest degree possible. Several vendors offer update management tools to assist with these tasks (see Chapter 17 for additional information). However, it is not wise to rely on a single installation or verification process when remote systems are involved. A secondary installation and verification method should be developed to ensure success should the primary deployment mechanism fail. This is particularly important for security or other priority updates with short deployment timeframes. Planning for remote system updates must always include contingency plans, including automated update rollback and

There is no single best process and it is likely that any process established today will change in the future as new requirements are realized. Organizations must settle on a process that accomplishes their change management goals within the context of their organizational structure and business practices. The primary purpose for defining and diagramming the process is to ensure that it is comprehensive—that all necessary steps and precautions are taken to maximize business benefits and minimize business impacts. The second purpose is to identify all the parties involved in or impacted by system changes, including business groups, users, and other consumers of system outputs, as well as administrative and support personal, vendors, and contracted service providers. This information is needed before process roles, responsibilities, and timelines can be established. The final benefit derived from process definition is reliability and consistency. A well-defined process provides a consistent, repeatable framework for implementation that reduces ambiguity and erroneous behaviors.

Timelines for accomplishing these tasks should also be defined in the form of service level agreements (SLAs). An SLA ensures that sufficient time is allotted for program activities and sets reasonable performance expectations for program participants.

Change Management Policy: Roles and Responsibilities

Processes work best when everyone involved understands their role, what they are responsible for, and the timelines they have for meeting those responsibilities. The organization section of the policy defines the roles, responsibilities, and organizational relationships of the business and technical entities involved in change management. The primary purpose of the section is to identify program roles, establish organization context, and provide a high level of understanding of role responsibilities. It is not intended to provide role-specific procedures or requirements. These should be developed as policy supplements and referenced by this section. This allows role requirements, responsibilities, and compliance timelines to be easily updated without reissuing the entire policy. For further information on the development of these supplements, see the "Roles and Responsibilities" section of this chapter.

The following is an example of the types of information that would be contained in this section.

> Executive management is responsible for ensuring due diligence in the protection of our information resources and ensuring our compliance with regulatory, legal, and contractual requirements. Other responsibilities for change management are assigned as follows:

- The chief information officer (CIO) has primary responsibility for the implementation of this policy. The CIO shall create and chair the change advisory board. The CIO shall designate a change manager to oversee the CM program and emergency change managers for each IT technology.
- The change manager is responsible for the day-to-day operations of the change management program, including CM policies and standards, change request processing, stakeholder notifications, change advisory board meetings, change status reporting, and program improvement.
- System owners are responsible for the identification and proposal of system updates. System owners shall ensure that change management notification and contract lists are properly maintained and that escalation resources are available to resolve change request issues.
- Support engineering is responsible for the preparation and scheduling of all system changes. Support engineering shall prepare and submit a change request once the required change parameters (i.e., schedule, back-out plan, etc.) have been determined.
- The change advisory board is responsible for the timely review and approval/rejection of system change requests. The change advisory board shall ensure that all system stakeholders are notified and have sufficient time to respond to proposed system changes.
- Emergency change managers are responsible for reviewing and approving/rejecting emergency change requests for their designated technologies and, whenever possible, shall ensure system stakeholders are notified of emergency changes prior to their implementation.
- System administrators are responsible for implementing and verifying system changes, reporting results, and closing out change requests. System administrators shall….

Change Management Policy: Authority

Any policy that cannot be enforced will be ignored. The authority section gives the change management program and its designated agents authorization from management to enforce change management policies and requirements. The section must mandate the compliance and participation of all parties in both the change request and change review processes. It should also (when necessary) outline the escalation procedure and authorization requirements for overriding any policy requirements. It is recommended that override authority require, at a minimum, the approval of the executive manager responsible for the change management program.

Change Management Policy: Compliance and Reporting

This section defines the methods that will be used to verify and report on program operations. The scope section defined what systems and actions require change management approval; the compliance and reporting section determines what constitutes adherence to those requirements. Compliance and reporting makes it possible to measure program effectiveness, identify issues, and adjust program operations to improve efficiency and compliance. It also provides a way to demonstrate process value and justify program costs.

There are no hard-and-fast metrics for change management. Each organization must determine what constitutes success for its program and IT environment. Some metrics to consider include:

- System failures/outages—There are three primary causes of system failure: malicious software (i.e., viruses, worms, etc.), operator error, and flawed system changes. Anyone that has been involved in IT operations knows that stable systems—those that have been operating successfully for a sustained period of time—do not suddenly start failing unless they experience a hardware failure, are under attack, or run out of disk space. All other failures are the result of system operator errors or erroneous changes. A large number of non-hardware-related failures is a good indication of ineffective configuration and change management practices.
- Failure duration—Reversing erroneous system changes can be difficult, especially if the changes were made without a rollback plan in place. This tends to result in long failure durations due to time-consuming troubleshooting and full system restores.
- Emergency requests—A large number of emergency change requests is a sure indicator of an inefficient or ineffective change management process. With the exception of security, there are very few instances where emergency changes must be made to a system. Most emergency requests are the result of poor planning or laziness; that is, support personnel do not take or do not have the time to submit change requests through normal channels or they refuse to do so because emergency requests require less time and effort. A small number of emergency requests is normal; a large number points to serious problems with change and CM processes.
- Exemption or extension requests—Like emergency change requests, a large number of exemption or extension requests is also indicative of change management process problems. A good change management program should facilitate, not delay, change. Exemptions bypass change requirements entirely and should only be granted for limited times and for short durations. This is equally true of extensions. Frequent exemption or extension requests and long-term exemptions or extensions are a sure indication of change management problems.

■ SLA adherence—Change requests should be consistently accomplished within the timelines set by the SLA. Long approval times and requests that remain open for long periods of time represent hard failures of the program that must be addressed.

Measurement and reporting intervals also need to be defined. Measurement intervals must be set to provide enough data points for a meaningful evaluation. Reporting intervals must be set so participants receive the information they need to successfully execute their change management responsibilities. When possible, status reports to participants with open change requests should be sent out daily and summary management reports issued monthly.

Change Management Policy: Communications Plan

It is also a good idea to include a communications plan in the program policy. Change management requires the coordination of changes across multiple owner- ship, geographic, time, department, and even company boundaries. In addition, various IT entities may be involved at different stages of the change process (i.e., planning, engineering, deployment, etc.). It is the responsibility of the change man- agement program to ensure all parties receive the information they need to suc- cessfully fulfill their responsibilities within the established timelines. Creating a consistent set of communications channels between the various entities is one way to ensure this obligation is met.

The plan must include horizontal channels between program participants as well as vertical channels for reporting program status to management. This also includes communications to supporting functions that may need to review pro- posed changes. For example, information security needs to be notified of proposed changes so potential security risks can be evaluated. Another key entity is the help/ support desk. They need to be aware of upcoming changes and potential issues so they can prepare troubleshooting and escalation procedures. Facilities may need to be notified when system upgrades increase power or cooling requirements. Legal may need to review changes that affect contracted services, and human resources may need to review changes that alter job responsibilities.

The plan should also define who is responsible for generating the communica- tion, the destination of each communication, as well as how often each commu- nication is sent. Some communications (e.g., monthly reports) are sent at regular intervals, others may be triggered by certain events. For example, the submission of a change request might automatically generate notifications or review requests to system stakeholders.

It is critical that the communications plan establish in-band and out-of-band emergency communication channels. Changes have been known to cause serious failures requiring immediate responses. Sometimes these failures adversely impact normal communication channels; having alternate out-of-band channels ensures the required information can be communicated to the responsible parties. In most instances this simply means an accurate contact list containing the cell phone or pager numbers of key systems support personnel and the help desk lead.

Roles and Responsibilities

It is the responsibility of the change management program to ensure that all parties involved in the change process receive appropriate notification so they have sufficient time to review and prepare for the change. At the same time the change process must not become a bottleneck that impedes necessary system changes. Defining roles, responsibilities, and timelines, and creating organizational alignment helps provide a reasonable balance between these requirements.

Change management roles cross a number of technical and business boundaries within and sometimes outside the organization. Organizational alignment creates the accountability structures necessary to manage change across these management realms. It defines the (dotted-line) relationships between realm roles and the change management authority, and sets up the protocols that will be used to communicate change management requirements, requests, and reporting across the enterprise.

Different change management roles will exist within IT and business groups depending on the systems within their control and the relationships of those systems to other entities. Discovering all the roles involved can be difficult given the diversity and integration of systems. The best source of role information is system and business owners. They should be included in the preparation and review of the roles and responsibilities section of the change management policy to ensure that all stakeholders and their notification and approval requirements are identified. Involving system and business owners in the definition of these components also promotes adoption of the policy. It is difficult for people to argue against compliance with something they helped define. Table 13.2 provides examples of some of the roles, responsibilities, and timelines involved in the change management process.

It is helpful to maintain a series of one-page role and responsibility summaries. These are single Web or document pages outlining the specific responsibilities and associated timelines for each change management role. They can also provide links to other resources that further explain change management requirements or to tools used to facilitate the process. These summaries provide a quick and easy way to get people up to speed on their responsibilities and quickly locate the documentation, forms, and tools they need to fulfill those responsibilities. A sample system owner summary is contained in Appendix B.

Table 13.2   Change Management Roles, Responsibilities, and Timelines

Role	Responsibilities	Timeline
System owner	Receive, evaluate, and approve proposed system changes.	System owner shall evaluate and approve proposed system changes in accordance with quarterly release management and security management requirements.
System engineering	Plan, engineer, and test proposed system changes.	System engineering shall plan and test system changes in accordance with quarterly release management and security management requirements.
System support	Initiate change requests, schedule and deploy changes, record results, and close change requests.	System support shall initiate, schedule, and deploy changes in accordance with quarterly release management and security management requirements. Close all change requests within 3 days of completion.
Emergency change managers	Review, verify, and approve emergency change requests.	Emergency change managers shall approve or reject emergency changes within 24 hours of submission.
Change manager	Review, verify, and approve routine and low priority change requests.	Within 72 hours of submission the change manager shall review and approve routine change requests and notify all stakeholders and change advisory board members of all other submissions.
Change control board	Review, verify, and approve change requests.	Change advisory board members shall review and approve or reject RFCs within 1 week of the request being placed on the change advisory board meeting agenda.
Information security	Propose system updates to remediate security vulnerabilities. Review potential security impacts of requested changes.	InfoSec shall propose changes as needed and review the potential security impacts of RFCs before the next scheduled change advisory board meeting.
Business unit	Review proposed system changes for potential impacts to business operations and contractual, legal, or regulatory compliance.	Business unit stakeholders shall review RFCs for potential impacts to business operations and contractual, legal, or regulatory compliance before the next scheduled change advisory board meeting.
Data consumer/ supplier	Review proposed system changes for potential impacts to downstream systems or operations consuming or supplying data to the system.	System data consumer of supplier shall review RFCs for potential impacts of systems consuming or supplying data to this system before the next change advisory board meeting.

Managing Change

Change management consists of a series of activities or tasks starting with a request for change (RFC) followed by change classification, authorization, deployment, and review. Change can be initiated by any number of parties involved with the system as a result of new business requirements, the need for new products or services, vendor updates, system performance or reliability improvements, and security patches. Whatever the source, it is the responsibility of the system owner to review these potential changes with the business and system engineering teams to determine cost, scheduling, and resource requirements. Once these elements have been defined and the necessary resources budgeted, the proposed change is handed over to the system engineering group for deployment planning, packaging, and testing. It is during this phase that the RFC is developed and entered into the change tracking system.

Change Request

The RFC initiates the formal change management review and authorization process. For efficiency and tracking purposes, electronic RFC submissions are recommended over paper-based forms, but both methods should be supported. There are two types of RFCs: individual and bulk. An individual change control request covers a specific system or systems; a bulk request covers a class of systems, for example, "all call center workstations." The main purposes of an RFC are to identify the system or systems being changed, describe the work being performed, specify implementation timelines, and identify potential impacts and contingency plans.

Depending on the organization, the RFC may also contain information on prerequisites, sequencing requirements, and other caveats; contact and notification information; and contractual, regulatory, and legal requirements. When a change is the result of a vendor notification, such as a security bulletin, the description of the work should include or reference that notification and any additional sources of information to which the notice points. It is far better to provide too much information with an RFC than to have the RFC rejected for too little.

The primary difference between an individual and a bulk request is in the identification of the systems to which the RFC applies. An individual change request contains specific system identifiers. A bulk request contains a class of systems that, depending of the type of change, can be associated with a particular location, hardware, operating system, or application. For example, the call center support group might submit a request to update "all call center workstations," the server engineering group might submit a bulk request for all servers running Windows 2000 SP2, and the desktop support group might submit a request for all systems with Visio installed. While a bulk request may not identify the individual systems, it should approximate the number of systems subject to the change.

The work description should contain a list of the exact changes that will be made to the identified systems. The changes should be identical for all the systems listed on the RFC. Combining different types of changes to multiple systems on a single RFC makes it difficult for the change authority to evaluate the request and will likely cause the RFC to be rejected. The description should also contain an overview of the deployment plan followed by the deployment schedule. For example, a bulk deployment might describe a phased implementation over a period of days or weeks, whereas an individual deployment might describe changes on a single day in different change windows. If the deployment is constrained to a specific timeline due to SLA, policy, or regulatory requirements, this must be clearly stated in the deployment plan. The deployment plan should be followed by the proposed change schedule. The following example of a Structured Query Language (SQL) server change deployment overview contains specific scheduling constraints and a proposed change schedule:

> The update will be applied to individual SQL servers during their normal maintenance windows and to clustered servers in two maintenance windows offset by a minimum of 2 hours. Updates will commence on Saturday Jan. 11 and must be completed by 6 a.m. Monday, Jan. 13.

System name	Change date	Window	Time
Atlanta data center			
HR-SQLSVR01	Saturday, Jan. 11	1	12 a.m.–2 a.m.
ENG-SQLSVR01	Saturday, Jan. 11	1–6	12 a.m.–8 a.m.
HQ-SQLSVR01A	Sunday, Jan. 12	2	1 a.m.–3 a.m.
HQ-SQLSVR01B	Sunday, Jan. 12	4	3 a.m.–5 a.m.
IT-SQLSVR01	Monday, Jan. 12	2	2 a.m.–4 a.m.

The scheduling information is critical to evaluating potential conflicts and prioritizing implementations. While it may not be possible to predict the exact date and time a change will be applied, it is essential that the RFC contain reasonable scheduling estimates. Note that the engineering SQL server above contains a range of update times on Saturday morning.

The final component of the RFC is information on the potential impacts of the change and the contingency plans for dealing with those impacts. This section should always contain contingencies (rollback plans) for update and system failures. The section should identify potential impacts to all system stakeholders. This includes those directly impacted by the change (system users) as well as downstream consumers of system data. This information is essential for proper review of the RFC. Any party potentially affected by the change should have the opportunity to review the proposed change for potential issues.

The primary sources of information for the RFC come from the initial update screening process in the identify phase and the early planning activities of the evaluate and plan phase. This is supplemented with system-specific information from the configuration management database (CMDB), including system owner and administrator information, hardware and software inventories, and location and criticality data. Appendix C contains a sample RFC template.

Change Tracking System

Change requests, like trouble tickets, need to be tracked to completion. In fact, many organizations use their trouble ticketing system to track change requests because the majority of these systems allow for the electronic entry of requests, automated notifications, status tracking, closure, and retention. The purpose of the tracking system is twofold. First, it provides a structured way to move RFCs through the approval process, and second, it provides a record of system changes and results. It is best to use an automated as opposed to a manual system for tracking changes.

The key features a tracking system should provide are:

■ Electronic RFC entry
■ Automated assignment
■ Automated notification
■ Status reporting
■ Escalation
■ Closure
■ Change reporting

A Web page or electronic form (e.g., Infopath) for creating and submitting RFCs is best. RFCs contain a lot of information, and entering it once on paper and having someone transfer it to the tracking system is very inefficient. Electronic submission with automated assignment moves the RFC directly to the approving authority for processing. Automated notifications to system stakeholders is also a valuable time saver. System owners are responsible for maintaining notification lists for each system. Typically these are email lists that can be used by the assignment mechanism to send stakeholders copies of the RFC for review. It is important for the notification to specify a drop-dead date for submitting issues to the approving authority.

The change initiator (typically the system owner) needs to be able to track the status of the change request. As mentioned earlier, it is recommended that a daily status report on open change requests be issued to system owners, but there should also be an ad hoc query capability that allows for complete viewing of all actions and information entries for a specific RFC. Request status reporting also allows the approving authority to quickly review incoming RFCs and escalations. This helps the approving authority efficiently manage and prioritize the change authorization process.

The change tracking system should also have an escalation mechanism. The system owner must be able to change the priority of an RFC when conditions, such as the public release of an exploit, change the implementation timelines. Finally, the system must provide an easy method for the people making and verifying changes to report on the results and close the RFC.

There are a couple of other system capabilities to consider as well. Try to pick a system with good reporting capabilities and one that is compatible with other system management and inventory tools. This facilitates system query and reporting functions. For example, an organization with an asset inventory database, CMDB, and a change management database using a common SQL server back end can easily join those databases to generate extensive system configuration and change reports.

Change Classification

The change initiator or system owner should assign a priority to the update as part of the RFC submission process. This facilitates the processing of change requests by allowing the change authority to focus on the most important/critical change requests first. It is best to have a limited number of predefined classifications for RFCs. There are a number of different factors that influence classification, but they all come down to impact. Whether it is new functionality that will improve business processes, security patches to prevent compromises, or updates for system reliability or performance, they can all be measured in terms of impact. Table 13.3 contains four RFC classifications and accompanying descriptions.

Zero-day exploit patches are one example of an emergency update, but emergency changes might also be requested to repel attacks or to limit the spread of virus or worm infestations. Security updates are usually given high classifications because the time between the release of a security patch and the release of an exploit can be as little as 7 to 10 days. Other examples of high priority updates are software or hardware failures that cause excessive downtime or require extensive amounts of

Table 13.3 Request for Change Criticality Classifications

Class	Timeframe	Description
Emergency	24 hours	The system is at immediate risk of failure or compromise
High	7 days	The system is at high risk of failure or compromise
Medium	30 days	The system is at moderate risk of failure or compromise
Low	90 days	The system is at low risk of failure or compromise

rework. High classifications are usually reserved for host and server systems, but can apply to workstations if the failure applies to an entire class of systems.

Medium is the most common classification. A medium change is typically a change to system functionality required to meet new business requirements, integrate systems, or patch security vulnerabilities without known exploits. Medium priority changes are always associated with a timeline for completion.

Low priority changes are not tied to a timeline, they are simply part of the standard quarterly or biannual update cycle; updates to improve system performance or capacity fall into this classification. Fixes to minor bugs that do not affect the functionality of the application (e.g., fixing a misspelled word) are another example.

The classification given an update may also be governed by the technologies used to track or deploy the update. For example, if your update management system only supports three classifications, it makes sense to match the process to the technology.

The initial change classification reflects the system owner's assessment of system-specific impacts. The change authority then evaluates those impacts within the context of all proposed changes and the overall impact these changes represent to the entire IT infrastructure. The type and classification of the change in the RFC feeds into the authorization process.

Change Authorization

Change authorization is the approval (or rejection) of an RFC. Depending on the type and classification of the change, the authorization can take place at the change manager, project, or change advisory board level. Allowing the change manager to authorize routine and low priority changes facilitates the change control process and reduces the number of changes that must be evaluated by the change advisory board. However, it is important to note that sometimes minor changes can have significant implications. Therefore it is important for the change manager to do a critical evaluation of the potential threats and impacts of the proposed change and when in doubt refer the change to the change advisory board.

Change Advisory Board

The change advisory board is responsible for the timely review and approval or rejection of system change requests. The change advisory board serves as the focal point for the management of system changes and is the ultimate authority for deciding which proposed changes actually get made. Therefore it is important that the members on the change advisory board accurately reflect both the business and technology aspects of the organization. The following is a representative example of change advisory board members:

- Executive sponsor
- Change manager
- Customer/end user representative
- Line of business or marketing representative
- Engineering leads (network, desktop, server, etc.)
- Security analysis
- Software development lead
- Quality assurance lead
- Documentation lead

The executive sponsor or change manager should chair the change advisory board meetings. It is the chairperson's responsibility to ensure all viewpoints are fairly heard and evaluated as part of the change authorization process. The customer/end-user and line of business/marketing representatives provide the business impact perspective and the other members provide the technological perspective for their various disciplines. Occasionally change advisory board membership may be expanded to support specific business or IT initiatives. For example, the project manager for a major acquisition or the lead for a major IT upgrade may be included to provide perspective on how proposed changes impact their projects. Stable membership is also highly desirable. Familiarity with change advisory board processes, member expertise, and pervious changes helps reduce RFC processing time and ensure better change outcomes.

Change Advisory Board Meetings

Change advisory board meetings should be regularly scheduled—weekly is the most common interval—and convened whenever emergency or other immediate change requirements must be evaluated. Meeting attendance need not be in person; phone conferences are acceptable, provided all parties have or can view the meeting materials. It is recommended that the change advisory board meet early in the work week because this provides additional planning time for system support personnel between the change authorization and available implementation change windows. It is the change manager's responsibility to schedule and facilitate these meeting. The change manager collects the RFCs, sends out the appropriate notifications, and schedules the change for evaluation by the change advisory board. For efficiency, the change manager may choose to group a series of change proposals together so they can be evaluated as a single change. Change advisory board members should receive a summary of the proposed changes they will be evaluating at least one business day before the change advisory board meeting convenes. The summary should include the systems to be changed, the change priorities, and proposed dates for the change. The summary should also provide a reference pointer to the actual RFC. A quorum of members is required to authorize changes; at a minimum a quorum should consist of the change manager, engineering, security, and quality assurance leads.

The change advisory board meeting should not be longer than 2 hours. The purpose of the change advisory board meeting is to approve, reject, or reschedule proposed changes; it is not to review or debate them. While it is the responsibility of the change advisory board to verify that all system stakeholders have been notified and have had sufficient time to respond to proposed changes, stakeholders and change advisory board members are provided with a list of requested changes so they can complete their evaluation of those changes prior to the start of the meeting. Stakeholders can submit their evaluation comments to the change manager or choose to attend the change advisory board meeting in person if they deem it necessary. The change manager must have a process in place to accommodate stakeholder (or for that matter any interested party) attendance that includes a way for the interested party to request attendance at the change advisory board meeting that will be reviewing the RFC in question, as well as a scheduling mechanism that ensures the interested party is notified of the time and place of the meeting, the agenda, and the results.

The notification process should be proactive; the requesting party should not be required to visit a Web site or other posting site to find this information. They should receive an email, page, or other similar message. The message should clearly state when and where the review will take place and what action the recipient must take if they are unable to attend (e.g., send a representative, request a deferral, etc.). Proactive notification avoids situations where the interested party does not attend and then comes back and requires a rescheduled review because their interests were not properly represented. This type of exception to the normal RFC process generates a lot of unnecessary work for everyone concerned. In contrast, if the interested party is notified and does nothing to ensure its interests are represented at the RFC review, little reason will exist to force another review.

The meeting should be a simple roll call of member approval, rejection, or proposed rescheduling for each RFC, including the accompanying reason(s). Board members may also suggest the bundling of a group of changes into a single change or an alternate priority rating for a change.

Change Evaluation

When an RFC is submitted it is circulated to the stakeholders identified in the RFC as potentially impacted entities for their comments. The change advisory board members evaluate the change based on the stakeholder comments received and their knowledge of the particular business or technology area they represent. Some areas of consideration include:

■ Impact on business, manufacturing, or IT operations
■ Impact on legal, regulatory, or contractual obligations

- Impact on the security of IT systems and data
- Workload impacts on IT and help desk personnel
- Impacts on end users
- Impacts to systems consuming outputs from the system being changed
- Thoroughness of predeployment testing
- Viability of the rollback plan/procedures
- Alternatives and workarounds

The goal is to identify the level of risk the change represents to the operational integrity of the IT infrastructure and the business, and to determine if the change timeline and preparation is sufficient to warrant approval, rejection, or rescheduling.

Sample Scenarios

The following scenarios cover the most common system changes and evaluation requirements:

- Critical or important security patch—This is a change to mitigate an eminent threat to the confidentiality, integrity, or availability of the system or system data. The scope of this type of change can be small (only a few systems) to very large (all Windows desktops and servers). The evaluation must focus on the deployment timeline and weigh the need to protect systems and data against compromise and the potential impact of the change deployment to system and business operations. Alternative mitigation measures are particularly important to this evaluation. If the threat can be mitigated by other means (e.g., by blocking the exploit at the router) additional time can be dedicated to testing, rollback, help desk, and operations planning to reduce potential impacts to end user productivity and business operations. For large deployments, the viability of the rollback procedure is also critical. Should the update cause significant operational failures, there must be a stable way to restore systems to their previous operational state.
- Critical or important functionality patch—This type of change resolves a serious problem with the operational integrity of an application or system; for example, a problem that keeps an application from starting properly or a driver flaw that causes a network card to intermittently disconnect from the network. These issues are usually small in scope but have substantial end user and business impacts. There is seldom an alternative to patching, so the evaluation must balance the business need and timelines against the potential impacts to IT operational integrity and security.
- Improved stability or reliability update—These changes resolve issues with defective components that cause periodic system lockups, crashes, or other failures. They are similar in scope to the critical functionality patches above,

but less critical to business operations, and often have workaround solutions available. Consequently the evaluation is less concerned with the deployment timeline and can focus on the potential impacts of the change to system security and operation, the thoroughness of testing, and potential impacts to system data transfers.

■ Improved functionality update—This type of change provides additional system or application functionality that is needed for business or operational reasons. The scope can be small (adding a module to an existing application) to very large (adding a browser plug-in to all desktops). While it is needed functionality, it is not critical; the evaluation should focus on the potential impacts of the change to system security and operations and the thoroughness of testing. For large deployments, rollback procedures must also be considered.

■ Periodic vendor maintenance release—These changes often come in the form of patch bundles or service packs and represent an incremental change to the application or operating system. Maintenance releases make massive changes to systems, adding functionality, improving reliability, and tightening security, but they are seldom critical to business or IT operations. The deployment scope is usually large, involving an entire class of workstations or servers. The primary focus of the evaluation is on the thoroughness of the testing and the viability of the rollback procedures. These changes are usually done in phases (as opposed to mass deployment), so timelines and scheduling are also important considerations; a long deployment has the potential to overlap critical business processes.

Approving, Rejecting, or Rescheduling Changes

During the change advisory board meeting the board must make a decision whether to approve, reject, or reschedule each proposed change. The action should be based on agreement of all the change advisory board members present at the meeting. Approvals require no additional action unless they are made over the objection of a stakeholder, in which case the reason for overriding the objection must be noted in the approval. Occasionally the change advisory board may need to approve an RFC over the objection of a stakeholder or change advisory board member. This should only be done when the risks to the enterprise for not completing the change is greater than the risks associated with the objection. With the exception of approvals, all other board actions must be accompanied with an explanation.

The board must provide its reasons for rescheduling a change, including its assessment of the risks related to the scheduling change. The submitter (change initiator) has the option to accept the rescheduled time or resubmit the RFC with a newly proposed schedule. The change advisory board may reject any RFC for a number of reasons, including incompleteness, stakeholder's objections, or change advisory board member's evaluation. Whenever an RFC is rejected, the board must provide the reason(s) for the rejection and recommended corrective action. The new status of the RFC is recorded in the change tracking system by the change manager so the change initiator and any other interested parties can monitor the progress of the RFC. At a minimum the tracking update should include the date when the change was accepted, rejected, or rescheduled; the reason(s) for the action (required for rejections and reschedules); and recommended corrective actions for all rejections.

There is one additional action the change advisory board may take. When a change is scheduled far enough in the future, the board can defer the review to a future meeting. This also allows additional review time for the stakeholders and change advisory board members. Deferring the review does not change the status of the RFC, but the change tracking system should be updated to reflect the change in the review date.

Change Development

It is possible for an RFC to be approved before all the planning and test procedures for the change have been completed. This really depends on how the vendor packages its updates. Most updates from Microsoft are packaged as MSI files that are ready for installation so little development work is required. Other patches, however, can require substantial development work to package the files, registry changes, and other configuration updates. Keeping the change development status along with the approval status helps stakeholders and system support personnel prepare for and prioritize upcoming changes without having to check multiple systems. Changes that have reached approved and released status are ready for deployment; all others are still pending. The field can also be used to track the deployment status after the update has been released; for example:

- Scheduled—a change window for deployment has been established
- In progress—the patch is actively being deployed
- Suspended—deployment has been halted to address an issue with the update or deployment
- Completed—change completed and ready for review
- Rescinded—change was backed out for failure, compatibility, or other reasons

When deployment planning is completed the status field is changed to test. This alerts system support personnel that the update package is ready for system-specific tests and deployment. When testing is complete the status is changed to release to reflect the update's progression into the deployment phase.

Change Review and Reporting

This portion of the change management process takes place during and after the update deployment is complete. The review process determines whether or not the change has produced the desired results (i.e., met the requirements of the RFC). During deployment, the progress of the change is monitored by system support, system engineering, and help desk staff for faults, failures, or other indications the deployment is not progressing successfully. At this point the deployment team may choose to suspend or rescind the update until any deployment issues can be resolved. The deployment status in the tracking system is updated to reflect this decision.

Whether an update completes successfully or not, the change is subject to review by the change manager. This includes both normal and emergency changes. Typically these reviews are brief, especially for routine or common changes such as antivirus signature updates. For such a review, the change manager may simply check the date of the signature file on his or her own system or request a status on the change from the AV coordinator. Some other review steps may be warranted for larger deployments; for example, a conference call with key stakeholders to identify any issues that need to be followed up and to determine the overall satisfaction/success of the change. It is vitally important that emergency changes be reviewed as soon as possible after the change is made. Emergency changes are usually deployed with very little testing and therefore represent a much higher risk to systems. A quick review can help catch unanticipated problems and reduce any potential impacts.

Help desk tickets and logs are another great source of information on change results and can help pinpoint issues or weaknesses in the process. For example, a large number of calls about changes in system behavior or the user interface indicates the need for better deployment communications. Calls concerning missing or erroneous functionality indicate a need for better testing procedures.

Failures, suspensions, and other major issues with a change warrant a thorough review by the change manager in conjunction with the update planning and evaluation team, system engineering, and security (if the update was security related). The goal of the review is to identify the root cause(s) of the issue so processes and procedures can be modified to ensure these are addressed and do not become issues in future releases. Another goal, especially if the change was security related, may be to get the issues resolved so the deployment can be completed as quickly as possible. Table 13.4 identifies the different stakeholders and the types of information that should be reviewed with each.

When the review is complete the change manager can close the RFC. A closed status indicates that no further actions are required for that RFC. However, a closed status does not mean that the change met all the objectives of the original change request; other actions may be required, including the submission of additional change requests to address the objectives that were not met.

Table 13.4　Review Subject Assignments

Team	Review subjects
Network engineering	Technical issues, bandwidth, and performance impacts
System engineering	Technical issues, system performance, and capacity impacts
Security team	Technical issues; network, host, or application security impacts; performance impacts on security controls and devices
Operations group	Operational issues, required workarounds, impacts to directory, backup, time, etc., resources
Help desk	Increases in support calls, recurring/common issues
Partner	Technical issues, SLA impacts, and fines

Conclusion

In summary, the primary goal of the change management program is to ensure that the business receives optimal benefit from changes to the IT environment by ensuring that changes are accomplished in a consistent and reliable manner, minimizing impacts to business processes and productivity. The process includes receiving RFCs; evaluation of change risks and impacts; approval, deferral, or rejection of requests; and postmortem reviews of completed changes. To be successful a change management program must have well-defined requirements, clear roles and responsibilities, good processes, established timelines, excellent communications, and, above all, active participation and support from everyone involved.

Chapter 14

Update Testing

The evaluate and plan chapter referenced the need to test updates and deployment packages for proper operations and compatibility with existing system configurations. Every update deployment consists of three or more components that must be tested, including the update, the manual and automated deployment procedures, and the rollback procedures. These tests must be conducted for each version of the update as well as each platform the update will be applied to. This means an update that applies to three different versions of the software on three different versions of the operating system requires nine test runs; multiply this times the number of different platforms and system configurations in the organization and you could end up with hundreds of test scenarios.

This chapter is designed to help you organize and streamline your testing efforts, including test planning, test facilities, testing roles and skills, test strategies, and test automation. While the chapter is aimed at larger organizations, many of the techniques and methods discussed can be applied to smaller organizations with equal effectiveness.

Test Strategy

There are three primary test strategies: centralized, dispersed, and outsourced. Most organizations will use a combination of these strategies based on the ownership, configuration, location, and criticality of the target system. Centralized testing makes the most sense for testing standardized system builds and applications. Dispersed testing makes sense for specialized configurations (i.e., one-off systems), custom applications, and for systems with high criticality or business impact. Systems outsourced to external organizations such as hosting sites may have a portion or all of the testing performed by the outsourcer, depending upon the contract terms and the type of update. For example, the hosting site may be responsible for all operating system update testing, while a local support group may be responsible for updates to the applications loaded on the system. Alternatively, an organization may choose to outsource testing for a particular technology stream (e.g., all workstation configurations). It is unusual for a company to outsource all update testing. The diversity of equipment, configurations, data sensitivity, and criticality inevitably result in the need for some testing to be conducted by internal support personnel.

A centralized testing facility with a dedicated staff offers a number of advantages, including better coverage, greater efficiency, more consistent results, and lower costs. Centralized testing allows for a higher degree of test automation. This improves the efficiency of the test process, allowing more tests to be conducted within a given timeframe. It is easier to keep a dedicated test environment synchronized with the production environment, and this also improves the consistency and viability of test results. Ultimately this equates to fewer deployment failures and substantial cost savings.

Cost can also be a disadvantage, depending on the size of the organization. Maintaining a dedicated test environment with all the associated production hardware and an expert staff can be costly. Selling your testing services to other divisions or organizations is one way to defray these costs. It is also difficult for a centralized testing function to maintain the knowledge or expertise required to cover every specialized system and custom application within the organization; some testing will have to be conducted by the people supporting these technology streams.

Dispersed testing has the advantage of being able to cover specialized systems and customized applications, including systems where data sensitivity, system criticality, or location precludes centralized testing. Some gains in efficiency from running tests in parallel may also be realized. Achieving consistent results is the biggest disadvantage.

Testing conducted by local support teams seldom has the rigor of a dedicated test function, and good test skills are not common among support personnel. Consequently, dispersed testing tends to cover fewer items and have less consistent results. Written test procedures and checklists can improve results, provided they are properly prepared by someone with test expertise. Unless a common test lab is maintained for all the technology streams, diverse testing results in multiple testing facilities with various degrees of compatibility with the production environment, or even worse, tests are conducted on production systems. These factors increase the risk of deployment failures and the costs of dealing with those failures.

Combining the two strategies provides the best overall results. Centralized testing can cover all the common system functions, making it unnecessary for the technology streams to repeat those tests. This improves testing efficiency by reducing the amount of testing that must be done. Efficiency is also increased because testing can be conducted in parallel. Once the evaluate and planning function has acquired the update and tested its basic functionality, the update can be released to all the technology streams for specialized testing while the centralized team tests the common functionality. This is especially valuable when the testing timeframes are short.

The expertise of the centralized test team can also be leveraged to improve testing methods and procedures and for support personnel training. Furthermore, the centralized test environment can be leveraged for testing by the various technology streams.

Organizational differences in the way workstations, servers, hosts, etc., are managed may result in multiple centralized testing groups built around these technologies. While this natural separation of duties appears to make sense, it can increase the cost of testing unnecessarily, especially when it increases the number of testing facilities and test personnel. Whenever possible, centralized testing should consist of a single test facility and a staff of test personal trained to cover as many technologies as possible. A single test facility provides a much higher degree of consistency in testing and test results (see the "Test Facilities" section for additional details).

Testing alone is seldom outsourced; it is usually part of a larger workstation or server support contract that includes system updating. If your organization plans to outsource testing, make sure the agreement covers the following areas:

- Test coverage
- Test types
- Test priority
- Test timeframes

Each of these topics is covered in detail later in the chapter.

Test Planning

The evaluate and plan phase defined the need to test; test planning determines what is going to be tested (test scenarios), who will perform the tests, and the types of tests that will be conducted. Testing, like most other disciplines, follows the 80-20 rule. Good planning results in less effort, better results, and less retesting; poor planning results in more effort and unreliable results that could jeopardize deployments and put business operations at risk.

Test planning is largely driven by the timeframes and resources available for testing. Unlimited time and resources allow for exhaustive testing, whereas short timeframes require prioritized and focused efforts. Testing requires a certain amount of rigor in order to produce reliable results. It also requires a specific set of skills that are not commonly held among information technology (IT) staff. However, testing is based on a certain number of repeatable processes that lend themselves to automation. A good testing process will take some time to develop and to train test personnel, but once it is up and running, tweaking and updating tests requires a relatively minor amount of effort.

Test Scope: What Is Going to Be Tested?

The evaluate and plan phase should have identified the systems that require testing based on the software and software versions specified in the update release documentation. This is a necessary part of the change request process. However, a request for change (RFC) may be a blanket request covering an entire class of systems, so it will be necessary to break this down into specific systems and platform configurations (scenarios) before constructing the test plan. The first division is the type of system: workstation, server, host, etc. The second division is the platform configuration (i.e., the hardware, installed applications, etc.). The type of system and its configuration drives the number and types of tests that will be performed, as well as who will perform them. A good source for this information is the configuration management database (CMDB) and software inventory systems. These should contain a list of all of the systems that have the version(s) of software identified in the update release notification. Another good source of information is system builds. Generally builds are created around common hardware and software configurations. Table 14.1 shows an example of the testing scope for Microsoft Update Bulletin MS06-011.

This information is usually sufficient to determine the types of tests to be conducted and who will do the testing. In the scenario in Table 14.1, the exchange team will need to test the two 2003 EE servers, the desktop support team will test the 30 XP SP1 systems, and so on.

Test Assignment: Who Will Do the Testing?

A number of factors contribute to test assignment. Testing may be assigned to a centralized testing group, dispersed to the various technology streams, or outsourced.

Table 14.1 Test Scope for MS06-11

Deployed software	Quantity	Update required
XP SP1	30	Yes
XP SP2	4080	No
Windows Server 2003 Standard Edition	6	Yes
Windows Server 2003 SE SP1	40	Yes
Windows Server 2003 Enterprise Edition	2	Yes
Windows Server 2003 EE SP1	14	Yes
Windows Advanced Server 2000 SP4a	4	No

Table 14.2   Test Assignments

Technology	Test assignment
Base Windows XP	Central test team
Base Window Server 2003	Central test team
Oracle Database Server	Operating system – Central test team
	DBMS – Database support team
Exchange Server	Operating system – Central test team
	Messaging support team
Siebel Application	Operating system – Central test team
	Application support team
Hosted Web Server	Operating system – Hosting site personnel
(Windows 2003)	Application – Web application support team
Microsoft Office Suite	Central test team
One-off/Special Function	System owner
Kiosk	Kiosk vendor/partner

The location, sensitivity, and criticality of a system may also affect test assignment. For example, a system located on a limited access segment such as a demilitarized zone (DMZ) may need to be assigned to the security group or another entity with the requisite permissions.

The main point is to know the limitations and capabilities of each testing team so tests can be assigned to achieve the most comprehensive results. The CMDB may provide the ownership information necessary to make assignment decisions. System management systems and compliance monitoring systems are other viable sources. Table 14.2 contains an example of testing assignments by technology types. Note that the majority of the testing is assigned to the centralized testing group.

What Types of Tests Will Be Conducted?

The final element of test planning is to determine the types of tests that will be conducted and the order in which they will be conducted. Test timelines may not allow for all the tests to be completed before the update must be deployed. Test suites need to be prioritized to ensure critical functionality is verified first. Each system will require a minimum of three test suites: one to test system functionality after the update is installed, one to test the operation of the deployment package, and one to verify the rollback package. Previous test experiences with problematic systems can also drive the types of tests conducted. Systems that consistently fail when updated warrant additional testing.

Functionality (operational) tests have the highest priority, followed by compatibility, performance, language, and other tests. The tests are outlined here an covered in detail later in this chapter. Functionality testing includes basic system functionality (the system boots, attaches to the network, communicates with network services, etc.), basic user functionality (users can log on, execute programs, etc.), and standard application functionality (i.e., applications included in standard build images). These tests are followed by extended application functionality for commonly deployed applications such a Microsoft Project and Visio, and specialty application functionality for limited deployment applications such as accounting and human resource programs. Functionality tests cover the ability of the system or application to initialize, communicate with its components and support services, and interact with users. This testing also includes standard maintenance processes such as system backup and restore. An example of functionality testing for a human resources application would include the ability of a user to execute the human resources client on their local system, log on to the program, and retrieve records from the human resources database server. Only under extreme circumstances, such as an actively circulating exploit (i.e., a zero-day exploit) should an update be deployed before functionality testing is completed.

Compatibility testing is the second priority once the base functionality of the system or application has been confirmed. Compatibility testing verifies the functionality and interoperability of the remaining system and application components. For example, functionality testing confirms front-end systems can communicate with back-end servers; compatibility testing confirms that all the components using that connection function properly. Compatibility testing also confirms dependencies between systems such as data feeds, connections to message queues and legacy systems, and so on. Depending on the size and complexity of the system or application and the extent of the testing, these test suites can become very large and require large amounts of time to execute. It is important to complete as much compatibility testing as possible prior to deployment; the best practice is to prioritize compatibility tests to ensure the most important (or most commonly used) functionality is tested first. Another way to increase the coverage of compatibility testing is to break the test suite into modules that can be executed in parallel.

One of the keys to the success of functionality and compatibility testing is understanding what needs to be tested and constructing tests that verify only those items. For example, if the base functionality of the system has been confirmed by a centralized testing group, there is no need for the technology stream to duplicate those tests. This is equally true of vendor testing. If the vendor performs compatibility testing with other products (e.g., a Microsoft XP update tested with Internet Explorer [IE]), there is little reason to repeat those tests unless the your configuration is radically different from the standard configuration. It is also possible (although somewhat more difficult) to reduce the amount of testing by comparing the changes listed in the update manifest to the components being used by the system or application. For example, if an update makes changes to the CryptoAPI and your application does not use the CryptoAPI, there is little reason to test those functions. However, this requires a thorough knowledge of all the system modules, services, and libraries your application uses, as well as all the modules called by these and subsequently called modules. Detailing this information can be time consuming, but being able to target testing to specific items makes the effort worthwhile.

The remaining tests should be completed in an order best suited to the production environment. If performance impacts are a concern, performance testing should be completed next. If international deployment is important, language testing would be the next logical choice.

Deployment and Rollback

Once you have verified the update works properly on the system, the only remaining things to test are the deployment and rollback components. If the update was manually installed on the system for compliance testing, the manual installation procedure has already been tested. Since the update needs to be removed from the system to test automated deployment operations, the manual rollback procedure can be confirmed as part of this task. Next, execute the automated deployment and rollback methods (remember there may be multiple methods) and verify the update is properly distributed to, installed on, and removed from the system. In addition to observation, the primary sources of information for verifying these processes will be the log files and system events generated by the deployment agents and applications.

Test Facilities

Industry best practices always recommend that testing be done in a dedicated environment to prevent tests from adversely impacting production systems. The primary goal of testing is to identify and resolve issues before the system or application is placed into production. Performing testing in the production environment is the antithesis of this goal. Organizations may choose to do pilot deployments in conjunction with or in lieu of testing, but testing should never be done in the production environment. There is simply no way to anticipate how testing procedures or an untested update might impact other systems or services. Microsoft Knowledge Base article Q315697 is a great example: if one of the test procedures caused Active Directory to create or re-create a large number of objects, the Domain Controller might stop processing logon and key distribution center (KDC) requests, causing network operations to slow to a crawl.

The size and equipment of a test facility depend a lot on the size of the organization, available resources (floor space, equipment, and personnel), and the criticality of their systems. For example, a small e-commerce company may require exhaustive testing before deploying updates to critical Internet sales servers. Regardless of size, a few general rules apply to all test environments:

■ Isolated—The test environment should be logically isolated from the production environment. Access to the test environment from a production segment should be limited to remote desktop, Telnet, or terminal server connections. Some means of transferring files into the test environment should also be provided. Outbound connections from lab systems into the production environment should never be allowed.
■ Logical replicate—The test environment should be a reasonable replication of the production environment, including the Active Directory domain and directory structure, time, Domain Name System (DNS) and Dynamic Host Configuration Protocol (DHCP) services, storage systems, print devices, backup and restore facilities, and so on.

Note: High-cost equipment might be the exception to this rule. Maintaining a second mainframe or a $50,000 tape library system may be price prohibitive. If these connections cannot be simulated in the test environment, some connectivity from the lab environment to these production devices may be justified. Rather than open outbound ports on the firewall, try to make these dedicated connections via a virtual local area network (VLAN) or a direct cable connection to a dedicated network interface on the production device. This eliminates the possibility that lab systems might accidentally or incidentally interact with production systems.

■ Network replicate—The test environment should also be able to replicate the physical characteristics of the production network, including network segments (backbone, distribution, wireless local area network [WLAN], virtual private network [VPN], etc.), and network devices (switches, routers, firewalls, modems, etc.).
■ Physical replicate—It is equally important to equip the test environment with the same class of systems used in production. Significant differences between production and test hardware can skew results and lead to deployment failures. This does not preclude the use of virtual machines for infrastructure components or functionality testing. However, compatibility and performance testing are closely tied to production hardware.

It is nearly impossible to get reliable test results unless the test environment is a reasonable facsimile of the production environment. Table 14.3 contains a sample list of hardware. If you intend to do performance testing you may need to acquire additional systems in order to simulate the peak loads on the system under test.

In addition to the production hardware listed in Table 14.3, the lab will also require machines for test orchestration, including servers to store the test suites, system rebuild images, test tools, test controllers that will execute the tests, and a system to collect test results and track bugs. A networked printer with copier

Table 14.3   Test Facility Hardware

Network

Network cards

Firewall, RAS server, VPN concentrator, etc.

Routers, switches, hubs, wireless access points, etc.

WLAN simulator

Infrastructure servers: DNS, DHCP, WINS, Active Directory, RADIUS, etc.

Print servers: Jet Direct, etc.

Data storage systems: RAID, SAN, CDR, USB drives, etc.

Reference platforms

Servers: application, file and print, SQL, Web, etc.

Workstations: desktops, laptops, etc.

Mobile devices: Blackberries, PDAs, smart phones, etc.

Printers from supported manufactures (HP, Epson, Xerox, etc.)

Other supported peripherals: scanners, fax servers, etc.

DVD burner

capability is also helpful. And do not forget the needed racks to mount all of this gear, tables, chairs, benches, and keyboard, video, mouse (KVM) switches, as well as power protectors, uninterruptible power supply (UPS), cooling, fire protection, and so on.

Software

The test facility also needs a complete library of the software currently in use within the organization, including operating system and application distribution source files, to facilitate system builds and configuration. Dumping the content of source disks to a network share will make them available to network capable systems, but make sure you have copies of the distribution media (i.e., CD, DVD) available for building new or stand-alone systems in the test facility. You can also facilitate system builds by keeping a library of standard production builds and virtual machine images. The software library should include every version of every operating system and application currently in use (including localized versions), as well as installation media for all test tools and utilities used in the lab. Table 14.4 contains a sample list of these items.

Do not forget to maintain the appropriate license keys as well. Writing the license keys on the distribution disk, storage sleeve, or case is a simple way to keep license keys readily available. Also check with your vendors to see if they provide nonproduction/test licenses at reduced or no cost.

Table 14.4   Test Facility Software

Operating systems

BSD Unix

Mac OS X

Microsoft Windows Server 2003 SP1 Standard and Enterprise Editions

Microsoft Windows 2000 SP4 Server and Workstation

Microsoft Windows XP SP2 Professional

Sun Solaris

All service packs, resource kits, admin toolkits, etc., for the above

Workstation applications

Antivirus, Adobe Reader, WinZip, etc.

Microsoft Office Professional Edition

Mail/messaging clients: Outlook, MSN Messenger, Notes, etc.

Browsers: Internet Explore, Firefox, Navigator, etc.

All service packs, updates, etc. for the above

Server applications

Database engines: Microsoft SQL Server, Oracle, MySQL, etc.

System management systems: SMS, Altiris, Tivoli, etc.

Web server software: Apache, IIS, SharePoint portal services, etc.

Lab software

Load generators and performance monitors

System build and update tools

Programming and scripting tools

Test orchestration: execution, results tracking, reporting, etc.

Reference Materials

Finally, the test facility should have a good library of reference materials for each of the technologies and applications used in the lab, including configuration and operation manuals for network devices, firewalls, servers, workstations, network services, applications, and test utilities. A good smattering of programming references for script development as well as some classic "how to" test books is also recommended.

Not only is it important to outfit the test environment to emulate production, it is equally important to keep it that way. Any changes made to the production environment must be reflected in the test lab, otherwise the reliability and effectiveness of lab testing will decline.

Staffing

Two principle skill sets are required for testing: test engineering and test operations. A test engineer is a senior-level analyst with solid network infrastructure knowledge, including a good understanding of network services operations (DNS, DHCP, Active Directory, Windows Internet Naming Service [WINS], etc.) and intermediate development skills. It is the test engineer's job to develop the test plans and procedures the organization requires. The task begins with a thorough analysis of the technical architecture of the production environment from both an infrastructure and application services perspective. The test engineer must understand the interactions of the systems and applications to be tested with the infrastructure, including what infrastructure components and services control or influence these interactions. For example, the test engineer must understand how connections between the systems are made. Is DNS or a local host file used to look up host addresses or are Internet Protocol (IP) addresses hard coded into applications? What protocols and services are used for these connections (Transmission Control Protocol/Internet Protocol [TCP/IP], Point-to-Point Tunneling Protocol [PPTP], Internet Protocol security [IPSec], Remote Procedure Call [RPC], etc.)? What bandwidth is available and what control points (firewalls, load balancers, routers, switches, etc.) do the connections traverse? This information is required for test planning as well as test setup.

The test engineer must also understand the current load on production infrastructure components in order to construct test scenarios that emulate those loads during lab testing. They must also understand the criticality of production systems and the testing timelines available in order to prioritize testing. These elements are determined through a series of baseline tests. The test engineer gathers a variety of performance indicators from production systems and network devices to determine the normal and peak operating parameters for each. For example, monitoring the packet rate and size makes it possible to determine the average bandwidth utilization on a local area network (LAN) or WAN link as well as the peak bandwidth utilization that can be expected. Monitoring central processing unit (CPU), memory, and paging operations in a server provides similar results. Baselines are needed primarily for performance testing. In order to accurately measure the impact of an update on network or system performance, the appropriate load must be placed to these components.

It is also helpful for the test engineer to have a historic perspective of problematic system hardware, operating system versions, and software so additional tests can be constructed to cover these peculiarities. Furthermore, the test engineer must understand what testing scenarios the test facility supports and what test skills or additional system support will be required to execute these scenarios in order to properly plan test execution. Legacy and outsourced systems are a good example; it is unlikely the lab will have the skills or permissions required to test these systems. Test planning requires that the engineer know when and to what degree external or specially skilled resources will need to be engaged.

The test engineer is also responsible for test automation, including determining what can be automated, the tools that will be used, and developing the scripts and configurations required for that automation. This requires some intermediate programming skills in scripting languages such as Perl, Visual Basic, and Java, as well as some knowledge of Web languages such as PHP and ASP. Good writing and communications skills are also a plus. The test engineer must be able to accurately convey test requirements, plans, and procedures to all personnel involved in test execution and results evaluation.

Operator/Tester

The second essential skill set is as a test operator. The test operator is responsible for test setup, configuration, and execution. This requires good network and system administration skills, including how to:

- Configure network devices (routers, firewalls, routers, etc.)
- Configure network services (DNS, directory services, DHCP, etc.)
- Build server and workstation systems
- Install and configure operating systems
- Install and configure system services (Web services, performance monitors, system management agents, test tools, etc.)
- Install and configure system software (Office, Outlook, Instant Messenger, antivirus, etc.)

The position also requires a good understanding of system and network hardware, including how to cable components and how to install and configure peripherals such as disks, disk controllers, networking cards, and so forth.

Expertise in all these areas is not required. Lab personnel should be able to rely on the expertise of production personnel to assist with the initial installation and configuration of components. What is required is sufficient skill to configure the component parameters required for test execution. These can include reserving IP addresses in DHCP, configuring forward and reverse lookup records in DNS, entering systems and users into the Active Directory, configuring local and domain policies, and so on. The position also requires good troubleshooting skills. When a test fails, it is very important for a test operator to be able to find the root cause of that failure. Testing is an evolutionary process. Test cases will not cover every configuration or usage scenario; there is always the potential that the failure was caused by the testing process and not the component under test. In order for testing to be effective and productive, the test operator must to be able to distinguish between the two.

Most organizations do not have sufficient software testing requirements to justify a full-time test staff, and given the skill requirements, it is not hard to see why hiring a skilled staff could be difficult. Instead, most organizations use production and development personnel for testing. This is a sensible approach, with one significant caution. Production personnel certainly have the administrative skills required to set up, configure, and execute tests, but they typically lack the skills required to develop test plans and automate test procedures. This results in a lot of manually executed processes that reduce test efficiency, coverage, and reliability. Organizations that choose this approach must ensure that some members of the test team receive test development and automation training. Another alternative is to contract or outsource test engineering tasks.

Test Development

The first goal of testing is to verify the basic functionality of the system or application, followed by system compatibility, interoperability, and performance. Test development is the process of turning goals into actionable testing targets and procedures. This includes developing the test cases and test suites needed to meet the requirements defined in the test plan. To illustrate this process, let's consider the requirement to verify basic system functionality after an update has been installed. The first thing that must be defined is, What is basic functionality? This may vary, depending on the role of the system, but essentially this is the functionality expected from the system after initial installation. In other words, Is the system usable? The second thing that must be defined is, What proofs are needed to verify basic functionality? Again, these will vary by role, but every system must be able to boot, initialize system services, attach to the network, and interface with users. These proofs constitute our basic functionality test suite.

Test Procedure: Turning Goals into Targets

Test Suite

A test suite (something referred to as a test set) is a group of the test cases needed to fulfill a test requirement. Table 14.5 defines the proofs required to verify basic system functionality. These proofs are broken into the individual test cases needed to verify each one.

Test Case

A test case or test scenario consists of "a set of test inputs, execution conditions, and expected results for testing a particular objective" (Institute of Electrical and

Table 14.5   Basic System Functionality Proofs

Proof	Description
System boots properly	The system can initialize from a powered off (cold boot) or powered on (warm boot) state.
Note: Not all updates require a reboot after installation. Nonetheless, the ability of the system to initialize after the update has been installed must be confirmed.	
Configured services start properly	All system services configured to start automatically during the boot process initialize and execute properly.
Network initializes properly	Network cards and protocols are initialized, assigned, and configured correctly.
System communicates properly with infrastructure services	The system can communicate properly with required network services with infrastructure services including DHCP, DNS, Active Directory, print services, etc.
Users have access	Local and domain users have the ability to log on and access system resources.
Logs clear of critical errors	System logs are free of any critical errors related to any of the above processes.

Electronics Engineers/American National Standards Institute [IEEE/ANSI]). A single test case may be one of many test cases required to verify a particular functionality. Test cases should identify the utilities, scripts, tools, and associated parameters required to generate and evaluate test results. Table 14.6 illustrates some of these techniques.

System logs are a great secondary source of information. Test cases should always attempt to interact directly with the object being tested. When this is not possible, checking logs may be the only way to determine the pass/fail status of the test. For example, the event record below shows a dynamic DNS registration failure, which may indicate problems with infrastructure component communications:

```
Event Type: Warning
Event ID: 11165
Source: DnsApi
Description:
The system failed to register host (A) resource records
```

The application event log can be checked for this error using the ELOGDMP utility found in the Windows Server resource kit. The syntax is:

```
elogdmp <TargetSystem> Application | Find /V "Event ID: 11165"
```

Table 14.6 Sample Test Case Execution

Condition to be tested	Execution details	Expected result	Pass/fail	Tools required	Comments
System cold boot properly	1. Power on the system	Reply from 192.168.15.1; bytes = 32; time = 1 ms; TTL = 64		PING.exe	Assumes echo responses are not disabled on target system.
	2. Wait approximately 5 min. 3. Open a command window and execute 4. Ping 192.168.15.1				
All services initialize properly	1. Open a command and execute	Scripts displays no errors		CScript ServicesStart. vbs script	Ignore security center errors, the service starts automatically, performs its checks, and shuts down. The functionality is not critical.
	2. CScript ServicesStart.vbs with the following parameters: /S <TargetSystemName>; /I TestMasterID; /P <TMPassword>				
User can log on	1. At the target system console, log on as Testmaster	System displays a standard user desktop		None	Also verifies connectivity to the domain controller since Testmaster is a domain account.

It is also possible on Windows systems to use WMI to query the event log. The following code uses the WMI to query the security event log for type 560 errors.

```
Set objWMIService = GetObject("winmgmts:" &_
"{(Security)}!\\" & strComputerName & "\root\cimv2")
Set colLoggedEvents = objWMIService.ExecQuery _
("SELECT * FROM Win32_NTLogEvent WHERE _
Logfile = 'Security' AND " & "EventCode = '560'")
```

Most testing involves repeatable processes that can easily be automated. The following section contains a number of things to remember about test cases and case automation.

Test Automation

Automated testing consists of six common tasks:

- Test configuration—This task can consist of any number of elements, including configuring the target system, setting up accounts, installing test software, editing configuration files, etc. Each test suite should contain a list of the prerequisites required to execute the suite. The test configuration task ensures those prerequisites are met prior to test execution.
- Set permissions—This task sets the appropriate permissions for the execution of the test. Tests related to operating system functionality are usually executed with administrative privileges, but it is poor practice to execute service or application tests with administrative credentials. This task ensures tests are executed in the same user context that the target service or applications would use in production.
- Send input and capture output—Test cases can contain one or more inputs. This task ensures all inputs are tested and the results of each test are captured for evaluation. Depending on the test environment, inputs might be keyboard entered at the console or remotely using a remote desktop or remote control program. They might be submitted directly to the system command process or a system service or application programming interface (API) using a script or remote execution utility. Capture also depends on the test environment; it can include displaying results on the console, redirecting outputs to a file, or writing results to a database.
- Validate and report results—This is commonly known in test circles as the oracle function. Actual results are compared to expected results and the outcome reported. In most case the results are reported as pass or fail. Reported results should always be written to permanent storage. They provide evidence the test was conducted and provide for further review if necessary. It is up to

the test engineer to decide whether or not the results will control additional test execution. It is reasonable to stop execution of a large test suite when a test case fails or when the failure of one test case will cause the remaining cases to fail. Otherwise it is better to let the entire case or suite execute. It is far more efficient to deal with all the resulting failures at the same time then to fix one and rerun the test.

■ Take appropriate action—If all of the test cases pass, there really is not any follow-on action that needs to be completed. Failures require an evaluation to determine the root cause. Was the failure a result of the update or a flaw in the test scenario? If the update is bad, forwarding the issue to the vendor is appropriate. Otherwise a decision must be made to ignore the test error or fix the test flaw and rerun the test.

■ Test teardown—The final task is test teardown: returning the test environment to the state it was in prior to test configuration and execution. This is probably the biggest weakness in most test environments. Changes made to the test systems and associated services are not reverted and end up affecting the execution and results of subsequent tests.

Automated testing should be designed to minimize direct interactions with the target machine. The test operators should be able to execute and monitor tests from a test controller or console system. Results can be captured on the console or, if multiple consoles are used, to a centralized results system. The diagram in Figure 14.1 shows a simple test lab configuration using test consoles and a results system.

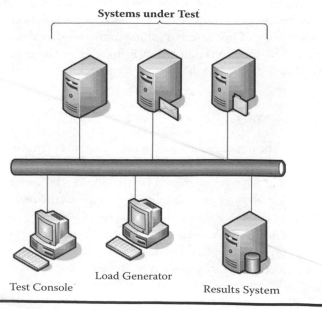

Figure 14.1   Simple test lab configuration.

The results system has multiple roles in this setup. It provides file services for build images, test scripts, and testing tools. It also receives, processes, and stores test results. The load generator creates the appropriate network traffic and system loads to simulate the production environment. The test console schedules and executes test cases, and may, depending on the circumstances, receive and forward test results to the results system.

Test Tips and Tricks

Only Test What Needs to Be Tested

One of the keys to the success of functionality and compatibility testing is understanding what needs to be tested and only constructing tests to verify those items. For example, if the base functionality of the system has been confirmed by a centralized testing group, there is no need for the technology stream tester to duplicate those tests. This is equally true of vendor testing. If the vendor performs compatibility testing with other products (e.g., a Microsoft XP update tested with IE), there is little reason to repeat those tests unless the configuration you are using is radically different from the standard install. It is also possible (although somewhat more difficult) to reduce the amount of testing being done by comparing the changes listed in the update manifest to the components being used by the system or application. For example, if an update makes changes to an API the application does not use, there is little reason to test that function. However, this requires a thorough knowledge of all the system modules, services, and libraries your application uses, as well as all the modules called by these and subsequently called modules. Detailing this information can be time consuming, but being able to target testing to specific items makes the effort worthwhile.

Prioritize Your Tests

Test suites should be organized to test the most critical system functions first and progress downward to minor or seldom used functionality. Functionality (operational) tests should have the highest priority, followed by compatibility, performance, localization, deployment and rollback, and so on. The goal is to successfully complete the critical tests within the designated test timeframe to reduce the risk of business impacts during deployment. This does not mean testing stops just because an update gets deployed. Testing should continue until all tests have been completed and all identified issues are resolved. Test suites and test cases should also be prioritized based on downstream effects. If the failure of a front-end component would cause all subsequent tests of downstream components to fail, it makes no sense to execute tests for these components. Figure 14.2 is a simple illustration of

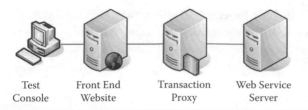

| Test | Front End | Transaction | Web Service |
| Console | Website | Proxy | Server |

Figure 14.2   Downstream test scenario.

this concept. If the transaction proxy in this test scenario fails, all communications to the Web service server will fail, so testing the Web service server before testing the transaction proxy could end up wasting precious test time.

Functionality testing, which includes basic system functionality (system boots, attaches to the network, communicates with network services, etc.), basic user functionality (users can log on, execute programs, etc.), and standard application functionality (applications included in standard build images), should always be conducted first. These tests should be followed by extended application functionality for commonly deployed applications (e.g., Microsoft Office, Adobe Photoshop, Visio, etc.). Next comes specialty application functionality for limited deployment applications such as accounting and human resource programs. Functionality tests cover the ability of the system or application to initialize, communicate with its components and support services, and interact with users, including standard maintenance processes such as system backup and restore.

Compatibility testing is the second priority once the base functionality of the system or application has been confirmed. Compatibility testing verifies the functionality and interoperability of the remaining system or application components, including component communications, data feeds, and connectivity to message queues and legacy systems. Compatibility testing should also be prioritized to ensure the most important (or most commonly used) functionality is tested first.

The remaining tests should be completed in an order best suited to the production environment. If performance impacts are a concern, performance testing should be completed next. If international deployment is important, language testing is the next logical choice.

Maximize Coverage

The amount of testing that can be accomplished prior to deployment is limited by the deployment timeframes. The faster tests can be executed, the better the coverage. Combining tests is one way to increase coverage. For example, using a Ping test to confirm a system has booted successfully also shows the TCP/IP stack on the network card is working and the system can interact with DHCP (if it is configured to use DHCP). This is much more efficient than testing these functions individually. Executing a successful Ping from the target system using a hostname also demonstrates the system can perform DNS lookups correctly. Another way to increase coverage is to execute test suites or portions of test suites in parallel using multiple test consoles. Most systems have more than enough memory and CPU power to execute simultaneous tests.

Use the Best Tools

There are many different ways to get information from a system, including system services like Simple Network Management Protocol (SNMP) and Windows Management Instrumentation (WMI), management agents, and graphical user interface (GUI) and command line utilities, and third-party tools. Pick tools that return consistent, accurate results. There is nothing worse than using a tool that intermittently causes test failure. Try to find tools that return just the information that is needed. It is difficult to filter through large amounts of information to find a particular result and inevitably this leads to unnecessary test failures. For example, it is much more efficient to use the WMI query capability to extract specific events from the event logs than to dump the entire log and filter through it for those events.

Minimize Target Interactions

Ideally all test cases should be executable from the test console. It should not be necessary to directly access the target system to execute tests or gather results. In addition to utilities that provide remote access to system information there are a number of different ways to execute commands on a target system, including remote control scripts, Telnet scripts, Remote Desktop Protocol (RDP) automatic executions, and utilities like Sysinternals PSExec. There are just as many ways to retrieve the results: writing to network file share, sharing a folder or disk on the target, trivial file transfer protocol/ file transfer protocol (TFTP/FTP), Web-based Distributed Authoring and Versioning (WebDAV), and others, including the file transfer capabilities of remote control applications.

System management and monitoring systems can also be used to gather this information. For example, Microsoft SMS has a software inventory function that can copy files to an SMS repository. There are also a number of centralized logging systems that can capture and consolidate system logs, including UNIX syslog and the Audit Consolidation Service in Microsoft Operations Manager. The next section provides even more ways to remotely interact with systems. Well-designed tests should allow the test operator to initiate the test suite, walk away, and return to review the results.

Leverage System Automation

Some operating systems and services have capabilities that can be used to facilitate test automation. For example, all systems provide log-on script execution and many can be configured to execute startup and shutdown scripts. These scripts can be used to initiate test cases and to transfer results to the results system. Combining script execution with an automatic log-on capability allows test executions to continue automatically after system reboots or user log-offs. For example, the following VBScript function configures a Windows system for automatic login:

```
'********************************************************************
'* EnableRestart()
'* Purpose: Configures auto login and restart of the script
'********************************************************************
' Configure system for auto login using TempAdmin during REBOOT
Public Function EnableRestart()
    EnableRestart = false
    Const CIMRegistryProvider = "StdRegProv"
    Dim objRegistry : Set objRegistry = wmi_.Get(CIMRegistryProvider)
    Const WinLogonKey = _
"SOFTWARE\Microsoft\Windows NT\CurrentVersion\Winlogon"
    WriteStringToRegistry(objRegistry, HKEY_LOCAL_MACHINE, _
        WinLogonKey, "DefaultUserName", "TempAdmin")
WriteStringToRegistry(objRegistry, HKEY_LOCAL_MACHINE, _
        WinLogonKey, "DefaultPassword", "pass@word1")
WriteStringToRegistry(objRegistry, HKEY_LOCAL_MACHINE, _
        WinLogonKey, "AutoAdminLogon", "1")
WriteStringToRegistry(objRegistry, HKEY_LOCAL_MACHINE, _
        WinLogonKey, "ForceAutoLogon", "1")
WriteStringToRegistry(objRegistry, HKEY_LOCAL_MACHINE, _
        WinLogonKey, "DontDisplayLastUserName", "0")
    'Create the Restart batch file and set it to RunOnce
Dim fs
Set fs = CreateObject("Scripting.FileSystemObject")
    Dim hBat
Set hBat = fs.OpenTextFile("Restart.Bat", ForWriting, True)
    Dim currentPath : currentPath = fs.GetAbsolutePathName(".")
    hBat.Write("CD """ & CurrentPath & """" & vbCrLf)
    hBat.Write("cscript """ & wscript.ScriptName & """" & vbCrLf)
    hBat.Close
    ' Set RunOnce Parameter
    Const RunOnceKey = _
        "SOFTWARE\Microsoft\Windows\CurrentVersion\RunOnce"
WriteStringToRegistry( objRegistry, HKEY_LOCAL_MACHINE,_
    RunOnceKey, _
        "HardenScript","""""&CurrentPath&"\Restart.Bat"&"""")
    End Function
```

Note that in this example the RunOnce registry key is used so the script is only executed the first time the system resets. Placing the script in the Run registry key would cause it to run every time the system starts. Active Directory group policy objects (GPOs) can also be used to cause Windows systems to install or execute software during system startup, log-on, or policy refresh. Other examples include placing test scripts into directories that are always executed during startup or using keystroke emulators to simulate keyboard command entry.

Leverage System Logging

Not only do system logs provide error information on system processes that can be leveraged for testing, they also provide a means for capturing and transferring results information. Every system provides a means for writing error messages to system logs. The following Visual Basic code writes the results of the Netbios test case (TC06) for workstation six (WS006) to the local application event log:

```
Const EVENT_SUCCESS = 0
Set ShellObj = Wscript.CreateObject("Wscript.Shell")
ShellObj.LogEvent EVENT_SUCCESS,_
"TC06:WS006 FAIL Netbios protocol installed."
```

The code below writes the same results to the event log on the results system:

```
Const EVENT_SUCCESS = 0
Set ShellObj = Wscript.CreateObject("Wscript.Shell")
ShellObj.LogEvent EVENT_SUCCESS,_
"TC06:WS006 FAIL Netbios protocol installed.","\\ResultsServer"
```

Assuming all test cases use this logging capability and format, filtering a dump of the result system's log on the name "WS600" would produce a list of all the test cases this workstation failed.

This piece of Perl script uses the Sys:Syslog library to write messages to the syslog daemon:

```
use Sys::Syslog;
openlog($program, 'pid', 'user');
syslog('info', "TC06: FAIL Netbios protocol installed.");
closelog();
```

The resulting message is

```
May 20 10:15:05 ws006 testmaster[914]: TC06: FAIL Netbios
protocol installed.
```

The PERL Parse::Syslog library can be used to query Syslog for records containing "WS600" in the host field.

One Piece at a Time

Do not attempt to test everything in a single script. Construct your test cases and test scripts in small blocks of code and call them individually. The difference in execution time is not significant compared to the time you will save troubleshooting script errors. This approach also makes it easy to eliminate a test case that is generating false positives; just comment it out in the calling script.

Watch your P's and F's

That's permissions and firewalls. Nothing will break your testing efforts faster than incorrect permissions and firewalls. When building modules, verify the permissions required to execute them on the target. If client firewalls are in use, configure an exemption for your test consoles. If there is a firewall between the target and test console do the same.

Conclusion

Every update deployment consists of three or more components that must be tested including the update itself, the deployment procedures, and the rollback procedures. Tests must be conducted for each version of the update as well as each platform the update will be applied to. In many organizations software testing is not a common activity; consequently IT organizations often struggle with test planning and testing processes. Nonetheless, a good test program is essential to ensure disruptions to critical business processes during update deployments are minimized. The test planning, test facility, roles, skills, strategies and automation techniques and methodologies presented in this chapter provide organizations large and small with the basics for building a solid testing program.

Chapter 15

Patch/Update Management: Deploy Tasks

The final quadrant in the update management process is deploy (Figure 15.1). Deployment focuses on the tasks and activities required to deliver and install a software update into the production environment. The evaluate and plan phase has prepared the update for deployment and acquired the necessary change management approval to deploy it. The goal of the deploy phase is to successfully deliver and install the approved updates to the targeted production systems. Tasks in this phase are focused on deployment preparation, delivery of the update, installation of the update, and verification that the update deployment was successful.

This phase is the second part of the deployment timeline defined during the identify phase. Typically the activities in the deploy phase are carried out by the individual support groups for each technology stream. In other words, the desktop support group performs or monitors these tasks for desktop systems, line of business owners perform them for their applications, and so on. This is not always the case; the use of a centralized software deployment system such as Microsoft's System Management Server or Altiris 6 Patch Management Solution can reduce the required interaction of the individual support groups substantially.

Deploy tasks should constitute the remaining portion of the overall deployment timeline. For example, if the timeline for deploying the update is 7 days, deploy tasks should commence on day 4 or 5 and be complete by the end of the overall deployment timeline (Figure 15.2). Good communications, accurate monitoring, and quick response capabilities combined with a high degree of automation are critical to the success of these tasks, especially for critical and emergency changes.

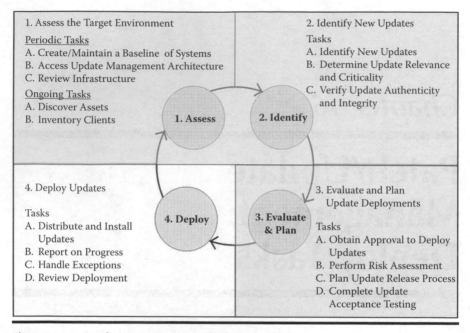

Figure 15.1 Update management deploy quadrant.

Deployment Preparation

The majority of the deployment planning, including deployment procedures and scheduling for update delivery, installation, verification, and (when necessary) roll-back, was completed in the evaluate and plan phase. What remains is to prepare the production environment for the rollout. This involves:

- Production staging
- Selecting target groups
- Training service desk and technical staff
- Backing up critical systems
- Communicating the rollout schedule to system owners, support personnel, users, customers, and other interested parties

Production Staging

Production staging moves the update material developed and tested in the lab into the production environment so it can be deployed. The actions required to complete the staging process will depend on the number of deployment techniques used; at a minimum this is two. The update planning process should have produced at least two deployment procedures for each update: one manual and one automated. Manual deployments typically involve the interactive copying and delivery

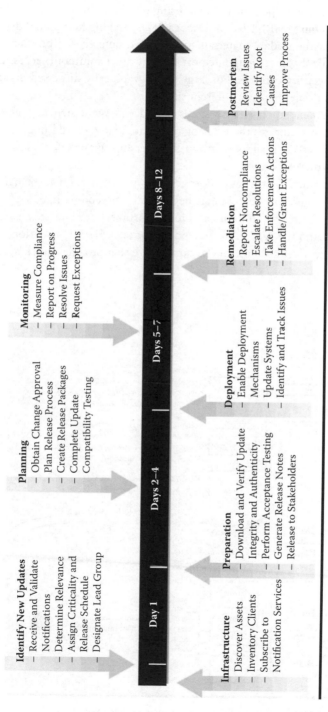

Figure 15.2 Update deployment timeline.

of update materials to the target system using file shares or portable media such as universal serial bus (USB) drives, CDs, or DVDs. Staging for manual deployments simply requires the update materials to be placed onto shared production stores. This can be a file share on an update portal or any other commonly accessible media with suitable security controls. For large or geographically dispersed organizations this may be multiple shares at different sites.

It is recommended that these stores have a consistent structure and naming convention. This facilitates the locating of update materials and makes it easier to control access based on support group membership. Figure 15.3 shows a sample update store structure.

There are a couple of things to note about this structure. First, the naming convention is very consistent; each update begins with the vendor's update ID, followed by the criticality rating (C for critical, I for important, L for low, etc.), a description of the update, and the version of the update package. Each installation package is accompanied by a release note of the same name that provides quick access to the

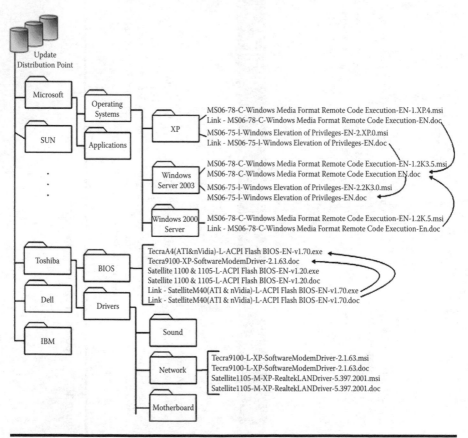

Figure 15.3 Sample update distribution store structure.

update details should additional information be needed. Also note the use of short-cuts (pointers) and compression to conserve storage space and facilitate backup.

Setting the appropriate rights on these stores is also crucial. The ability to write update packages to these stores must be tightly controlled to prevent the introduction of a package with malicious code. If an attacker or malicious user can substitute an update package with one that contains a worm or backdoor, they can easily compromise security, especially if that package is installed with administrative privilege. Furthermore, only authorized support personnel should be able to read files from this store; users should not be able to directly access the packages in this store. The potential for a user to select and install the wrong update and damage their system is too great. It is far better to restrict access to qualified support personnel. Organizations with specialized software may choose to further restrict access to certain subfolders; for example, only database administrators having access to the updates in the Oracle folder. This prevents someone with system administration privileges from inadvertently installing an application-specific update.

Using security groups to assign permissions at the folder level is the easiest way to provision permission. Once the permissions are assigned to the security group, the list can be populated with the names of support personnel or support groups that have those rights. Packages written to those folders inherit the folders' rights, automatically granting the appropriate access level to the packages for group members. This also makes it possible to use the same security groups to control manual and automated deployment. In other words, the same group that allows support people to read and deploy packages in the automated management system can be used to control access to packages on the store used for manual deployments.

The second type of production staging supports automated deployment systems such as Windows Server Update Service (WSUS), Microsoft System Management Server (SMS), and Altiris Server Management. Staging involves importing the packages into the management system and configuring the necessary commands and advertisements to distribute and install the package on target systems. It is best to import the exact packages that were developed and tested in the lab to maintain the greatest reliability and security. If you maintain a lab/test environment that closely mirrors your production environment there should be little reason to change package content when it is moved into production. Import procedures vary considerably from product to product. Consult the vendor's document; it is the best source of information on how to import and configure packages for automated deployment on their system.

There is one potential convergence point that should be paid attention to. System management applications have to maintain stores for the packages they manage. Sometime it is possible to configure these stores so they can be used as distribution points for manual and automated deployments. This eliminates the need to maintain duplicate copies, which can produce substantial storage and backup savings.

Select Target Groups

Most organizations schedule update deployments in stages to limit the potential effects of an update failure on business operations. The exception to this methodology is emergency updates, which have too short a deployment window to make staged deployment practical. When an update package is scheduled to be deployed in stages, the target groups must be identified as part of the deployment preparation. Despite the best testing methods, there are going to be times when updates cause system failures, so it is prudent to first deploy the update on a limited basis, verify proper functionality, and then continue the deployment in increasingly larger target sets.

A target group consists of some number of systems that will receive the update during a particular deployment time period (e.g., a day or a change window). The selection of target groups may be dictated by the type and nature of the release. For example, a security release may target the most vulnerable or critical systems first and progress to less critical systems. Selecting a group of targeted systems for a manually deployed update may be subject to the availability of staff who are qualified to perform the update. An effort should be make to get a good sample of system types and software versions in the initial target group, as this increases the likelihood that problems will be discovered early in the deployment. Basing the widespread deployment of an update on the success of an initial deployment to a target group not representative of the enterprise computing environment is asking for trouble. Most system management applications provide a way to dynamically create a collection of systems that can be used for target groups. Having a consistent staged deployment method also allows these groups to be created in advance. Target groups are discussed further in the "Distribute and Install" section of this chapter.

Training

The evaluation and planning process identified the training requirements related to this update. The deploy phase is responsible for ensuring that all identified parties in the deployment plan receive the training necessary to support the deployment and any postdeployment issues that may arise.

Training for today's dispersed information technology (IT) organizations can be challenging, but the ultimate success of some updates will depend on how well users and support personnel understand how to operate and support the updated product. For major upgrades to system or application software, this training will likely be handled by the company's training group. Training for smaller updates should be incorporated into the deployment communications and procedures. In most instances this will consist of some basic operational instructions in the deployment notification coupled with troubleshooting and problem resolution information for support personnel. One of the best resources for this type of information is testing; exceptions and potential failures are usually discovered during performance and compatibility testing. Ideally this information should be provided to support personnel when the package is released for production deployment. A Web-based knowledge base is an excellent way to capture and distribute this type of information, and built-in search capabilities facilitate the location and updating of information. A well-maintained knowledge base can significantly reduce the turn-around time for service requests. Discussion group aliases and indexed newsgroups are two other tools capable of providing searchable deployment and troubleshooting information.

Some other training alternatives include lunchtime brown bag sessions, Web casts, and streaming media presentations. The key is to provide a standardized methodology best suited to the needs of the intended audience. Most administrators and support personnel do not have the budget or time to travel to training sessions, and streaming media may not be a good alternative for traveling personnel or those on low bandwidth connections (e.g., home office users).

Backup

There is absolutely no excuse for not being able to restore a system to a fully operational state should an update fail. A full backup is the only certain way to ensure this can be done, but backups have become such a normal part of IT operations that people simply assume good backups exist for their system. This is a bad assumption when changes with potentially large impacts are going to be made to a system. Support personnel must verify that a complete backup of the system exists prior to the update being installed. A complete backup means all the operating system, application, and utility files and system data necessary to completely restore a system to its fully operational state have been saved. This may require reviewing one or more backup records; one if a complete backup of the system was done, several if incremental backups were done. A complete backup is preferable because it makes restoring the system easier. A system restore from incremental backups requires restoring pieces of the system from multiple backup stores. This usually takes more time and effort than restoring from a single source.

Quick restore alternatives, such as file system state capture (restore points), are excellent ways to quickly restore systems back to their original (preupdate) state. These mechanisms are often used in update rollback procedures, but they are not a substitute for backups. When these alternatives exist it is still recommended that a complete copy of system files and data be made before the system is updated. All update procedures and checklists should include "full backup of the system completed" as a prerequisite for update installation.

Communicate Rollout Schedule

"Communicate, communicate, communicate" is the update process equivalent of the "location, location, location" adage for retailing. If you want the process to be successful you must have clear and consistent communications with all the people involved. The update management process only works when everyone involved is tracking on their tasks; good communication provides the information needed to stay on track.

Administrators should be informed about proposed update release dates when the change request is submitted and should be updated when the schedule is confirmed by the change advisory board. End users should receive consistently formatted information concerning the deployment, what steps they should take to protect their data, and who they should contact if they have a problem. If the deployment is outside of normal business hours, make sure the users know they should leave their computers on overnight on the specified installation date. Users should receive this notice twice, once 3 to 5 days before their systems are updated, and again the day before the change is made. An easily identifiable email subject line such as

Subject: SECURITY UPDATE – IMMEDIATE ACTION REQUIRED

should be used to alert the recipient to the nature, importance, and urgency of the notification.

For administrators, the email should provide installation instructions, including the location of the update materials, timelines for deployment, and reporting steps. It should also point to other sources of information that can assist them with their deployment and verification tasks.

Distribute and Install

The evaluate and plan phase defines the methods used to place an update on the system so it can be installed based on the update infrastructure the company has in place (see Chapter 6). During the deploy phase, these methods are triggered and carried out in accordance with the established deployment timelines. In most instances distribution will begin as soon as the update has been released. Keep in mind that delivery does not automatically imply installation. Distribution is only the act of making the update available to the installation mechanism either from a physical location on the target system or a logical location on the network such as a shared network drive.

Distribute

Once the request for change (RFC) is approved the distribute tasks can begin. There are two primary distribution methods: network and courier. Most systems will receive updates via a network connection, but there are instances where network delivery is impractical or impossible. For example, it is impractical to deliver a large patch bundle or service pack to a user on a low-speed or dial-up connection, and it is simply impossible to use network delivery for a nonnetworked (stand-alone) computer. This does not mean these systems do not require updates. Many portable systems (i.e., laptops, desktop PCs) are high value industrial espionage targets. They must have critical security patches installed to ensure the sensitive data they hold is properly protected. In fact, any system in use (including a stand-alone system) is subject to attack and compromise and must have critical security patches installed and antivirus signatures regularly updated. In addition, periodic updates to increase functionality, improve reliability, and fix application bugs are also required. The distribute function must take all these situations into consideration.

Network-based delivery is fairly straightforward; it requires connectivity and privilege. In other words, the target system and the package store must be able to connect to each other and have sufficient privilege to read the update package from the store and write it to the target. This works fairly well in pull distribution scenarios because most security mechanisms do not limit outbound (target initiated) connections. But for push-style deployments network address translation (NAT), firewalls, and other protective measures can interfere with inbound connections initiated by the management system or other support mechanism.

Connectivity also implies the necessary bandwidth and connection duration to deliver the update in a timely manner. This is seldom an issue with target systems that are directly connected to the corporate network with high-speed connections, but it can become problematic in dial-in, virtual private network (VPN), and shared media situations. For example, it takes approximately 10 bits of transmitted data to move 1 byte of update data from the store to the target system. So dividing the transmission speed by 10 provides a reasonable approximation of how many bytes can be transferred across a connection in 1 second. Dividing that result into the size of the update package results in the approximate time required to deliver the package (assuming the entire bandwidth of the connection is available for this one task). In other words, on a 100 Mbps local area network (LAN) connection it would take approximately 10 seconds to transfer a 100 megabyte update from the store to the target—100 MB/(100 Mbps/10) = 10 seconds—not much of an impact on a high-speed full-duplex LAN connection. However, on lower speed connections, the same transfer would take 100 seconds on a 10 Mbps wireless connection, 600 seconds on a 1.5 Mbps cable modem or digital subscriber line (DSL) connection, and close to 18,000 seconds (4 hours) on a 56 kbps dial-up connection. The distribution mechanism must be able to take into account the available bandwidth as well as the potential that the duration of the connection may not allow for the entire transfer to take place. A dial-in user is unlikely to remain on line for 4 hours at time. If the distribution mechanism restarts a disrupted transfer at the beginning of the file, the dial-in user would never get a 100 MB update installed.

Most commercial system management products use agents that are bandwidth aware and able to resume transfers at the point where they were interrupted. Microsoft's Background Intelligent Transfer Service (BITS) is an example of this type of transfer mechanism. BITS uses all the available bandwidth on the connection that is not being consumed by other processes to transfer data from the store to the target, and should the connection be interrupted, BITS will resume the transfer at the point of the interruption. BITS also leverages Hypertext Transfer Protocol (HTTP) technology to facilitate transfers across firewalls and proxies. Unfortunately, these types of functions are not common in standard transfer methods.

Standard transfer methods such as Trivial File Transfer Protocol (TFTP), File Transfer Protocol (FTP), and file shares (Network File System [NFS], Server Message Block [SMB]) can be scripted to deal with connection interruptions, but they are not designed to resume the transfer from the point of interruption. Consequently the standard versions of these mechanisms are not well suited for large transfers across VPN or dial-in connections. However, there are a number of software companies that offer enhanced versions of these protocols that resume transfer capabilities.

Privilege is the second major element of update distribution. The transfer agent must have the necessary rights to read information from the package store and write the package to the target. Four factors are involved in this interaction: the credentials of the target system, the credentials used by the target application, the credentials of the store, and the credentials used by the store application. Again, most commercial management systems have native mechanisms for dealing with these factors. The agents installed on target systems typically run with system privileges, so creating folders and writing files to the local file system is not an issue. For agentless scenarios, the management system will use an appropriately privileged account on the target that was created as part of the management system setup. Commercial management systems usually provide privilege management for the package store as well. This can include general access to the storage site as well as specific access to individual packages. Most standard transfer mechanisms only manage a portion of these requirements.

For example, in a client pull scenario, the FTP service account on the package store has appropriate privilege needed to access package files. It can also enforce access rights to stored packages based on the credentials provided by the FTP client application on the target system. However, this control does not extend to the client. In order to create and write files on the target, the FTP client must be given the appropriate rights to the file system on the target as well. This is equally true of file shares; access can be granted to the client based on log-on credentials or group membership, but sufficient privilege to write files on the target must also exist. This is where privilege can become an issue. If the application that is pulling the package files is running under a low privilege account, it may not be able to create files on the target system, and elevating the privilege of that account could raise security concerns. This is the same situation with push deployments. If a shared storage location is created on the target so the push mechanism on the distribution store can write files to the target system, this may also be a security concern, especially if the shared location is open to everyone. Providing the least privilege required to accomplish the reads and writes is the best practice, and anonymous access to either the package stores or stores on the target should never be granted.

The mechanisms that trigger the distribution must also be taken into consideration. Commercial systems will have some type of advertisement mechanism that will initiate the transfer of a particular package to a set of target systems. This will need to be managed separately when standard transfer mechanisms are used.

Scheduled executions, startup executions, and log-on scripts are three such triggers. Scheduled executions are applications or scripts that are periodically executed by a scheduling application like Cron or Windows Task Scheduler. The application then checks for updates via a Web site, Web service, file share, or other means. An example of this process might be a script that checks for new updates on a central server and then transfers them to the local system for installation. The same principle applies for startup scripts, except the script is only executed when the system is booted. The disadvantages of these methods are they are difficult to centrally manage and require script development and maintenance. Log-in scripts provide a better alternative because they are usually located on a server and are easier to manage. However, log-on scripts are only executed when a user logs on to the system. While this is a fairly common occurrence on workstations, log-ons to servers can be infrequent, so there is no guarantee the update will be installed within the required timeframe. The event monitoring function in Windows Management Instrument (WMI) provides another technique for triggering installations. The function can monitor changes to a file (e.g., one containing a list of required patches) and begin processing updates whenever the file is changed (see EventLogMon.vbs in the "Tools" section of Chapter 17).

Summary

Table 15.1 summarizes the network distribution mechanisms, triggers, and required store and target privileges for update distribution. It is best to have a primary and secondary delivery system; for example, a system management application as the primary and some scripted processes to ensure delivery should the primary fail. The primary method should be enabled first and the distribution monitored for some period of time before the secondary method is enabled. For example, in a 7-day distribution timeline, the management system's automated distribution might be the only distribution mechanism used for the first 4 days, with the log-on script secondary method enabled for the final 3 days to pick up systems that failed the primary distribution. This keeps the two methods from competing with each other during the initial distribution. When the secondary method uses scripts, it is best to configure the script to do a quick check for the required updates and only call

Table 15.1   Network Distribution Parameters

Method	Trigger	Target privileges	Store privileges
Client agent pull	Polling interval	Same as agent	Read to package shares and files
Server push	Scheduled or event driven	Write to local disk system	Same as transfer service
Logon script	User logon	Same as user	Read to package shares and files
Client script	Scheduled	Same as user or scheduler service	Read to package shares and files
Event monitor	Event driven	Same as user	Read to package shares and files

an installation script when needed. This reduces the time required to execute the script, allowing the log-on process to complete faster.

Courier Distribute

Courier distribution involves a number of manual tasks, but it is necessary for stand-alone systems and for large update distributions to systems with low-bandwidth connections. First, the distribution must be prepared; this includes the media as well as instructions to the user on how to perform the update. Some system management systems such as Microsoft's SMS directly support removable media (i.e., CD, DVD, floppy, etc.) distribution and will help with the media creation step. Then the distribution must be duplicated to cover all the targeted systems. There are several good reasonably priced duplication systems available. Depending on the number that must be reproduced, a commercial duplication service may be more efficient. Keep in mind that all this activity must take place inside mandated update timelines. Instructions for what to do with the media when it is received must also be created and duplicated. Whenever possible, try to print the instructions on the media label. Leverage automatic start features like Autoplay to eliminate the need for long instructions. The final media preparation piece is packaging (i.e., placing the media in an addressed shipping envelop). Larger courier services usually supply the envelopes for free. It is also necessary to maintain a database of the names and addresses of the people getting the update in order to generate address labels. There are dozens of good label-making programs. Once everything has been packaged there is one more thing to consider, the courier service.

There are two things to consider when choosing a courier service: coverage and speed. If your organization is widely dispersed it will be necessary to find a courier service(s) that covers each location. For short duration deployments, speed is important. If the update must be deployed in 4 days and it takes 2 days to prepare the distribution, the courier service must be able to deliver the update media within 2 days or the timeline will be missed. A third factor to consider is tracking. You will need a way to determine if the update arrived at the destination on time. The final factor is cost. Wide coverage, reliability, and high performance usually come with a high price. It is up to your organization to determine what cost level is acceptable and balance that with your security goals and requirements.

Security Considerations

There are a couple of security concerns that must also be addressed around distribution. Some delivery mechanisms such as TFTP and FTP do not have good security attributes. TFTP has a very simplistic authentication model based on the clients media access control (MAC) address; FTP uses a userID and password. In both instances the credentials are sent in the clear. Although it is difficult to capture transmitted data on a switched network, it is not impossible. The greater concern is the security of the update packages themselves. As noted earlier, when update packages are poorly protected an attacker or malicious user can replace a legitimate package with one containing a virus or other malware. Most commercial system management systems provide package integrity protections, including versioning controls and digital signatures, to prevent tampering; mechanisms such as TFTP and FTP do not. It is possible to mitigate this by explicitly setting access controls at the file share, folder, and file levels. The default permissions for these containers are not secured.

Distribute Summary

Proactive technologies are the preferred delivery methods of updates, but agents and standard protocols can also be used for push-style distributions. It is smart to employ and develop procedures for multiple automated methods so the failure of a single method does not require manual intervention. It is also a good idea to have a method in place to verify the delivery was successful. Good, rather than required, because a failed delivery will also result in a failed installation being reported. While servers and workstations usually use the same delivery mechanisms and procedures, they often require very different installation procedures.

Install

Once the package distribution is complete, installation can begin. Installation consists of the procedures and methods used to deploy the update package on the target system. There are two primary types of installations: automated (those accomplished by a service or agent) and manual (those performed by a user). Three critical parameters govern the success of the install process: installer privilege, available disk space, and file usage. It is also important to take into account the method used to install the package.

Most packages are designed to be installed by an installer application, such a Windows Installer (.MSI packages), Altiris Wise (.WSE packages), or Linux RPM. Installers simplify the installation process by providing the common processes (directory creation, file copy, ALC configuration, etc.) needed for reliable software installation. The other commonly used method is a self-executing package where the installer and the update are bundled into a single executable. A good example of this is an executable WinZip file that extracts all the files to a temporary directory then executes the setup.exe file. The term installer is used in this section to denote the installer application; "installation package" is used to denote self-executing packages.

Automated Installation

Automated installation is the preferred package installation method. Automated installation is fast, consistent, and minimizes administration overhead. It also gives personnel the ability to schedule installs for specific maintenance windows, defer system reboots, and recover from (retry) failed installations. There are three commonly used methods for automated installations: agent, installer, and self-executing. Agent-based installations utilize the system management agent to install the update package, the installer method uses an installer application or a script to install the package, and the self-executing method simply executes the package. In some instances these methods may be combined; for example, instead of building installation processes into the agent, the agent is used to execute the installer or self-executing package. No matter which method is used, the installation will require appropriate permissions to complete successfully.

Privilege/Permissions

Most management system agents used for automated software installation will run with sufficient privilege to complete the installation successfully. For example, the SMS agent runs on Windows systems under the SYSTEM account so it has administrative privileges to all systems resources. There are several other agents on the system that can also be used to install packages. Job scheduling agents often run with administrative privilege, as do log-on script processors. For example, the group policy agent on Windows systems executes with SYSTEM permissions, so group policy objects can be used to install applications. In other instances the installer or the self-executing package will need to run with elevated privileges. The only notable exception would be an application designed to be used by a single user. It can be installed directly into that user's home directory without elevating privileges.

There are a number of different methods for elevating privileges, depending upon the operating system you are dealing with. Installers or self-executing packages for UNIX systems can be run with root privilege using the set user ID (SUID) attribute. On Windows systems, the Windows installer can be set to run with elevated privileges by enabling the "Always install with elevated privilege" policy. This policy causes the Windows installer to use SYSTEM permissions when installing software on the system. The best way to install self-executing packages is with an agent.

Caution: There is a potential security risk associated with the execution of installer software with elevated privileges. Since the user has the ability to execute the installer application and the installer will install any package submitted to it with administrative privileges, it is possible for a malicious user or attacker to create an installation package that elevates account permissions, installs malicious software, destroys system files, or otherwise compromises system security or integrity.

Another possible way to elevate privilege is to use system utilities like Unix "SU" and Windows "RunAs." The downside of using these utilities is they require the user to enter the password of a privileged account or the password must be stored somewhere on the system for programmatic entry (in which case it is subject to discovery and compromise).

Most installations will require some elevated privilege to complete successfully even when the application runs with user privilege. Therefore it is important to have an installation process that provides the necessary permissions and, ideally, in a way that is transparent to the user.

Available Disk Space

Running out of disk space during the installation can crash or cripple a system and it can be difficult to recover from the error. Just as the distribute process requires sufficient disk space to store the package on the system, there must also be sufficient disk space to install the package. This includes the temporary storage space required to unbundle the package and expand compressed files and the permanent storage space required by the update or application. Disk utilization requirements should have been calculated when the package was created and the installation package configured to check for the required temporary and permanent storage space before unbundling or expanding any files in the package.

If the installation package does not support an "available disk space" function then manually checking for sufficient disk space will be required. Watch out for self-executing packages; installer functionality is often reduced to keep package sizes smaller, so they may not perform available disk space checks.

File Usage

The final factor for the installation phase is file usage. If a file is in use by the system, it may be locked and consequently cannot be changed. This situation will cause the installation to fail. File usage issues should have been identified during the packaging and testing processes. Another usage scenario that must be considered is cached files. Some executables and libraries (e.g., dynamic link libraries [DLLs]) may be loaded into cache memory. It is not possible to execute the updated version of the application until the old file versions are cleared from the cache because the system gives precedence to files in the cache. File caching issues should have been identified in the packaging and testing phase.

Whenever possible, the installer should be configured to deal with file usage conflicts, including pausing or killing the processes (and restarting them once the file has been updated), locking a file that needs to be changed, and flushing older file versions from the cache once the new versions have been installed. If the installer does not have this capability, the installation procedure may require the manual shutdown of services or applications prior to installation execution. A forced system reboot may also be required to clear older versions from the cache.

Manual Installation

Manual installation can be viewed from two perspectives. The first is manual execution. This typically involves executing the installation package from the system console and observing the installation process through to its completion. This is a common practice for server updates. The update is distributed to the system, but the system administrator manually initiates and actively monitors the installation. This ensures updates are not installed outside of designed change windows or before all the prerequisite testing and verification processes have been completed. Alternative manual installation methods include executing the installation using a remote console connection or a remote execution utility such as PSExec from SysInternals. Manual execution is also a common scenario for courier delivered updates. The user must take some action to trigger the automated installation process—this could be as simple as putting the distribution disk into the CD/DVD drive.

The other manual installation technique is manual operations. This involves interactively making the system changes the installation package would make. In other words, copying the individual files to the appropriate directories, updating configuration and registry settings, setting ACLs, etc. This is okay for small updates (changes to one or two files) but it is not practical for large installations because it is too time consuming and too prone to error. The method is usually reserved for system troubleshooting or restoration if both the installation and back-out procedures fail.

Installation Triggers

One or more events can trigger an installation, including manual execution, a machine or user log-on, a GPO refresh, a scheduled job execution, or a command from the system management service to the client agent. How and when the installation is triggered really depends on the urgency of the deployment, the criticality of the system, and your change management policy.

Most installation triggers will be time based, configured to trigger installations during allotted system change windows. Most system management programs can be configured this way. Scheduled jobs can also be configured to trigger installations inside specific change windows, and system administrators can manually trigger installations as well. Time-based triggers are preferred for most installations, especially for critical or high impact systems.

Event-based triggers, such as user or machine log-ons, GPO refreshes, etc., are suitable for situations where immediate execution of the installation is desired. Emergency deployments often use event-based triggers to ensure systems are updated as quickly as possible. For example, placing an installation trigger in a log-on script ensures every system receives the update when any user of the system logs on. Event-based triggers are also suitable for installing updates to workstations and other low impact devices.

Primary and Secondary Deployment

It is wise to have multiple mechanisms in place to deploy updates to ensure the best possible coverage; for example, a system management system with client agents as the primary deployment mechanism and log-on scripts as the secondary method. Should the primary deployment mechanism fail (i.e., agent not installed, agent disabled, etc.), the secondary deployment mechanism can take over and install the update. If that fails there is always manual installation. The primary deployment mechanism can be viewed as the orderly time-triggered deployment mechanism, the secondary as the forced (immediate) deployment mechanism, and manual deployment as the last resort. Activation of the different deployment mechanisms should be staggering across the deployment timeline so the primary and secondary methods are not competing with each other. For example, Figure 15.4 shows a 7-day deployment timeline; the primary mechanism is triggered at the beginning of the deployment, the secondary on the fourth day, and manual deployment on the final day. All three methods remain in place through the remediation phase. Redundant mechanisms do not guarantee that every system will automatically be updated, but they do increase coverage (thus reducing risk) and cut down on the number of manual installations that need to be performed by support personnel.

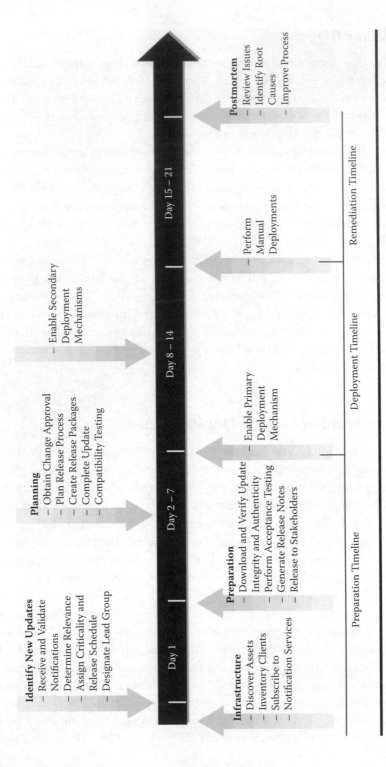

Figure 15.4 Deployment mechanism timelines.

Pilot Deployments

Some organizations choose to do pilot deployments as an additional testing step or as a testing alternative. There are a number of different approaches:

- Deploy to low value or low impact systems—The theory behind this approach is simple: if the update has issues, the impact will be minimal and the issues can be resolved without impacting critical systems. If no issues are noted then the update is safe to deploy to other higher impact systems. The approach is simple to carry out and can be consistently applied. It does increase the likelihood that major issues with the update or the deployment package will be discovered, however, subtle differences in system configurations between the pilot machines and other systems could still result in unexpected failures. This type of deployment is most often used with servers, but it is suitable for workstations too. It is a reasonable alternative to in-depth update testing in small to medium IT environments. It is not recommended for large or complex environments.
- Deploy to a random or representative sampling of systems—This approach accounts for differences in system configurations by deploying the update to a representative set of systems. The systems can be predefined or chosen at random. The approach increases the likelihood that major as well as subtle configuration-related issues will be identified. The approach is fairly simple to implement and statistically sound; a random sample of 100 systems in a population of 10,000 will produce a coverage probability greater than 95%. As good as this is, it still leaves 5% of the configurations untested. This type of deployment is an excellent alternative to in-depth update testing for workstations because the number of potential failures is small and so are the resulting impacts. It is not recommended for servers.
- Deploy to a high tolerance group of users (i.e., IT)—This approach attempts to minimize impacts to the general user population by deploying the update on systems with user expertise or where the organization has a stake in the success of the update management program (usually an IT group). The approach is simple to carry out, can be consistently applied, and has one big advantage—these systems tend to be some of the most complex configurations in the organization, so major and subtle issues with the update are likely to be identified. On the downside, these systems will usually not have mainstream business applications installed, so it is possible for fairly high impact issues to be missed. This type of deployment is suitable for workstations and departmental servers. It is a reasonable alternative to in-depth update testing in small to medium IT environments and a supplemental test in larger environments.
- Deploy to component systems—Another approach used primarily for server deployments is component deployment. When redundant systems are clustered or placed behind load balancers, the update can be deployed to one of

the component servers. If no issues are noted it is reasonably safe to assume the update can be successfully deployed to the remaining systems. Since the systems are redundant, any deployment or update issues will have little impact on overall system availability or performance. While this approach is simple, it may be difficult to consistently apply. Some updates could cause systems to get out of sync with each other, resulting in inconsistent operations. For example, if an update changes the data elements being managed by the system, the pilot component would work fine with the new elements, but the other components would not. Generally updates to redundant components must be done in separate change windows. This approach simply lengthens the timeframe between component updates so potential issues can be identified.

Deploying to Build Environments

Updating build environments is another important part of the deploy phase. How updates are incorporated into build images will vary depending on the technologies in use. For example, the slipstream process can be used to update distribution images of Windows products. The files on the product CD are copied to a writable file system and updated using the Update.exe slipstream option. The process is simple and allows updates to be incorporated quickly. Other technologies may require loading, updating, and resaving of system images. No matter what technology is used, there are a couple of key points to remember:

- The build process should never result in a system being brought on-line in a production environment without all required updates installed. In other words, at a minimum the build process must include the installation of all critical updates before the system is placed into production. Even if the system is set to be updated immediately, the time required to install the updated is more than sufficient for a worm or virus to be propagated to the system. This has been a common scenario during worm attacks: systems get infected, are rebuilt and placed on the network, and are reinfected before the update can be installed.
- Updates should be deployed into the build environment using the same deployment timelines as production systems. The exception would be test images; all other build images should be treated like production systems. When updates to the build environment lag behind production deployments, it creates a potentially dangerous situation where systems with known flaws and vulnerabilities are intentionally being introduced into the production environment.

Update deployments to the build environment are often overlooked, but they are critical to the overall patch compliance of the organization. It should not be possible to build a noncompliant system! Keeping the build environment in sync with production system update requirements reduces risk and helps maintain overall operational integrity.

Monitoring and Reporting

During the distribution and installation of the updates it is necessary to monitor and report on the deployment. The goal of monitoring is to verify the updates are being applied successfully. Reporting provides an overall view of deployment progression.

Verifying Successful Installation

Tracking the success and failure rates of the distribution and installation processes is critical to the overall success of the deployment because it drives subsequent deployment decisions, including expanding the deployment scope, activating secondary deployment mechanisms, halting the deployment, or initiating a rollback.

How the deployment is monitored depends on the technologies used for distribution and installation. If you are using a system management system for the deployment, it will be your first source of information on distribution and installation success. Some of these systems report the status of updates to a monitoring console in real time, others require periodic reports to be run against the configuration database.

The error messages and logs generated by system management agents, distribution systems, and installers are excellent sources for detailed success and failure information. However, without a centralized logging or reporting mechanism, the information can be difficult to access. Error messages are usually displayed on the system console and can only be accessed by someone physically at the system or remotely connected to the console. Log files are usually written to the local hard disk in a number of different places. Furthermore, they may not have consistent naming conventions and may require special permissions to be accessed. Consequently these sources are more often used for debugging failures than for reporting installation status.

A good compliance or vulnerability scanner is your next best source of information. These devices perform periodic queries against a system to verify the update has been installed or the vulnerability the update addressed is no longer present. The status is usually displayed on the scanner's console or available through a reporting function. The advantage of using a scanner is that it can be targeted to scan the update status of a specific range of systems. However, the status is only going to be as current as the scanning interval; this could be near real time (scan this system now), an hour, or a day if it takes the scanner that long to scan all the devices. Scanners and compliance monitors are discussed in greater detail in Chapter 16.

Another good source of success and failure indicators is operations monitoring systems like HP Openview and Microsoft Operations Manager (MOM). These systems typically monitor the operational health of servers, services, and applications. While these systems may not be able to report on the status of the installation, they can report on adverse deployment results, including performance hits, service malfunctions, error events, and reboot failures.

Monitoring help desk calls provides similar information about system failures, malfunctions, and performance hits. An increase in system crash reports or a consistent pattern of user complaints is a good indication of distribution or installation issues. The nature of the complaints is also a good way to evaluate the effectiveness of predeployment communications.

Reporting Deployment Progression

Monitoring the installation status of individual systems is important, but understanding how the overall deployment is progressing is also a necessity. It will drive your deployment scope, secondary deployment activation, and escalation decisions. It is also important to provide individual stakeholders (system administrators, application owners, etc.) with a ready view of the deployment status of their systems across the deployment timeline. These reports are really just a summary of the status information gathered by the monitoring process combined with some system ownership information.

Most system management systems will have reporting mechanisms capable of generating these reports and some have built-in publishing capabilities as well. If the monitoring process is updating status in the configuration management database, reports can be generated directly from the database using a compatible reporting application such as Crystal Reports or SQL Reporting Services. Reports can also be constructed manually if necessary. Ideally status reports should be sent to stakeholders every day during a deployment. Reports should be reviewed daily to identify departments, groups, or administrators that are lagging behind on the deployment so assistance can be provided. In addition to stakeholder reports, management reports on deployment status also need to be generated. Reporting is covered in greater detail in Chapter 16.

Handling Issues and Exceptions

It is inevitable that issues are going to arise during deployments. No amount of planning and testing is going to cover every possible failure scenario, so your deployment process must include procedures for dealing with them, including verifying issues, measuring impacts, granting exceptions, halting deployments, and performing rollbacks.

Verifying Issues

When the deployment is generating a large number errors or help desk calls, an investigation should begin immediately to determine the cause. Monitoring systems are not perfect nor are end user perceptions always accurate. Issues must be verified before any action is taken.

Determining Impact

Once an issue has been verified, an evaluation of its impact is needed to determine the best course of action. Impact to the business, security, and the deployment should be evaluated. If the impact is minor (only affecting a small number of systems or minor functionality) it may be sensible to allow the deployment to continue and deal with the affected systems individually. A medium impact issue might cause the deployment to be halted for a particular class of systems (e.g., all the systems with the affected application installed). Major impacts should produce an immediate halt to the deployment. Halting a deployment confines the issue to a set number of systems, allowing the update management team and stakeholders to identify and resolve the issue so the deployment can continue. When the impact of the issue causes the loss of critical functionality, updates will also need to be rolled back on the affected systems.

Rolling Back Deployments

When an update deployment causes system failure or the loss of vital system functionality, the update must be removed. The planning process includes the creation of a rollback procedure. Once the decision has been made to rescind the update it must be quickly communicated to the stakeholders so active deployments can be canceled and rollback procedures activated. Installation logs, error messages, and events should be captured as part of the rollback process. These will facilitate the resolution of the issue. Rollbacks should be tracked to ensure they are completed in an expedient manner. The goal here is to restore the system to its original functional state as quickly as possible.

Note: For critical or important security patches, halting or rolling back an update deployment does not change the deployment timeline. The system vulnerability still exists and the associated risks must be mitigated. It would be prudent to investigate other available mitigation controls in case resolution of the issue pushes the deployment past acceptable timelines.

Granting Exceptions

Occasionally, for unforeseen reasons, a system simply cannot be upgraded within the established timelines. This may be due to update incompatibilities or critical business processing requirements (e.g., the finance server during tax time). The deployment process must include a procedure for handling these exceptions to the standard deployment process. The procedure should include a formal request process that includes other mitigation controls that will be used to mitigate the risk. The request should require senior management approval. Exceptions should be kept to the shortest term possible and renewals should require the completion and approval of a new application. For example, if the financial reporting period is causing the delay, the exception should end on the same day the reporting period does. If incompatibilities are the issue, exceptions should be no more than 30 days. That is more than sufficient time to identify and resolve the issue if the issue is actively being worked on. Longer terms usually mean the issue is not being actively worked on until the last 2 weeks of the exception.

Review Deployment

The final deployment task is the postdeployment review. The review should be conducted with system stakeholders as soon as possible after the deployment completes, but no later than 30 days. The purpose of the meeting is to identify areas where the update management process can be improved. The agenda should include the following:

- A discussion of the planned versus the actual results
- A discussion of the root causes of identified issues
- A discussion of the risks posed by the release
- A discussion of lessons learned
- Suggestions for improving results

Based on these suggestions, there are a number of potential follow-up actions, including updating procedures, updating documentation, and adding the lessons learned to the update management knowledge base.

Conclusion

Deployment is the final phase in the update management process. Deployment focuses on the tasks and activities required to deliver and install updates on production systems. This phase occurs during the second portion of the deployment timeline established during the identify phase. The activities in the deploy phase are carried out by the individual support groups for each technology stream.

Successful deployments are based on effective stakeholder communications, accurate monitoring and reporting, and the ability to quickly respond to and resolve any issues that come up. Given the short deployment timeframes required for security updates, a high degree of automation is also critical to the success of these tasks.

standards, and requirements. You cannot measure what you do not know about. A complete and accurate inventory of systems and systems ownership is an absolute necessity for successful compliance management. The majority of these data are collected as part of the configuration and update management functions, but the "trust but verify" principle also applies here. The compliance management program should maintain a separate database of systems that the compliance program independently verifies.

Baseline requirements are primarily derived from company policies, standards, and requirements, although industry and government regulations as well as vendor best practices are also drivers. It is not possible to measure unless there is a reference point to measure against. Therefore the policies, standards, and requirements function must provide these baselines before the compliance process can be initiated. This is not to imply that compliance management processes cannot be put into place without these essential elements; they certainly can be, but the overall effectiveness of the program will be severely limited without a solid inventory and defined baselines.

Compliance management processes periodically check systems and reports on their adherence to established baselines. The results can be used to identify critical security risks, drive remediation efforts, improve controls, and prioritize spending. These benefits can only be realized if the program is comprehensive, accurate, and enforceable. Attempting to establish a compliance management process without these elements is not going to be successful in the long run.

Baseline Compliance Process

The compliance management process consists of the six major tasks and four supporting functions depicted in Figure 16.2. Two of the supporting functions (risk and asset management program, and policies, standards, and requirements) were addressed in the previous section, along with the compliance management database—an independent collection of assets, baselines, and measurement results. The monitoring and scanning infrastructure is covered in Chapter 17.

We will go over the remaining elements in detail in the following sections. It is also helpful to understand how the compliance process parallels the update management process across a common timeline. Figure 16.3 depicts this relationship.

The discovery phase as well as the criticality and release schedule determinations are collaborative efforts between the update management and compliance management teams. Once the deployment schedule has been determined the compliance team starts working on the measurement techniques required to validate compliance. For example, the compliance team might review the update manifest for changes to file version, date, or size that can be checked to verify a successful update installation. As soon as the appropriate measurement techniques have been determined the team updates the compliance scanning tools and tests the functionality (accuracy)

Symantec/Norton Ghost

Symantec/Norton Ghost is one of the most popular system imaging, deployment, and management solutions around. Ghost can provide file-based and sector-based imaging as well as personal/user state migration. The enterprise version includes a centralized console to simplify the management of both Windows and Linux images. Ghost also incorporates multicasting capabilities, so images can be deployed to multiple system simultaneously. Ghost has been upgraded to include an easy edit and update mechanism for existing image files to reduce the amount of time required to maintain images. For additional information on Norton Ghost see http://www.symantec.com/index.jsp.

Microsoft SMS Operating System Deployment Feature Pack

Operating System Deployment (OSD) is a free downloadable extension for SMS 2003. OSD uses ImageX and WIM image formats for zero-touch upgrades and desktop deployments. It helps desktop administrators create a Windows OS desktop image and automate the deployment. Using the OSD Feature Pack you can deploy new systems using the Windows PE preboot environment and upgrade existing systems without reformatting or repartitioning disks.

The SMS 2003 OSD Feature Pack includes a package creation wizard to simplify the creation and configuration of OS deployments. The OSD Feature Pack provides a seamless way to manage the provisioning and deployment of desktop images. For additional information see http://www.microsoft.com/technet/sms/sms2003_default.mspx.

Microsoft ADS

Microsoft ADS is a service that can be used to push software, including the OS, to bare metal Preboot Execution Environment (PXE) booted machines. This is a service add-on to the 2003 Windows server. It is a very simple but powerful way to push software in an automated fashion to a large number of machines. This type of PXE push also exists in the Altiris software. For more information see http://www.microsoft.com/windowsserver2003/technologies/management/ads/default.mspx.

Hardening Tools

Microsoft Windows Security Tools

Windows OSs include a number of security tools for local and domain security policy management (Table 17.2). It is recommended that these tools be used in conjunction with the Microsoft Security Configuration guides. For enterprises, the same setting can be conveyed to domain-joined systems using group policy objects

Table 17.2   Native Windows Security Management Tools

Security tools	Description
Local security policy	A tool to edit individual security settings for your local computer.
Security templates	Microsoft provides a series of templates to strengthen the security setting of a system. The templates are customizable and can be applied to a local computer policy or imported into a group policy object.
Security configuration and analysis	A tool to analyze or configure the security on a computer using a security template.
Security settings extension to group policy	A tool to edit individual security settings on a domain, site, or organizational unit.
Secedit.exe	A command-line tool to automate security configuration tasks.

(GPOs). For more information on how to use the SECPOL and GPO management console plug-in see http://www.microsoft.com/technet/security/default.mspx.

Microsoft Security Tools

Microsoft also offers a number of other free security tools for managing updates, assessing security state, and detecting malicious software. See http://www.microsoft.com/technet/security/tools/default.mspx.

UNIX/Linux Hardening Scripts

Most UNIX-style systems use a script to harden OS parameters. One of the best known scripts is the Bastille hardening program. Bastille provides an assessment capability that measures the system's current state of hardening as well as a series "lock-downs." Bastille is available for Red Hat, SUSE, Debian, Gentoo, and Mandrake Linux distributions, as well HP-UX. At this writing it was also being ported to Mac OSX. Bastille is available from http://www.bastille-linux.org/.

YASSP (Yet Another Solaris Security Package) was a very popular Solaris hardening package. YASSP was originally written by Jean Chouanard of Xerox in concert with a host of other Solaris experts. The tool includes a number of useful precompiled security tools. The key features of the package include:

- Improving file permissions (Casper Dik's "fix-modes" package)
- Cleaning of the Solaris package database
- Tuning of Solaris network parameters (Jens-S. Vöckler's "nettune")
- Hardening of other system parameters for typical bastion host usage

YASSP has been replaced by Sun's Security Toolkit, available from http://www.sun.com/security/.

UNIX Security Tools

The National Institute of Standards and Technology (NIST) maintains a good list of UNIX-related security tools at http://csrc.nist.gov/tools/tools.htm.

CMDB Tools

Computer Associates CMDB r11

Computer Associates (CA) CMDB r11 is designed to help IT organizations manage their IT system configuration information and relationships across the entire enterprise. CA CMBD r11 encompasses both the change and configuration controls needed to ensure that the impact of configuration changes to the availability of core business services is minimized. CA CMDB r11 is a unified data repository that simplifies the management of configuration information. It automates a full range of operational tasks with Information Technology Infrastructure Library (ITIL)-based processes that reduce operational risks. These features include:

- Confederation of IT configuration sources—the ability to pull configuration information from sources across the enterprise
- Reconciliation—the ability to produce consolidated multiple data elements in to single data instance
- Visualization—the ability to dynamically show relationships and dependencies between systems

These features help place IT-related configuration information into a business priorities context as well as providing complete visibility into CI settings, attributes, relationships, and dependencies. For more information and CMDB white papers see http://www.ca.com/us/.

Update and Compliance Management Tools

This section covers tools that can be used for update and compliance management.

Update Management

Microsoft Windows Server Update Services

Microsoft Windows Server Update Services (WSUS) 3.0 is a free update service designed to help system administrators deploy Microsoft product updates to

Windows-based computers. WSUS provides a local version of the Microsoft Update Web site. It includes an automatic check and download of updates for Microsoft OS and Office products. Client computers can be configured to automatically download and install updates from any WSUS server. For additional information on WSUS see http://technet.microsoft.com/en-us/wsus/default.aspx.

Microsoft SMS Software Update Services Feature Pack

The SMS Software Update Services Feature Pack is an add-on to the SMS designed to inventory, track, and deploy software updates to Windows systems. It includes a security update inventory tool, an office inventory tool, and a distribute software update wizard. The package also includes a number on Web-based reports. For detailed information about each tool see http://www.microsoft.com/technet/sms/20/downloads/featurepacks/suspack/default.mspx.

PatchLink Update

PatchLink Update is an agent-based software update and scanning solution that works with Windows- and UNIX-based systems. The solution includes prepackaged update downloads to facilitate update deployment. PatchLink Update also provides continuous network monitoring for vulnerabilities: "PatchLink Update provides rapid patch management, allowing you to proactively manage threats by automating the collection, analysis, and delivery of patches throughout your heterogeneous enterprise to secure end-points." PatchLink also provides an inventory assessment features that identifies and reports all software, hardware, and services on your system. In addition to updates, PatchLink Update can also be used for general software distribution. Additional information on Update and other PatchLink system management solutions is available at http://www.patchlink.com/.

BigFix

BigFix produces agent-based services and solution packs for managing a number of IT operations, including policy enforcement, update management, network device discovery, hardware and software inventory, software provisioning, and more for Windows and UNIX systems. BigFix solutions consist of framework and solution packs that run on standard Microsoft Windows-based hardware. The BigFix Server provides centralized resources for managing data, policies, and content sent to client agents. Additional information on BigFix products is available at http://www.bigfix.com/.

Compliance Management

Microsoft SMS Desired Configuration Monitoring Feature Pack

The Desired Configuration Monitoring (DCM) package is an add-on to the SMS agent that automates configuration monitoring tasks by comparing the desired system configuration to actual settings. DCM supports the monitoring of desktops and servers. DCM can monitor both hardware and software settings, including any settings held in Windows Management Instrumentation (WMI), the system registry, and the Windows file system. It can also monitor application and service configurations such as the IIS, Active Directory, and SQL server. The package includes a user interface for defining and deploying configuration checks as well as a number of add-on SMS reports. The feature pack can be downloaded from http://www.microsoft.com/technet/solutionaccelerators/cits/mo/sman/dcm.mspx.

Microsoft Baseline Security Analyzer

Microsoft Baseline Security Analyzer (MBSA) is a free utility for assessing the update and security compliance of Windows systems. The tools are installed on the client machine and run locally. Assessment results are written to the user's document directory, where they can be downloaded by a log-in script or other method for analysis. The tool is designed to help small and medium-size businesses manage the security state of their IT resources. MBSA detects missing updates and common security misconfigurations. The tool can be downloaded from http://www.microsoft.com/technet/security/tools/mbsahome.mspx.

Configuresoft Enterprise Configuration Manager

Enterprise Configuration Manager (ECM) is an agent-based configuration monitoring tool that uses a CMDB-based approach to deliver superior performance and data accuracy. ECM has a central console for configuring scans, analyzing results, and producing reports. The system comes with analysis templates based on industry and government requirements including Health Insurance Portability and Accountability Act (HIPAA), Peripheral Component Interconnect (PCI), Sarbanes-Oxley Act of 2002 (SOX), Microsoft Solutions for Security (MSS) guides, SysAdmin Audit Network Security Institute (SANS) guides, etc. ECM collects thousands of asset and configuration data settings and stores them in a comprehensive CMDB. The CMDB can be leveraged for IT asset management, change management, and other IT operations. Additional information on ECM is available at http://www.configuresoft.com/ecm.aspx.

eEye Retina Network Security Scanner

Retina is a high speed agentless network vulnerability scanner with excellent system discovery capabilities. Retina detects network security vulnerabilities indicative of missing updates and security settings. The system also provides prioritized threat remediation guidance. Companies can leverage Retina results for security risk assessment and project risk management. Custom policy audits are also supported. For more information see http://www.eeye.com/html/Products/Retina/index.html.

Network Discovery Tools

Microsoft Nbtstat

Nbtstat is a Windows tool that displays NetBIOS over Transmission Control Protocol/Internet Protocol (TCP/IP) statistics, including the NetBIOS name tables and the NetBIOS name cache. The target can be the local computer or a remote host, but Nbtstat does not support scanning a range of IP addresses. This requires some minor scripting efforts. For example, the following command line will feed a list of IP addresses from a text file into the Nbtstat command. This example returns the system name table and media access control (MAC) address for a system named Products.

```
C:\ >nbtstat -an Products
Local Area Connection:
Node IpAddress: [192.168. 0.98] Scope Id: []
NetBIOS Remote Machine Name Table
Name Type Status
---------------------------------------------
PRODUCTS <20> UNIQUE Registered
PRODUCTS <00> UNIQUE Registered
MAC Address = 00-08-02-B2-AD-C9
```

Foundstone/Symantec SuperScan

SuperScan, a free utility from Foundstone, can be used to collect information about systems connected to your network. SuperScan is a graphical user interface (GUI)-based utility with a large number of discovery and scanning options as well as a set of compatible tools for gathering additional information about a device or network. For example, there is a Domain Name System (DNS) zone transfer tool, a Whois tool, and a configurable Windows Enumeration tool. SuperScan can be configured to use Internet Control Message Protocol (ICMP), TCP, and User Datagram Protocol (UDP) to discover systems. The tool is preconfigured with the most commonly used ports, but other ports can be added. The Windows Enumeration tool has an interesting option that allows you to enumerate a number of registry keys.

The keys are specified in a flat text file, so it is possible to use the option to check for installed software and patches. SuperScan is extraordinarily fast and accurate, but the report mechanism is weak; only Hypertext Markup Language (HTML) reports are supported. SuperScan is available at http://www.foundstone.com/us/resources-free-tools.asp.

SolarWinds SNMP Sweep

SNMP Sweep is part of the SolarWinds Network Management Suite. The suite contains a number of utilities for network discovery and performance management designed with an emphasis on speed, accuracy, and ease of use. SNMP Sweep can scan a range of IP addresses and show which IP addresses are in use and their DNS lookup names. If the systems have SNMP enabled and the proper community string configured in SNMP Sweep, the system name, location, contact, last reboot, and system description are also returned. SNMP Sweep can print results or export them into plain text, Hypertext Transfer Protocol (HTTP), or comma delimited files for reporting and consolidation. Additional information on SNMP Sweep and other SolarWinds tools can be found at http://www.solarwinds.net/.

Network Mapper

Network Mapper (Nmap) is a free open source utility for network exploration and security auditing. It was designed to rapidly scan large networks, although it will work equally well for single systems. Nmap uses raw IP packets in novel ways to determine what hosts are available on the network as well as their OS (including version), the services they are running, the packet filters or firewalls in use, and dozens of other characteristics. Nmap runs on most vendor platforms and is available in both console and graphical versions. Nmap is distributed under the terms and condition of the GNU project general public license (GPL). The following example displays the OS and version, and services running on a single system named Madell:

```
./nmap -A -T4 Madell.company.com
Starting nmap 3.40PVT16 ( http://www.insecure.org/nmap/ ) at
2004-01-03 02:56 PDT
Interesting ports on Madell (127.0.0.1):
(The 1640 ports scanned but not shown below are in state: closed)
PORT STATE SERVICE VERSION
22/tcp open ssh OpenSSH 3.1p1 (protocol 1.99)
53/tcp open domain ISC Bind 9.2.1
443/tcp open ssl/http Apache httpd 2.0.39 ((Unix) mod_
perl/1.99_04-dev [cut])
5001/tcp open ssl/ssh OpenSSH 3.1p1 (protocol 1.99)
```

```
6000/tcp open X11 (access denied)
8080/tcp open http Apache httpd 2.0.39 ((Unix) mod_perl/1.99_04-
dev [cut])
Device type: general purpose
Running: Linux 2.4.X|2.5.X
OS details: Linux Kernel 2.4.0 - 2.5.20
Uptime 3.45 days (since Fri Jan 03 1:32:40 2004)
Nmap run completed -- 1 IP address (1 host up) scanned in 51.24
seconds
```

The scan can be expanded to all systems on the network segment by adding a range parameter to the command: ./nmap -A -T4 Madell.company.com/24. By adding the /24 class C network mask, Nmap will scan all the systems on the segment Madell is attached to.

Services

Microsoft Network Access Protection

Network Access Protection (NAP) is Microsoft's version of the health policy validation system. It is not considered a single application, but a collection of technologies that provide a health check function. Microsoft NAP relies on the latest version of Windows Vista and Windows "Longhorn" server beta. The technology is in a beta format now and will not be fully supported until the server component is released to market. When considering activating NAP there are a few decisions to make.

In the planning stage of a NAP deployment, the main decision an organization has to make is how to enforce access. Access is given to end users via a radius server, but access is enforced by one of four connectivity solutions listed in Table 17.3. Each of the technologies are discussed in the technology section of this chapter, but in addition one needs to think about the security needs of the organization. The technologies give network access at various levels of the network stack. They also offer varied levels of security. The selection of an enforcement method should be based on a review of the organization and its needs. DHCP may be an option

Table 17.3 Network Access Protection Technology Options

Enforcement method	Remediation	Monitoring
DHCP	Systems Management Server	Microsoft Operations Manager
IPSec	Altiris	HP OpenView
802.1X		
VPN		

for an organization that is smaller and needs something not quite as technology intensive as the other options. 802.1X would be an option for an organization that already has a large investment in 802.1X enabled gear. IPSec is a good selection for a larger organization that is looking for a more secure enforcement method, or for an organization that already has IPSec deployed in the environment.

In the planning stage, an organization will need to select a method of remediation. The selection should be based on what is already in place for patch management, in addition to whether the solution in place is a NAP partner. As of now the amount of functionality and how they will perform the remediation function are unknown for the various partners.

An area that is also wide open is monitoring. Microsoft has its Operations Manager software that will be integrated into the solution. There are also many other vendors who have monitoring functionality. Most organizations will probably press their vendor of choice into adding NAP support so that they will not have to train new staff and deal with other changes. For the latest updates to the NAP framework check the Microsoft Web site at http://www.microsoft.com/technet/network/nap/default.mspx.

Cisco Network Admission Control

Network admission control (NAC) is Cisco's health check solution. It is very similar to Microsoft's solution, but it also relies on some of Cisco's hardware strengths. The enforcement method for NAC is either 802.1X or EAP. NAC is considered to be in its second phase. There are documents on the Cisco Web site that explain in depth the NAC framework, how it works, and who the partners are; see http://www.cisco.com/en/US/netsol/ns466/networking_solutions_package.html. The actual deployment details are currently not easily put into practice.

Notification Services and Resources

All major software vendors offer free proactive security update notification. Table 17.4 is only a sample; a much larger list of vendor notification services and Web sites is available for James Madison University (see http://www.jmu.edu/computing/runsafe/update.shtml#notifications).

There are also a number of free and commercial services providing consolidated update notifications. For example, Cassandra is a free service from Purdue University that allows you to set up profiles indicating the products of interest to you. Cassandra will then send email notifications to you when vulnerabilities associated with those products are reported. The service is best effort; there are no guarantees you will be notified of a vulnerability. You can sign up for Cassandra at https://cassandra.cerias.purdue.edu/main.

Testing Tools

IBM Rational Software

IBM Rational software provides a comprehensive set of test tools, including test automation tools, coverage tools, etc. The tools do not come cheap, but if your organization has the IT budget, your test lab should have the Rational suite in its arsenal of test tools. For more information see http://www-306.ibm.com/software/rational/.

Scripting Languages

Scripting tools are one of the easiest ways to build test scripts. Most OSs have built-in scripting capabilities; for example, Windows systems have native support for Visual Basic script and command line batch files. All UNIX system shells support script and both systems support additional languages such as PERL, Python, and Java. One of the biggest advantages to using scripting languages is the large pool of freely available test scripts.

- Microsoft maintains a repository of scripts on Technet at http://www.microsoft.com/technet/scriptcenter/scripts/default.mspx?mfr=true.
- Librenix maintains a repository for Linux shell scripts along with a number of good links to other programming resources at http://librenix.com/?inode=5446.
- The Oracle Resource Shop maintains a collection of hundreds of free SQL, Windows NT, Java, PERL, and UNIX shell scripts for Oracle database administrators (DBAs) and developers.
- The Open Directory project has a large number of links to scripting resources at http://dmoz.org/Computers/Programming/Languages/Scripting/.
- Hannu Valanen Ltd. maintains an excellent set of links to UNIX scripting resources at http://www.valtanen.com/unix/scripts/.

Simulators

PureLoad Software

PureLoad is a tool with a centralized management console that can be used to define the number of virtual users and usage scenarios, and to execute and evaluate test results. PureLoad can be used to test a wide range of applications, but it has specific support for Web application testing. PureLoad has a recording feature that allows you to capture a common Web usage session. The recording can then be used to simulate multiple users for load testing purpose. More information on PureLoad is available at http://www.codework.com/pureload/index.htm.

Shunra Virtual Enterprise

Shunra Virtual Enterprise (VE) provides high performance hardware appliances for network bandwidth and load simulation. Their solution includes capture, replay, analysis, and detailed reporting capabilities. "Shunra VE is extremely easy to install, configure and use, and it seamlessly integrates with your existing infrastructure and lab environment, right out-of-the-box." Shunra VE is essentially a bridge/routing device with the ability to change the speed of the network traffic traversing it to simulate throughput for wide area networks or to simulate congested local area networks. For more information see http://www.shunra.com/content.aspx?pageId=12.

Open Source

Additional open source load simulators can be found at http://www.opensource-testing.org/performance.php.

Mapping Tools

Sysinternals Process Explorer and Process Monitor

Process Explorer displays information on what files, registry keys, and other objects processes open, including what DLLs they load. Process Explorer has a handle mode that allows you to see the handles that the process has opened and a DLL mode that displays the DLLs and memory-mapped files the process has loaded. Process Explorer also includes a search capability so you can quickly find processes with a particular handle opened or DLL loaded.

Process Monitor displays the real-time usage of file system, registry, and process/thread resources. The program includes rich nondestructive filtering, comprehensive event properties, simultaneous logging of displayed items, and much more. "Its uniquely powerful features will make Process Monitor a core utility in your system troubleshooting and malware hunting toolkit." These tools and other Sysinternals tools are available at http://www.microsoft.com/technet/sysinternals/default.mspx.

VTrace – Jacob R. Lorch and Alan Jay Smith

VTrace is a free software tool designed to trace the things a computer does. Once installed, VTrace collects traces of file system, network, disk drive, and process activities, including threads and interprocess communications. VTrace is available from the authors at http://www.cs.berkeley.edu/~lorch/vtrace/.

Sarion Systems Research Apius

Apius is a commercial program for tracing Windows DLL calls issued from Windows programs. Apius gathers both the call and passed parameters. The data are stored in a database for simple context-sensitive analysis. Apius includes a smart analysis feature that eliminates the need for source code. Virtually any Windows application can be traced with Apius. Additional information on Apius is available at http://www.sarion.com/.

Packaging and Rollback Tools

Microsoft Sysdiff

Sysdiff is a Windows-based tool that can be used to check for differences between two systems, so it can be used to track the changes an update makes to the system. The process is straightforward. Create a baseline or before image of the system, apply the update, then compare the system to the original image. The process looks like this: use "sysdiff /snap baseline.img" to create a image of the system. After the update has been applied use "sysdiff /diff baseline.img changes.img" to capture the differences and then dump them to a text file using "Sysdiff /dump changes.img changes.txt."

The tool is very useful when the IT department uses a base image for building systems. The baseline.img can be created off the base build image and used to monitor changes to systems built with that image. This makes it possible to do periodic checks for what has been added to systems beyond the base build and helps troubleshoot system issues. For more information on using sysdiff for auditing purposes see http://www.oreilly.com/catalog/ntmaint/chapter/ch05.html. Sysdiff can also be used to image and deploy OSs. For further information on this feature see http://www.microsoft.com/technet/archive/winntas/deploy/depopt/advsysdf.mspx?mfr=true.

Macrovision InstallShield

InstallShield is an installation authoring tool for creating high quality, reliable software installations. InstallShield combines power and flexibility with an easy-to-use interface. InstallShield improves the end users' installation experience while avoiding installation failures. InstallShield supports Microsoft Installer (MSI) formatted files as well as its proprietary format. Additional information is available at http://www.macrovision.com/products/flexnet_installshield/index.shtml.

OnDemand Software WinINSTALL Desktop Management Suite

WinINSTALL Desktop Management Suite (DMS) provides an integrated solution for software packaging, distribution, inventory management, and patch distribution. Capabilities include MSI packaging, inventory-based distribution, multicast distribution replication, patch and antivirus update distribution, change management, OS deployment, software inventory, and centralized reporting. The DMS suite also includes native integration with Microsoft Active Directory, NT Domain, and Novell NDS to facilitate deployment targeting. Operations are managed from a central console. For additional information see http://www.attachmate.com/en-US/Products/PC+Lifecycle+Management/.

Reporting Tools

Crystal Reports

Crystal Reports is a tool that is used to configure and manipulate data from a database into easily consumable reports. It is a way to take log information and data from various points and turn it into something that can be presented to management. There is a trend in IT where groups are looking to format information output from logs and other sources into something that can help management make well-informed business decisions.

MS SQL Reporting Service

MS SQL Reporting Service is a tool like Crystal Reports for creating reports out of database data points. There are other services that leverage MS SQL into an even more focused report. An example is the Business Scorecard Manager, available at http://office.microsoft.com/en-us/performancepoint/FX101686301033.aspx. These reports take data and put it into a balanced scorecard format. Balanced Scorecard is a format that is gaining in popularity among IT organizations as a way to present information in a business centric mode.

Monitoring/Audit Tools

Microsoft Operations Manager

Microsoft Operations Manager is a server package that allows you to manage the log information on a wide range of servers. The administrator can then configure the software to act on various output. For example, if a specific server reported a critical error, the server could email an administrator the list of the failure to mini-mize downtime.

Open Source and Freeware Tools

Open source software tools can be helpful in filling in the gaps where purchased software may not completely do the job. A great resource for open source software is the Web site http://sourceforge.net/. There are many projects that may help you in your testing needs. The issue with open source software tools is that the user must be technically proficient. Many IT staff members rely on open source software to help get their jobs done.

Shavlik HFNetChkPro

HFNetChkPro is a tool by Shavlik that is focused on patch management. The tool will scan a network, look for systems, and check the patch level. It will then push the update to the clients that do not have the version that the tool is set to push. For more information see http://www.shavlik.com/.

Standards and Frameworks

Information Technology Infrastructure Library

The Information Technology Infrastructure Library (ITIL) is a set of British gov-ernment standards created by the Office of Government Commerce. The library is a set of books that outline the basic framework of the specific book topic. The current ITIL books are:

- *Software Asset Management*
- *Service Support*
- *Service Delivery*
- *Planning to Implement Service Management*
- *ICT Infrastructure Management*
- *Application Management*
- *Security Management*
- *Business Perspective*

Each book discusses the topic and industry best practices around each subject. The books do not go into each subject in too much detail, they are there to frame each subject and link the topics. The specifics are left up to the individual implementer. Many other frameworks and methodologies are ITIL based and go into much more detail on specific subjects. Because of its broad acceptance, gaining a background in ITIL will help when reviewing other standards and methodologies.

CoBiT

CoBiT is a management framework developed by the IT Governance Institute. The framework is focused on IT management, upper management, and board members, and focuses on measurement of IT operations. It shows management how to gauge success in IT functions. Adopting CoBiT helps IT management articulate to management its current performance. The framework features a maturity model that ranks maturity. Using the maturity model, an organization can model their maturity and identify weak points and know where they can make improvements.

International Organization for Standardization

The International Organization for Standardization (ISO) is an international group focused on technology and management standards. The standards that are published are very highly regarded and many times are government standards that are then adopted by the ISO. ISO 17799 is a great example of ISO adoption. ISO 17799 was a British standard (BS 7799) that was adopted by the ISO. Many companies and governments demand ISO certification from their contractors and partners. Larger organizations should be familiar with ISO standards if they want to do business with other large organizations or governments.

National Institute of Standards and Technology

The National Institute of Standards and Technology (NIST), a U.S. government standards board, has published multiple standards and guidelines. The 800 series guidelines are focused on information security. The documents are used by the U.S. government and government contractors. The Federal Information Processing Standards (FIPS) document set is a broader set of documents that focus on all information processing standards. A subset of FIPS and 800 series documents has been collected to support the Federal Information Security Management Act (FISMA). FISMA mandates a minimum level of information security for government agencies and contractors. All NIST documents are available for download from the NIST Web site at http://csrc.nist.gov/. Unlike other standards boards, NIST publishes all documents on their Web site free of charge.

Conclusion

This chapter lists many of the technologies and frameworks that have been mentioned throughout this book. Each has been touched on only briefly. For a more detailed review of any of the topics please go to the Web links listed throughout this chapter.

When reviewing one's own infrastructure, focus on the base technologies. Ensure that the technologies that are used in your environment are standards based when at all possible. Companies should insist that their vendors provide standards-based solutions. Vendors should also understand that the use of standards-based solutions creates goodwill with their customers. The use of standards shows that a vendor is confident enough in their solution that it stands on its own without the use of proprietary technologies to entrench their products.

The software that was reviewed is very heavy on management functionality. The management focus is in line with the book topics of configuration management and patch management. Many of the tools can be used for both management functions. The tools discussed will only be effective if they and the people that administer them are managed correctly. To correctly use the listed tools, an IT management team must have a solid IT strategy. IT policies should further this strategy. Strict enforcement of the policies via management tools and automation will ensure that an IT organization is successful in executing the management strategy. The translation of high level business goals into very specific IT automated policies will help an IT organization be successful in executing its strategy.

Standards and frameworks must be adopted by IT management to place structure around day-to-day operations. Many times, standards are more than what an organization requires, but they are always a great starting point for a custom framework. Most private organizations do not follow standards word for word, only government organizations are bound to standards. But just because they are not legally bound to standards does not mean that private organizations should not consider them when creating their own policies. Organizations will be best served if they adopt well-known and researched standards. By adopting standards, organizations show they have done their due diligence regarding specific policies. Using standards minimizes the exposure an organization may have to lawsuits. It is extremely difficult for an external party to prove negligence when an organization can prove they are using industry standards.

Glossary

Actuals: Test results. Actuals are the information returned by a test or series of tests. The actuals are compared against system or process baselines to determine compliance.

Baseline: The basis for a measurement. In this book, baseline refers to the minimum acceptable value for compliance with a specific requirement; values that equal or exceed the minimum are considered compliant.

Change: The introduction of a new component into the IT infrastructure or the addition, modification, or removal of an approved/supported component, including baseline hardware, networks, operating systems, or applications.

Change advisory board (CAB): A group of people representing the business operations and IT support functions who are responsible for assessing and authorizing changes to the IT infrastructure.

Change authority: The entity with the authority to approve changes. The CAB is the primary change authority; other entities may be granted change authority for low priority, emergency, or project-based changes.

Change authorization: The control process used to evaluate change impacts and risks and approve IT infrastructure changes.

Change classification: The assignment of a change priority based on urgency and the potential impact on users, security, systems, and business operations.

Change control: The processes and procedures used to ensure changes are made in a controlled and monitored way, including submission, evaluation, approval, implementation, and postimplementation review of the change.

Change development: The planning and development portion of the update management process that drives the development and submission of a request for change.

Change history: Records describing what changes were made to a system, when they were done, by whom, and for what reason.

Change initiator: The entity that initiates a request for change (usually the system owner or support team).

Change log: A log of requests for change raised during a project. The change log contains information on each change, its evaluation, decisions made, and its current status, including submitted, reviewed, approved, implemented, or closed.

Change management: The service management function that defines, manages, and enforces change control requirements to avoid the introduction of errors and minimize the impact of IT changes on business operations and productivity.

Change management process: The formal steps that each request for change must follow, including the steps to request, classify, authorize, develop, release, and review a change to an IT system or component.

Change manager: The person responsible for the overall management of the change management program in an IT organization.

Compliance: Conformance to a requirement. Compliance can be expressed as a binary result (i.e., "met" or "did not meet" a requirement) or a level result (e.g., fully compliant, partially compliant, noncompliant). Compliance is used to determine subsequent remediation actions.

Configuration management: The policies, processes, and infrastructure used to control updates to system hardware, firmware, software, and documentation.

Managed system: A system that is actively managed and maintained by the operations group; for example, servers or workstations that the operations group inventories, monitors, updates, or repairs.

Metrics: Measurement points. A metric defines what will be measured based on established requirements. Metrics can apply to multiple and disparate processes or systems, therefore metrics do not define how the measurement is accomplished.

One-off system: A system that the operations group is aware of but cannot manage with existing techniques and tools due to special performance, availability, or confidentiality requirements. A medical system used for life support is a good example.

Patch/update: A patch is an update to a piece of application code. In this book the terms patch and update are synonymous and they are used interchangeably.

Procedure: A series of tasks designed to achieve a particular goal for a specific situation or technology. For example, a backup procedure consists of configuration, scheduling, execution, and verification tasks designed to protect data from destruction. The tasks are based on the specific requirements of the backup application, system hardware, and the computer operating system.

Process: A series of high level tasks designed to accomplish a particular goal. Processes are generic in nature so they can be applied across multiple situations and technologies. Change management, for example, is a process consisting of change requests, evaluations, approval/denial decisions, scheduling, and verification tasks designed to implement changes with minimum risk or impact to business operations.

Program: The totality of people, processes, and technology employed to achieve a specific purpose; for example, a change management program.

Remediation: Actions taken to comply with a requirement. Remediation includes identifying the cause of the noncompliance and determining an appropriate course of action (solution) to resolve the issue. Remediation can include direct changes to the process or system, changes to surrounding controls or processes (e.g., addition of a firewall access rule), or acceptance of the risks associated with the noncompliance.

Rogue system: A system attached to the production network without the knowledge or consent of the operations group and not actively managed or maintained by operations. Examples of rogue systems include test machines, vendor and contractor laptops, home machines, etc.

Solution: The process, technology, training, and guidance used to resolve a problem.

Test: A measurement technique. Tests are the methods used to gather the actual data for a specific metric from a specific process or system.

Unmanaged system: A system that the operations group is aware of but does not actively manage. Examples of unmanaged systems include systems located in test facilities or staging areas, systems supplied and managed by third parties, and one-off systems.

Update management: The policies, processes, and infrastructure used to control updates to system software.

Appendix A

Request for Change (RFC) Template

I. INITIATOR IDENTIFYING INFORMATION

   1.1 Name: <<SYSTEM OWNER>>   Date Prepared:
      Dept: Phone #:   Email Address:
   1.2 Technical Investigator: <<SYSTEM ENGINEER/ADMIN>>
      Name: Phone #:   Email Address:
   1.3 Priority: Date Due: (if applicable):

If this change is subject to specific time constraints enter the date the deployment must start on.

II. DESCRIPTION OF PROBLEM/REQUEST/REQUIREMENT

   <<Summary of Requested Change>>

III. TECHNICAL INVESTIGATION

   3.1 System Scope
      Unique system identifier(s) for individual RFC
      Or class of systems for bulk RFC
   3.1 Prerequisites (if any):
   3.2 Assumptions (if any):
   3.3 Dependencies/Constraints (if any):
   3.4 Risks (if any):
   3.5 Benefits Analysis:
   3.6 User Impact Analysis (including data consumers):
   3.7 Other Impact Analysis:
      3.7.1 Development: <<IMPACT>>

3.7.2 Operations & Maintenance: <<IMPACT>>

3.7.3 Training: <<IMPACT>>

3.7.4 Other Program Activities: <<IMPACT>>
    e.g., Will this change impact quarterly or annual reporting runs?

3.7.5 Affect on Existing System Including:

    3.7.5.1 System hardware, software, and/or network footprint. <IMPACT>>

    3.7.5.2 Facilities and/or equipment. <<IMPACT>>

    3.7.5.3 User or administrator procedures and processes. <<IMPACT>>

    3.7.5.4 Operating environment. <<IMPACT>>

    3.7.5.6 Product form, fit, or function. <<IMPACT>>

    3.7.5.7 System performance. <<IMPACT>>

3.8 Time required to perform this Technical Investigation:
<<TIME IN HOURS>>

IV. DEPLOYMENT AND SCHEDULING

4.1 Deployment Overview

4.2 Proposed Change Schedule

System Name	Change Date	Window	Time
SAMPLE01	Saturday, Jan 11	1	12AM – 2AM
<<HOST ID>>	<<DAY>>,<<DATE>>	<<##>>	<<TIME>>
<<HOST ID>>	<<DAY>>,<<DATE>>	<<##>>	<<TIME>>
<<HOST ID>>	<<DAY>>,<<DATE>>	<<##>>	<<TIME>>
<<HOST ID>>	<<DAY>>,<<DATE>>	<<##>>	<<TIME>>

V. CHANGE ADVISORY BOARD RECOMMENDATION

5.1 Approval Date: <<DATE>>

5.2 Rejected Date: <<DATE>>

5.3 Rejection Description:
<<Reason of RFC rejection>>

Appendix B

System Owner Roles and Responsibilities

The system owner is the business person ultimately accountable for the functionality of the system. It is the system owner's responsibility to ensure that the system:

- Meets the business objectives for which it was created.
- Has sufficient funds for yearly operations and maintenance.
- Conforms to all IT standards, policies, and security requirements.

It is the system owner that determines the functional requirements for the system based on business objectives or reliability, performance, or security needs. The system owner reviews solutions meeting these requirements and proposes or approves system updates. The system owner may also participate in the procurement, development, and engineering of these updates.

As part of the change management program, it is the system owner or their specified designee who is responsible for:

- Ensuring that all changes made to the system are accomplished in accordance with change and release management policies and procedures.
- Ensuring system ownership and support contacts are accurate and up-to-date.
- Ensuring an accurate list of system users and data consumers is maintained for change notification purposes.
- Reviewing all change requests related to the system for potential conflicts with business or operational requirements.

- Notifying the change authority of potential issues and negotiate solutions.
- Requesting extensions or exemptions when changes cannot be accomplished in accordance with IT standards, policies, or security requirements.
- Reviewing change management reports for the system or systems owned.
- Participating in change management program improvement activities and policy update reviews.

IMPORTANT NOTE!
The system owner or their specified designee serves as the primary escalation point for all change management issues that cannot be resolved at the system support level. Therefore the system owner must ensure that someone within the business unit is always available to receive, process, and resolve change management escalations.

Appendix C

Update Management Process Diagrams

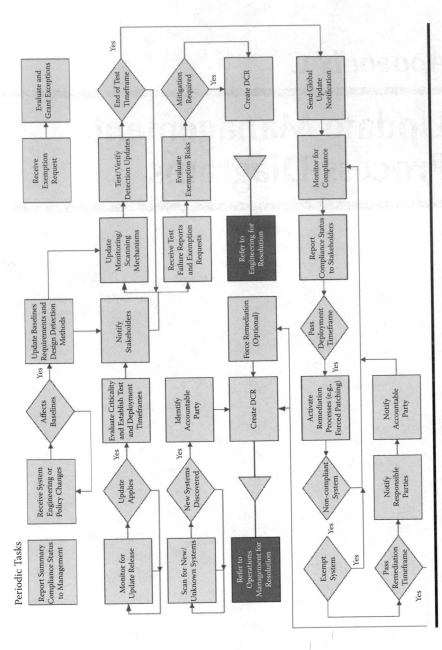

Figure C.1 Information security update management process stream.

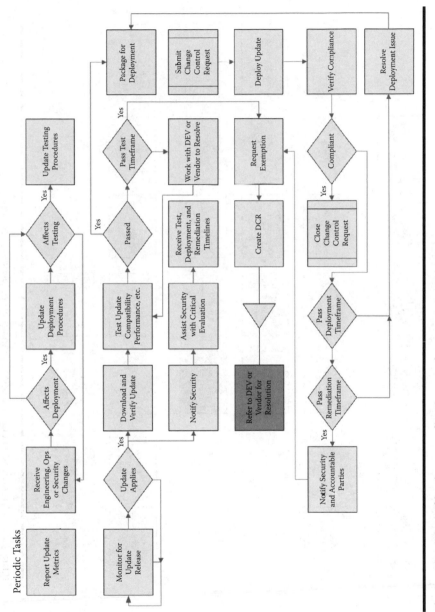

Figure C.2   Line of business applications update management process stream.

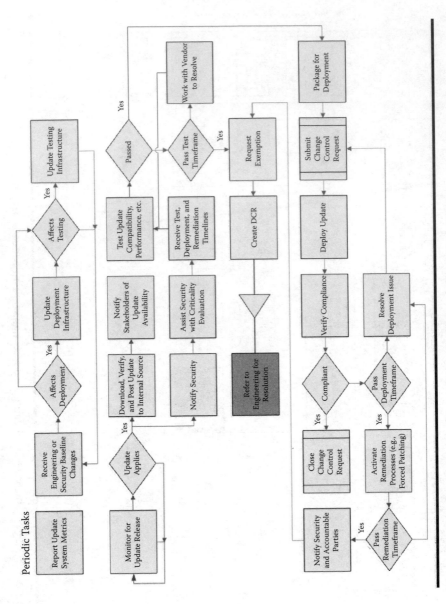

Figure C.3 Operations security update management process stream.

Index